BOSNIA AND HERCEGOVINA:
A TRADITION BETRAYED

D0067111

BOSNIA AND HERCEGOVINA: A TRADITION BETRAYED

ROBERT J. DONIA   JOHN V.A. FINE, JR.

With maps by John C. Hamer

Columbia University Press
New York

Columbia University Press
New York

Printed in Hong Kong

Library of Congress Cataloging-in-Publication Data

Donia, Robert J.
    Bosnia and Hercegovina: a tradition betrayed / Robert J. Donia.
John V.A. Fine Jr. ; with maps by John C. Hamer.
      p.   cm.
    Includes bibliographical references and index.
    ISBN 0-231-10160-0 ; ISBN 0-231-10161-9 (pbk.)
    1. Bosnia and Hercegovina—History. 2. Bosnia and Hercegovina—
Ethnic relations.   I. Fine, John V. A. (John Van Antwerp), 1939-
    II. Title.
DR1685.D66 1994
949.7142—dc20   .   94-162223
                                                     CIP

c 10 9 8 7 6 5 4 3 2
p 10 9 8 7 6 5 4 3

This work was typeset by John C. Hamer on a Macintosh 660AV
computer using Aldus PageMaker 5.0. The text employs the Adobe
Garamond font family altered to include the Serbo-Croatian diacritical
marks (č, ć, š, and ž). All of the maps are original diagrams created in
Adobe Illustrator.

For the innocent victims
of a tragic war

Acknowledgements

THE AUTHORS WISH to thank a number of our friends and colleagues who contributed to the preparation of this book. We are particularly grateful to John C. Hamer, who devoted his considerable creative talents and much time to preparing the maps, designing the layout, and typesetting the book. Christine Stuebner, a keen observer of contemporary Eastern Europe, collected and interpreted the data for tables relating to the modern period.

Balkan specialists Francine Friedman, Stan Markotich, Patrick Moore, and Duncan Perry offered valuable comments and suggestions after reading portions of the manuscript. Non-specialists Holly Avey, John Banks, Mine Ener, Anthony Kaldellis, and Stephen Rapp read early drafts and offered suggestions pertaining to clarity and style. We are particularly indebted to Elizabeth B. Fine and Jane Ritter, who read the entire text and proposed numerous editorial and stylistic improvements. Although the suggestions and proposals of these readers have greatly enhanced the final product, the authors alone are responsible for the interpretations appearing in the text and for any flaws and factual errors that remain.

The University of Michigan History Department generously allowed us to use its photocopying facilities, and its secretarial staff sent and received packages and faxes for us. Kelly Sahyouni of Fort Worth, Texas, patiently maintained the flow of communication among the authors and the publishers. The Center for Russian and East European Studies at the University of Michigan facilitated in various ways the preparation of the manuscript. The commitment and constant encouragement of our publishers, Michael Dwyer and Christopher Hurst, have sustained us throughout the preparation of this work.

April 1994   Robert J. Donia, *Fort Worth, Texas*
                              John V. A. Fine, *Ann Arbor, Michigan*

Contents

Guide to Pronunciation

THE LANGUAGE OF Bosnia and of the neighboring states of Serbia, Croatia, and Montenegro is Serbo-Croatian. It is a single language (with, of course, dialectical differences) written in two alphabets, Latin for Croatian and Cyrillic (the alphabet used also for Russian) for Serbian. We are rendering names in the Croatian form. The letters with unusual pronunciation for speakers of English are:

c	=	*ts* as in the word *tsar*
ć	–	*ch* (soft), found regularly at the end of proper names
č	=	*ch* (hard)
dj	=	*j* as in *jet*
dž	=	similar to *dj*, but a bit harder
h	=	guttural, as in the Scottish *loch*
j	=	*y* as in *yes*
š	=	*sh*
ž	=	*zh* as in leisure

To make matters more accessible, we have rendered Turkish words used in Bosnia with Serbo-Croatian spellings. Thus *sandžak* and not *sancak*. Since adding English plurals to certain Serbo-Croatian words is quite awkward, on a few occasions we use Serbo-Croatian plurals. Nouns ending in *a* have a plural ending in *e*, thus the plural of *Ustasha* (we also use this form as the adjective) is *Ustashe*, and the plural of *Kosača* is *Kosače*. Nouns ending in a consonant have a plural ending in *i*; thus the plural of *Pavlović* is *Pavlovići*, and the plural of *Miloradović* is *Miloradovići*. Inhabitants of Sarajevo are referred to as *Sarajlije*.

Introduction

ON APRIL 6, 1992, a crowd of demonstrators estimated at over 50,000 gathered in front of the Bosnian Parliament building in Sarajevo to demonstrate for peace in Bosnia and Hercegovina. The demonstrators were members of all three of Bosnia's largest nationalities: Serbs, Croats, and Bosnian Muslims. Directly across the street, from the upper floors of the ultra-modern Holiday Inn built for the 1984 Winter Olympics, heavily-armed Serbian militiamen fired randomly into the crowd, killing and wounding dozens of the peace demonstrators. This cavalier killing spree quickly dispersed the crowd and marked the demise of the few remaining hopes that moderation and compromise might prevail in Bosnia and Hercegovina.

The Sarajevo massacre of April 6 contained many elements that would recur in the Bosnian war in subsequent weeks and months. The victims were unarmed civilians who hoped for the preservation of a multiethnic Bosnian society which had roots and traditions dating back many centuries. The perpetrators were nationalist extremists, organized and heavily armed by political and paramilitary leaders intent on destroying Bosnia's multiethnic society and replacing it with the national supremacy of a single ethnic group, in this case the Serbs. Symbolically, the Sarajevo massacre stilled the voices of peace and mutual tolerance; the shrill shouts of ethnic hatred and national divisiveness triumphed by force of arms.

I

The war that began in Bosnia in 1992 encompassed death, atrocities, and terror on a scale unknown in Europe since World War II. The perpetrators of the Bosnian war seemed to know no bounds in the cruelty, brutality, and havoc they wrought on their adversaries and on the innocent inhabitants of the land. Television cameras captured some of the killings and brutality, and daily newscasts revealed the awesome depravity of the conflict.   Viewers around the world saw starving prisoners, victims of systematic rape, mutilated corpses, calculated destruction of homes and cultural monuments, mortally wounded victims of random shelling, and the results of ethnic cleansing. The daily images of warfare, coupled with the reality of United Nations troops in the area and the prospect of deepening involvement by NATO and the United States, were hauntingly reminiscent of the Vietnam War in the 1960s.

Bosnia, however, is no Vietnam: it is not a far-away land about which we, collectively, know nothing. The argument for "collective ignorance," so persuasively advanced by both critics and supporters of US intervention in Vietnam, is simply not valid for the lands of the former Yugoslavia. Inspired by Cold War fervor, the US Congress appropriated many millions of dollars in the decades after World War II to fund research centers and exchange programs so that Americans could know more about the lands where Communism held sway.

Yugoslavia, with its open borders and accessibility to outsiders, became the destination of choice for hundreds of Western students and scholars who studied all aspects of Balkan history and civilization.   Some of the best studies of Yugoslav and Bosnian society and history have been prepared by Western specialists and published in English. Many leading scholars and political leaders of the former Yugoslav lands have studied and taught at American universities. At the height of the Vietnam War, with 600,000 US troops engaged, the number of Southeast Asian specialists in the United States did not begin to approach the number of knowledgeable scholars in the 1990s who are familiar with the history and culture of Southeast Europe.

Despite a substantial reservoir of Western knowledge about Bosnia and Southeast Europe, public debate about policy options in the former Yugoslavia appears to us to be deeply mired in false dichotomies, flawed analogies, gross historical exaggerations, and well-worn shibboleths with little foundation in historical reality. Many of these myths are the product of nationalist propaganda spread by Serbian, Croatian, and Bosnian Muslim publicists, but they have been endorsed and repeated by those who mold or influence policy. Propaganda, historical precedent, and superficial analogies have been harnessed to justify a particular policy action or inaction. To those who oppose Western intervention, the analogies advanced are Vietnam, Beirut, and Northern Ireland. Bosnia is another "Vietnam quagmire," a hopelessly insoluble problem with no conceivable positive "endgame" for the United States and the West. For others, principally those favoring a more assertive Western role, the relevant analogy is Neville Chamberlain returning from Munich having deceived himself and others into believing that appeasement would bring lasting peace.

Bosnia lends itself to few simple analogies and no easy answers. Even so, one need not despair of understanding the roots of the conflict or of evaluating prospective policy alternatives to American and European involvement in Balkan affairs. In the search of understanding the complex situation and arriving at guideposts for action, an examination of historical traditions and past behavior provides insights into the sources of current events and illuminates potential solutions. At the very least it should help dispel falsehoods spread by propagandists and enable policy-makers to avoid foolhardy missteps.

Our intent in this volume is to explore the historical roots of Bosnian society from the arrival of Slavic tribes in the 6th and 7th centuries AD to the breakup of socialist Yugoslavia, and to identify the traditions and patterns of social and ethnic relations that have characterized Bosnian society throughout its history. We describe the major historical processes that account for the present-day ethnic composition of Bosnia: religious conversions in the medieval and early Ottoman periods; the subsequent evolution of distinct ethnoreligious communities; and the rise of political nationalism in the 19th and 20th centuries. We also trace the origins of the present conflict in Bosnia and describe, in overview, the course of the Bosnian war.

The history of Bosnia and its inhabitants intersects and sometimes blends with that of other South Slavs, so some of our inquiry leads us to treat Bosnia's relations with its neighbors. In the twentieth century, the development of a South Slav state — Yugoslavia — and its subsequent disintegration have profoundly influenced the lives of all inhabitants of Bosnia. Some of our account necessarily centers on Yugoslavia, for Bosnia's experience over the past seventy years is incomprehensible without an appreciation for its Yugoslav context.

As two historians who have studied the history of Bosnia, and who lived in Sarajevo at different times in the 1960s and 1970s, we have drawn upon our personal observations and experiences from that time as well as our historical research into the area. We are specialists on the medieval (John Fine) and modern (Robert Donia) periods of Bosnian history. Our

account, although historical in approach and broadly chrono-
logical in organization, frequently reaches back and forth in
time to draw comparisons and identify long-standing historical
traditions. Chapters 1-4, dealing primarily with the medieval
and Ottoman periods, were written by John Fine; chapters 5-11,
treating the modern era (1875-1994), were written by Robert
Donia.

This is not a conventional history. We have sought to
discern patterns rather than merely describe events, to charac-
terize developments rather than chronicle episodes, and to
identify the long-term traditions that transcend a single historical era. Furthermore, while we have not set out to provide a
detailed history of the war, our account is intended to shed light
on the sources of the Bosnian conflict that began in early 1992.
We fervently hope that the war, which continues at the time of
writing (April 1994), will end in peace for Bosnians of all ethnic
groups.

A Misunderstood Society:
Bosnia's Tolerant Past Betrayed

——— · ———

THE CONFLICT THAT began wracking Bosnia in early April 1992, when the international community recognized Bosnia's declaration of independence from a crazed and self-destructing Yugoslavia, has only partly been an ethnic one. The government of Bosnia, though often called in the press the Muslim government, has been representing those who want to keep Bosnia the entity it was as a republic within Yugoslavia. Promising equal rights to all nationalities and religions, it has been supported by much of the urban population of all ethnic groups. At the time of this writing in April 1994, most of the Sarajevo Serbs I know are, to the best of my knowledge, still in the city, supporting the Bosnian government. The Bosnian cabinet as of February 12, 1993, contained nine Muslims, six Serbs, and five Croats. One third of the Territorial Defense Forces then defending Sarajevo was Serb. Thus Serbs (and Croats too) have been on both sides. In so constituting itself, the Bosnian government has been representing a tradition of tolerance and coexistence that goes back many centuries. We shall explore the roots of that legacy in the following pages.

Croat and Serb chauvinists have wanted to depict the present conflict as an ethnic war to justify the territorial expansion of Serbia and Croatia, the two neighboring states that have both been actively involved in the warfare. The involvement of these two expansionist neighboring states has made the conflict an international war as well. But to call the Bosnian warfare "ethnic" demeans the Bosnian cause by making it seem as if the "Bosnians" too were just one more narrow ethnic group; moreover, labeling the Bosnians "ethnic Muslims" not only ignores the Serb and Croat Christians in the Bosnian ranks as well as the centuries of a common Bosnian identity that has continued to be felt by many under siege, but also helps stir up among ignorant locals unfounded fears of the Turkish (or Ottoman) past and of Muslim fundamentalism.

It is also important to underline the wrongness of all the proposed solutions along lines of partitioning Bosnia between its aggressive neighbors or of transferring populations to make three mini-states based on ethnicity out of Bosnia's territory. Throughout its long history (medieval, Ottoman, and modern) Bosnia has had its own very distinct history and culture, and this culture has been shared by people of all its religious denominations. Their famous and enormous medieval tombstones (the so-called Bogomil tombstones or *stećci*), for example, were built by members of all three of the Christian denominations then existing in Bosnia. And though Bosnia did interact with its Serb and Croat neighbors over the centuries, it had a very different history and culture from them.

Bosnia enjoyed its own medieval state and was a separate and legally defined provincial entity during its 400 years under Ottoman rule. It also maintained its own special status both under Austrian rule and as part of Yugoslavia. As an integral territory, including Hercegovina, Bosnia has had more durable and widely recognized borders through the centuries than either Serbia or Croatia. Serbia and Croatia have been laying claim to parts of Bosnia on ethnic grounds. However, at the various times when these neighbors were independent states or were

FIG. I.I — FOURTEENTH-CENTURY TOMBSTONE FROM ZGOŚĆE, NEAR VISOKO IN CENTRAL BOSNIA. EXHIBITED IN COURTYARD OF *ZEMALJSKI MUZEJ* IN SARAJEVO. DAMAGED BY SERBIAN SHELLING IN 1992.

provinces in larger enterprises, they have held only bits and pieces of Bosnia, and those only briefly. Furthermore, except for the three years of Ustasha terror during World War II, these brief interludes occurred over 500 years ago. Thus neither Serbia nor Croatia has any serious historical claims to Bosnia. Bosnia has been a coherent entity for centuries; and despite Serb statements to the contrary, there is nothing artificial about Bosnia. It is only the fanaticism of nationalists that insists that states must be based on ethnicity and be nation-states and that pluralism is artificial and unworkable. And these neighbors, and their local surrogates, have been doing their best to make facts fit their theory through demagoguery, hate-mongering, and vio- lence. But Bosnia — for centuries a pluralistic society — has shown over these centuries that pluralism can successfully exist even in a Balkan context.

Bosnia's distinctiveness has continued in many ways through the centuries and is shared by members of all three national groups. This special character and common sympathy among aware Bosnians of all three (and, if we include the Jews, four) backgrounds has existed particularly in the cities. In fact, since World War II, 30% to 40% of urban marriages in Bosnia have been mixed. These urban cultured Europeans, representing the best in Bosnia, never wanted partitions or ethnic cantons; the goal of many, if not most of them, even should it now be an unrealistic one, is still at the time of this writing a restored united Bosnia populated by people of all ethnic and religious back- grounds. Moreover, for those unfamiliar with the area, it is worth stressing at the outset that the three so-called ethnic groups of Bosnia all speak the same language (one which in the twentieth century we have come to call Serbo-Croatian) and have a shared historical past. The only difference among them is their different religious backgrounds. And I want to stress the word background, for to say "religions" would give the wrong emphasis. After fifty years of a very secular and secularizing Yugoslav state, few modern-day Bosnians (and certainly almost none of those leading any of the sides in the current war) are deeply religious. Their ways of life are the same, and when one meets a Bosnian, if one does not notice the personal name, one may spend considerable time with that Bosnian and then go on one's way, unaware of his ethnic identity.

Finally, before turning to the medieval and Ottoman (or Turkish) periods of Bosnia's colorful history, it is worth stressing that, despite its *ad nauseam* repetition in the international press, nowhere do we find evidence of the alleged centuries of hatred (whether religious or ethnic) among various Bosnian groups that has supposedly permeated their history. Though Bosnia in the Middle Ages fought wars against Serbia and against principalities under Croats, at no time did Bosnians fight civil wars along these or any other ethnic lines. In fact, few Bosnians ever referred to themselves as Serbs or Croats, and those who did were to be found in border regions. Since the Ottomans categorized people by religion, Bosnians did not use ethnic names under the Ottomans either, before their gradual appearance in the nineteenth century. However, at the start of the nineteenth century Bosnians were certainly conscious of being members of distinct communities defined by religion. Then, in the nineteenth century, Orthodox and Catholic Bosnians gradually and unevenly, under the impact of ideas exported by their neighbors in Serbia and Croatia, began acquiring the ethnic labels "Serb" and "Croat" respectively. Thus many Bosnian Christians had acquired an ethnic consciousness to further define their distinctiveness by the end of the Ottoman period. In some cases, and increasingly in the 1870s, this ethnic awareness was transforming itself into a nationalism similar to that being expressed at the time by Croats across the Sava or by Serbs across the Drina. As they spread, these new nationalist identities, for those who had acquired them, played a part, particularly in the 1870s, in movements of liberation from the Ottomans. Subsequently under the Austrians these national identities became more prevalent and were to play an increasingly important role in movements against Austrian rule. How-

ever, this nationalism was chiefly directed at the Ottoman and
Austro-Hungarian empires, rarely at other ethnic groups in
Bosnia (except insofar as their members supported the occupying governments). Though signs of it can be found from the
1890s, serious ethnic rivalry began only after the formation of
Yugoslavia in 1918, and in Bosnia it was mainly a spill-over from
the more serious, but also then brand-new, quarrel between
Croats of Croatia and the Serb-dominated interwar Yugoslav
state. For all practical purposes ethnic violence in Bosnia
erupted for the first time in World War II when Bosnia was
assigned to the fascist Croatian Ustasha state, which set about
stirring up ethnic hatreds and carried out genocide akin to what
is now called "ethnic cleansing." Tito's successful Partisan
movement and the state he created, one that sensibly did not
tolerate chauvinism, restored Bosnia's mixed population to its
traditional tolerance.

As we shall see, religious rivalry and violence were also not
part of Bosnia's heritage. Though Bosnia had three faiths in the
Middle Ages, their members tolerated one another. Civil wars
with a religious ingredient never took place. Only in the last five
years of the medieval state do we find Bosnia's sole example of a
locally directed religious persecution, and this was forced on an
unwilling Bosnian king by an intolerant papacy which made
persecution of a local denomination a condition for Western aid
against the Ottomans, who were poised to invade. During the
first century of Ottoman rule, a limited amount of tension
existed between Bosnian Catholics and Orthodox as they quar-
reled over possession of Church buildings and Church taxes; but
such cases were infrequent and short-lived, and did not lead to
fighting but were settled in court. The leading role of Islam in
the state clearly grated on Christians, and, as local Bosnians

converted to Islam, surely some of this resentment was felt toward them. However, once again the *position* of Islam did not emerge from local action, but was imposed by the conquering Ottoman Turks. Bosnians did not fight one another as members of religious groups at any time in the Ottoman period either. And when they rose up in various rebellions against Ottoman rule, though Bosnians were found on both the rebel and the Ottoman state sides, these wars were fought for and against a regime and the social order it imposed; they were not ethnic or religious clashes between Bosnian groups. After the creation of Yugoslavia, religious wars did not take place there either, except during World War II when religion was an ingredient of the policy imposed by the fascist Croatian Ustashe, which did provoke domestic responses along religious lines.

Thus one is not justified in saying "a plague on all their houses," on the grounds that these people are just reverting to a centuries-long past of ethnic and/or religious hatred and fighting. This is sheer myth. One finds no examples of such behavior in Bosnia's history before our own vicious twentieth century and, even then, this behavior was in great part instigated by the actions and policies of the Germans and the same chauvinist neighbors who, for their own ends, have incited and unleashed the horrors that are now destroying Bosnia.

2

Religious Toleration and Distinctiveness
of Medieval Bosnia

———— • ————

MODERN BOSNIA AND Hercegovina made up one of the six republics of former Yugoslavia. The modern republic is bounded by Dalmatia and the Dinaric Alps to the west, by the Sava River beyond which lies Croatia to the north, by the Drina River across which lies Serbia to the east, and by a mountainous border with Montenegro to the south. Called Bosna in Serbo-Croatian, it is named for the Bosna River which has its source just outside of Sarajevo and runs north into the Sava. In the early Middle Ages the region was divided into small units or counties; and the one centered around the source of the Bosna River was called the county of Bosnia. The leaders of this county came to be the most powerful local figures, and eventually their holdings were increased to include the territory that makes up the modern republic. By the thirteenth century this whole region had come to be called Bosnia. Throughout the rest of the Middle Ages, until the Turkish conquest in the last half of the fifteenth century, Bosnia was an independent state with distinct traditions that sharply distinguished it from its Serb and Croat neighbors, even though the Bosnians and these two neighboring peoples all spoke the same language.

SLAVIC MIGRATIONS

The Slavs settled in Bosnia (as well as Serbia, Croatia, and Montenegro) in the late sixth and early seventh century. They appeared in small tribal units, but were drawn from a single Slavic confederation — the Slaveni. Thus they were all one people, which means that the Bosnians come from the same Slavic base as today's Serbs and Croats. In the second quarter of the seventh century, the Croats invaded and asserted their overlordship over the Slavs (Slaveni) in Croatia and parts of Bosnia. In regions to the south and east of Bosnia, the Serbs came to predominate over the Slavs there. Whether these newcomers asserted their control over all the Slavs of Bosnia is unknown; it is also impossible to determine which parts of Bosnia fell under Serbs, which fell under Croats (other than the northwestern counties mentioned in Byzantine sources), and which remained under neither.

The Croats and Serbs were probably originally Iranians. At least linguists have concluded that both their tribal names as well as the preserved names of their leaders were Iranian. However, despite the nomenclature, the leaders and some or ·even all of their following could have been slavicized before their appearance in the Balkans. In time these later invaders were assimilated and, if they were not so already, slavicized by the more numerous Slavs. But the Iranian invaders provided the names for the resulting medieval populations of the territory that we now call Serbia, parts of Croatia, and possibly Montenegro. At first the Croats and Serbs did not form single states; different leaders controlled smaller county units called *župas*. The Byzantine emperor, Constantine Porphyrogenitus, writing in the tenth century, refers to eleven Croatian župas, four of which were in northern and western Bosnia.

EARLY HISTORY: FOREIGN RULE

Bosnia lay at a considerable distance from Rome and Constantinople, the two centers that produced written records. Thus we know little about it in the early Middle Ages. However, during most of the tenth, eleventh, and twelfth centuries, Bosnia found itself under foreign rule. But, since Bosnia is very mountainous, making communications difficult, one may wonder how much impact these foreign rulers and overlords had upon its inhabitants. In any case, in capsule format, Bosnians found themselves from the mid-tenth to the late-twelfth century under a succession of short-lived conquering states: in the tenth century, Bosnia was briefly part of the Serbian state under a ruler named Časlav; after he died in battle around 960, much of Bosnia was briefly incorporated into the Croatian state of Kresimir II; soon thereafter, in about 997, Samuel of Bulgaria marched through Bosnia and may well have asserted his overlordship over part of it. After the Byzantines defeated Samuel and annexed Bulgaria in 1018, Byzantium asserted its suzerainty over Bosnia; this lasted until later in the century when some of Bosnia was incorporated into Croatia and some into Duklja (basically modern Montenegro). The Bosnian parts of Duklja seem to have seceded from Duklja in about 1101; soon thereafter, in 1137, Hungary annexed most or all of Bosnia, only to lose it to the Byzantine empire in 1167. But, in 1180, Hungary reasserted itself and by treaty regained its suzerainty over Bosnia, a suzerainty it claimed throughout the remainder of the Middle Ages, although it was usually just nominal.

The nominal side of it became apparent immediately after 1180, when Bosnia's ruler, Kulin, began to assert his independence. Kulin bore the title of *ban*, the title regularly held by Bosnia's rulers (whether independent or under foreign overlordship) from the mid-twelfth century until 1377, when Ban Tvrtko assumed the title of king.

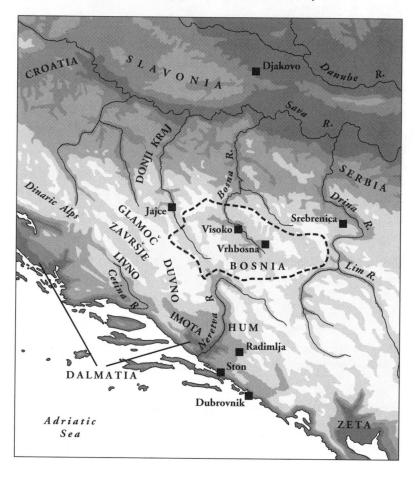

MAP 2.1 — THE EXTENT OF BOSNIA UNDER KULIN (C. 1200)

Although parts of Bosnia prior to 1180 had briefly found themselves in Serbian or Croatian units, neither neighbor had ruled the Bosnians long enough to acquire their loyalty or to establish any serious claim to Bosnia. And Bosnia seems to have been little affected by these foreign rulers. Kinnamos, a late twelfth-century Byzantine historian, reports that Bosnia of his day was not under the Grand Count of Serbia; rather the Bosnians had their own distinct way of life and government.

CONVERSIONS TO CHRISTIANITY

From the ninth century, Christian missions from Rome and Constantinople pushed into the Balkans; Rome won Croatia and most of Dalmatia, while Constantinople succeeded in Bulgaria, Macedonia, and eventually most of Serbia. Bosnia, lying in between, is often called a meeting ground between East and West. However, due to its mountainous terrain and poor communications, it was more a no-man's land between the two worlds. Before the middle of the eleventh century, despite jurisdictional rivalries, there was still a united Church. But the missions established lasting jurisdictional authority for their respective bishops over much of the Balkans in this early period. In so doing they determined which regions were to be Orthodox or Catholic after the Greek and Roman Churches split in the eleventh century. Bosnia, more superficially worked by the missions, along with Albania, did not end up permanently locked into either Church's camp but remained receptive to switches of faith.

In any case, though it was not to last, by the tenth century most Bosnians were probably nominally under Rome, having been converted by missionaries from the Dalmatian coast. In the twelfth century Bosnia's Catholic Church was under the Archbishop of Dubrovnik. However, its Catholicism was primitive; Bosnians did not know Latin and few were literate in any language. Thus surely there was much that the Pope would have found wrong in their Catholicism.

LOCALISM

Bosnia's mountains encouraged localism and division into various regions (e.g., the Podrina, Bosnia [the central part], Hum, Donji Kraj, etc.). Each region had its own local traditions and local nobility. These local traditions lasted throughout the Middle Ages and made the Ban of Bosnia's task of centralizing the country very difficult. Thus, periods of expansion were frequently followed by separatism. Different religious faiths, as we shall see, were also to dominate in different areas.

Central Bosnia, under Hungarian suzerainty, was governed by its ban; the regions to its north (but south of the Sava) were ruled into the fourteenth century by one or more bans of the same family also under Hungarian suzerainty. From 1168 to 1326 Hum (roughly modern Hercegovina) was separate from Bosnia under members of the Serbian royal family, the Nemanjić dynasty. Thus this region was under Serbian rule for an extensive period of time. The northern and central regions of Bosnia, as noted, were Catholic. However, Hum (except for its coastal regions around Ston, where there were also Catholics) belonged to the Serbian Orthodox Church and had its own Orthodox bishopric. From 1219, when the Serbian Church of Serbia became autocephalous (self-headed or autonomous in jurisdictional matters from, though still in communion with, the Patriarch of Constantinople), the Bishop of Hum was subordinated to the Archbishop of Serbia.

ESTABLISHMENT OF THE BOSNIAN CHURCH

The Hungarians, in the early thirteenth century, frustrated by Bosnia's assertion of independence, succeeded in making the flaws in Bosnia's Catholicism appear as heresy, giving them an excuse to meddle in the hope of reasserting their authority over Bosnia. When various ecclesiastical maneuvers failed, the Hungarians persuaded the Pope to declare a crusade and they invaded Bosnia, warring there between 1235 and 1241. They experienced gradual success, advancing as far south as Vrhbosna (modern Sarajevo) against stubborn resistance, until a Tatar attack on Hungary forced their withdrawal. The Hungarians then got the Pope to remove Bosnia's Catholic Church from the jurisdiction of the archbishop in Dubrovnik and subordinate it instead to a Hungarian archbishop. The Bosnians refused to comply, and drove the Hungarian-appointed bishop out of Bosnia. The official Catholic Bishop of Bosnia then took up residence in Djakovo in Slavonia (Croatia), where his successors remained throughout the Middle Ages, having no role whatsoever in Bosnia. The Bosnians, severing their ties with international Catholicism, then established their own independent Church, known as the Bosnian Church, in schism with Rome. Despite scholarly claims that the Bosnian Church was dualist, neo-Manichean, or Bogomil, the local evidence overwhelmingly shows that it retained its basic Catholic theology throughout the Middle Ages.

BOSNIAN EXPANSION UNDER KOTROMANIĆ

The Bosnian state became stronger under Ban Stjepan Kotromanić, who assumed office around 1318. He mended his relations with Hungary, and for much of his reign was basically an ally of the Hungarian king. He expanded his state by supporting Hungary against various Croatian nobles to Bosnia's north and west, taking for himself the territory west of his banate (the land between the Cetina and Neretva rivers) and Završje (including Imota, Duvno, Glamoč, and Livno). This territory was Catholic and had two Catholic bishoprics. The ban did not interfere with them, and they continued to function over their dioceses. After the death of King Milutin of Serbia in 1321, disorders followed among the Serbs of Serbia. As a result, Kotromanić was able to conquer Hum in 1326. Here, as noted,

MAP 2.2 — BOSNIAN EXPANSION UNDER KOTROMANIĆ (C. 1326)

most of the population was Orthodox. The ban did not interfere with Orthodox institutions either.

ESTABLISHMENT OF THE FRANCISCANS

Ban Stjepan Kotromanić next supported a Franciscan mission initiated in the 1340s against alleged "heresy" in Bosnia. There had been no Catholics — at least no Catholic clergy or organization — in the center of his state for nearly a century. By 1342

FIG. 2.1 — SEAL OF BOSNIAN KING OSTOJA FROM 1400

the Franciscan Vicariate of Bosnia was established; eventually its territory was to include all those parts of southeastern Europe where Franciscans worked.   By 1385 the Franciscans had four convents in Bosnia proper; another dozen were to be built before the Turkish conquest in 1463.   Throughout the Middle Ages and also the Turkish period (1463-1878), excluding a handful of court chaplains, the Franciscans were the only Catholic clergy in Bosnia proper.   By 1347 Stjepan Kotromanić had accepted Catholicism.   From then on, all Bosnia's medieval rulers, except possibly Ostoja (1398-1404, 1409-18), were to be Catholics.   Under Kotromanić, Bosnian mines (particularly lead and silver) were opened, paving the way for Bosnia's economic development and increasing its commercial contacts with the coast.   As a result, many merchants from Dubrovnik came; some settled, forming colonies.   These coastal merchants supported the Franciscans; the commercial towns that developed in Bosnia, dominated by these coastal merchants, were Catholic in character.

CHARACTER OF THE BOSNIAN CHURCH

What of the Bosnian Church? This institution was tolerated by the state even after the 1340s, when the Franciscan mission was established and the rulers became Catholic. Despite this toleration, the Bosnian Church did not play a major role in the state and was not a state Church. For most of its existence — other than occasionally allowing its leaders to witness charters — it had no political role. Such a role can be shown only early in the fifteenth century — particularly between 1403 and 1405 — when its leader, the *djed*, was an influential advisor at court. His influence at the time, besides whatever personal merits he had, was probably owing to the particular sympathy for his Church felt by Ostoja, the king at the time. Since after the 1340s all the other rulers of Bosnia were Catholics, it is not surprising that the Bosnian Church was not a major state institution. Though some scholars have argued that an alliance existed between the Bosnian Church and the nobility, this too is greatly exaggerated. Connections between the Church and specific noblemen can be shown for only about ten families; all these ties fall into the last seventy years of the state. For most of these nobles the known services rendered by the Church were limited to religious matters. For only a very small number did the Bosnian Church provide political or secular services (usually as diplomats or mediators of quarrels), and for only two families — the Kosače and Radenović-Pavlovići — did these ties last longer than one generation.

The Bosnian Church continued to exist — as a small organization in only parts of the state — until finally, in 1459, under papal pressure (papal aid against the Turks being conditional on persecuting the Bosnian Church), King Stefan Tomaš (1443-61) gave Bosnian Churchmen (presumably meaning the clergy) a choice of conversion or exile. Most accepted Catholicism — at least nominally — which shows that their morale was low. A minority sought refuge in Hercegovina with the ruler of that land, Herceg Stefan. Thus the Church, a weak institution throughout its existence, was weakened further on the eve of the Ottoman conquest. It disappeared entirely soon after that conquest, as its members were absorbed by Islam, Orthodoxy, and Catholicism.

Many scholars have depicted the Bosnian Church as dualist, calling it neo-Manichean or Bogomil. Domestic sources about that Church (both Bosnian and Dalmatian, in particular the rich documentation from Catholic Dubrovnik) do not suggest this. These sources show that, unlike the Bogomils or Western neo-Manichees, the Bosnian Church accepted an omnipotent God, the Trinity, church buildings, the cross, the cult of saints, religious art, and at least part of the Old Testament. Bulgarian and Greek Dualist Bogomils rejected all these items. Furthermore, had these Bosnians been Manichees, the cordial relations these sources depict between Bosnian Churchmen and both Orthodox and Catholic clerics and officials (including those from Dubrovnik and Hungary) could not have occurred.

THE SO-CALLED "BOGOMIL TOMBSTONES"

The most distinctive surviving cultural feature of medieval Bosnia and Hercegovina is the region's enormous, and often beautifully decorated, tombstones. In the late nineteenth century, scholars, seeing them as a specific cultural feature of Bosnia, concluded that they must be associated with Bosnia's other unique feature, the Bosnian Church. Believing that Church to be Bogomil, they labeled the stones "Bogomil tombstones." This label, convenient and appealing to nineteenth-

FIG 2.2 — MEDIEVAL TOMBSTONES FROM THE MILORADOVIĆ FAMILY
CEMETERY AT RADIMLJA, NEAR STOLAC IN HERCEGOVINA

century Austrian administrators — who sought to demonstrate
Bosnia's distinctiveness from its irredentist neighbors in Serbia
or Croatia — and also to the more recent local tourist industry,
remains common today. It is, however, totally inappropriate.
First, the Bosnian Church does not appear to have been Bogomil
or dualist. Second, inscriptions on a number of stones indicate
that they were erected by members of all three local denominations. Thus, those Catholics, Orthodox, and Bosnian Church
members who could afford it put up these stones. The knightly
elite was particularly prominent in erecting them. The most
varied and elaborate motifs were produced in Hercegovina. The
most famous cemetery there is at Radimlja near Stolac. In it
several stones portraying a warrior with a raised and enlarged

hand are to be found. Though often presented as the epitome of Bogomil art, this large-handed figure was no Bogomil; Radimlja was the family cemetery of an Orthodox clan, the Miloradovići. Thus, "Bosnian tombstone" is a far more fitting term, for the stones are a distinctive regional feature, produced by Bosnians and Hercegovinians alike, regardless of their Church affiliation. And after the Turkish conquest, many converts to Islam also erected stones which, despite being Turkish/Islamic in shape, continued to display various medieval Bosnian motifs and styles.

MEDIEVAL DISTRIBUTION OF DENOMINATIONS

Let us pause now to consider the identity labels that may be applied to medieval communities in Bosnia. If we exclude some people on the periphery of this expanded Bosnia (some in the north and west who might identify themselves as Croats and some in Hum who might call themselves Serbs or members of the Serbian Church), we do not find Bosnians calling themselves Serbs or Croats. If they wanted a major label, they called themselves Bosnians. We cannot say that they perceived this term as an ethnic one. More likely, it signified the geographical region they came from, indicated that they served the Bosnian state, or identified them as subjects of the Bosnian king. Often these people in Bosnia also used regional identity labels like Hum, Donji Kraj, etc.

When we turn to the geographical locations of the various religious groups, we find Catholics to the north and west of greater Bosnia — the areas Kotromanić annexed to his state — and, after the appearance of the Franciscans in the 1340s, we begin finding evidence of Catholics in the center of the state near the handful of Franciscan monasteries and in the commercial towns. In these towns, of course, foreign Catholic merchants and technicians connected to the mines were settled. We find Orthodox believers to the south and east, in Hum, and expanding gradually and on a small scale across the Drina into eastern Bosnia. We find the Bosnian Church in the center of the state with its institutions extending east to the Drina and south into Hum.

As the state expanded, the population did not move or mix to any significant extent. The distribution of confessions remained as just described throughout the Middle Ages. Rulers and nobles (unlike their contemporaries in most of Europe, including the nobility of Serbia and Croatia) were indifferent to religious issues. They intermarried and formed alliances across denominational lines; when it suited their worldly aims, they changed faiths easily. They made no attempt to proselytize for their own faiths or to persecute others, consciously resisting calls from the Pope or the Hungarians to persecute those of other faiths. The expansion of the state did not lead to the expansion of the Bosnian Church's area of operations, except for a small-scale push into Hum. Throughout this process, state expansion meant submission to the ruler by local notables, who continued to run their own areas. We do not find central administrators with entourages being sent out by the ban to govern far-flung provinces.

CHARACTER OF MEDIEVAL VIOLENCE AND WARFARE

Bosnia was involved in much warfare during the Middle Ages, both foreign and domestic. Its foreign adversaries were Serbia, Hungary, various neighboring Croatian nobles, and the Otto-man Turks. The domestic warfare took place among the nobles or between nobility and king; they fought over territory. Not once did medieval Bosnians fight one another as religious or ethnic groups.

Much of the violence in both the medieval and Ottoman periods was outright plundering and brigandage. Bosnia's mountains, with narrow roads running through passes, encouraged highwaymen, and thus brigandage was endemic, especially in Hercegovina. In that region, which has poor soil that discourages agricultural cultivation, pastoralism (primarily connected with sheep herding) was the predominant occupation in the more barren mountainous regions. There, families, organized as clans and tribes, raised horses as well as sheep and migrated in the course of a year over regular routes — which often needed defending — from the valleys in winter up to mountain pastures in the spring and summer. With their horses, they often led and guarded merchant caravans that traveled from Dubrovnik and other coastal cities through Hercegovina and Bosnia into the Balkan interior. While some clans led caravans, others found it more lucrative to plunder them, and one caravan's guards were another's plunderers. Organized as extended families, they fielded large mounted units which, in one way or another, lived off the passing merchants and fought for their pasture-lands and routes, which they defended through feuds. And when times were unsettled, as they were during the years of Turkish raiding and conquest, growing numbers of Bosnians retreated into the more secure mountains, establishing themselves against rivals by violence. Not surprisingly, armed clans rented themselves out, not only as guardians of caravans, but also as armed retainers for various noblemen and, at the time of the Turkish conquest, as auxiliaries to the Turkish armies. Some of these families received all sorts of privileges as a result, including the right to bear arms, despite their nominal Christianity, throughout the Turkish period. As among the Montenegrins and Ghegs of Northern Albania, the warrior ethos became deeply ingrained in many of the pastoralists, particularly among those of eastern Hercegovina; they frequently plundered or rose up against the local Muslim estate-holders and later opposed the Austrian state when they disliked its taxation and conscription policies. They are today playing an active part in the violence that is marking the end of Yugoslavia. As relatively uneducated armed hillsmen, with a hostility toward urban culture and the state institutions (including taxes) that go with it, they have proved susceptible to Serbian chauvinistic propaganda and have allowed themselves to be recruited into Serb paramilitary units. They make up a significant part of those who are today shelling Bosnia's cities.

ZENITH OF THE MEDIEVAL BOSNIAN STATE UNDER TVRTKO

Now, to return to Bosnia in the mid-fourteenth century: Kotromanić died in 1353 and was succeeded by his teen-age nephew Tvrtko I (1353-91). Kotromanić had established little state apparatus and generally left his vassals in outlying regions to administer their own lands. Thus Tvrtko lost control over much of his inheritance, but he succeeded in reassembling it by the early 1360s. Having reasserted his authority over the northern lands, he next began to meddle in the feuds of the Serbian nobility to Bosnia's southeast, and he was able to annex still more territory in 1374, including the Upper Drina and Lim regions. This gave him all of Hum and also most of what we now think of as the Sandžak. As a result of the acquisition of this Serbian territory and the extinction in Serbia in 1371 of the Nemanjić dynasty, to which Tvrtko belonged (for his grandfather had married the daughter of Serbia's King Stefan Dragutin Nemanjić), Tvrtko claimed the Serbian kingship. He was

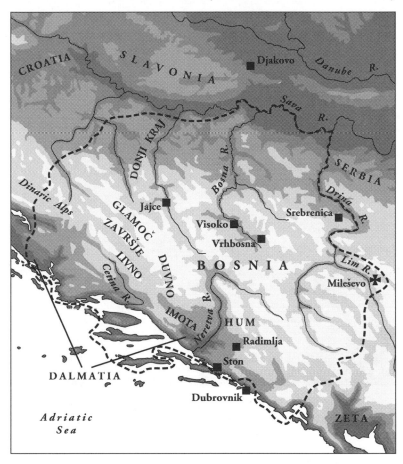

MAP 2.3 — THE MEDIEVAL BOSNIAN KINGDOM AT ITS GREATEST EXTENT
IN 1391, THE FINAL YEAR OF TVRTKO'S REIGN

crowned King of Serbia and Bosnia in 1377 at the Serbian
Orthodox monastery of Mileševo on the recently conquered
Lim. From then on, the rulers of Bosnia, instead of being bans,
were kings and bore this double title even though they held very
little Serbian territory. Tvrtko then participated in a civil war
over the Hungarian throne, which drew into the fray on one side
or the other many Croatian nobles. By playing his cards well,
Tvrtko succeeded in acquiring considerable Croatian territory,

FIG. 2.3 — ORTHODOX MONASTERY OF MILEŠEVO WHERE TVRTKO WAS
CROWNED AS FIRST KING OF BOSNIA IN 1377

including several Dalmatian cities. By 1390 Tvrtko had added
"Croatia and Dalmatia" to his royal title.

BOSNIA IN THE EARLY FIFTEENTH CENTURY

In the fifteenth century, feuds between king and nobles became
commonplace. More and more frequently the expanding Ottoman Turks involved themselves in these conflicts, as did the
Hungarians, occasionally allied with the rulers of Serbia. As a
result, on occasion, a frequently victorious Hungary assigned
territory on the Bosnian side of the Drina to the Serbian ruler
(especially the rich silver mine of Srebrenica); when Srebrenica

FIG. 2.4 — THE BELL TOWER OF ST. LUKE'S (JAJCE), A CATHOLIC CHURCH
BUILT IN THE LAST DECADES OF THE MEDIEVAL BOSNIAN KINGDOM

was lost, the Bosnians refused to recognize Serbian possession of
it, and many clashes occurred between Serbia and Bosnia over it.
Ethnic differences played no part in any of this warfare. Thus
matters of detail do not bear on present Serb or Croat claims.

FIG. 2.5 — HERCEG STEFAN'S FORTRESS OF BLAGAJ (MID-FIFTEENTH
CENTURY), NEAR MOSTAR IN HERCEGOVINA

In the 1430s the Franciscans increased their numbers and
activities in Bosnia, building several new monasteries. In this
and the following decade, a number of new Catholic churches
were erected, and many nobles accepted Catholicism. The
towns in which the Franciscans were actively operating, a high
percentage of whose populations were Catholic merchants from
the coast, were essentially Catholic. Despite Catholic gains, the
Bosnian Church, whose monasteries were chiefly rural, continued to be tolerated. The Orthodox Church maintained its
dominance in Hum even though the leading family of Hum
supported the Bosnian Church.

THE OTTOMAN CONQUEST

In the 1430s, too, as Ottoman pressure increased against Serbia,
Serb refugees began fleeing into eastern Bosnia; thus the number of Serbs/Orthodox in the region between the Drina and
what is now Sarajevo increased. In 1448 Stefan Vukčić Kosača

FIG. 2.6 — SKETCH OF JAJCE, MEDIEVAL BOSNIA'S LAST CAPITAL

of Hum, to assert his independence, dropped his title Vojvoda of Bosnia, which reflected his subordination to the Bosnian king, and took the title Herceg (Duke) of Hum and the Coast. The following year, he changed it to Herceg of St. Sava (a Serbian saint whose relics were at the monastery of Mileševo on the Herceg's lands). Soon his lands became known as

Hercegovina, a name the Turks also used; this name has lasted to the present. Meanwhile Ottoman pressure increased against Bosnia, and the Ottomans started picking off parts of eastern Bosnia. In 1451 they took Vrhbosna. That town, bearing the name it acquired under the Ottomans of Sarajevo, was to grow into the major city in Bosnia during the Turkish period.

In 1463, using the Bosnian king's increasing ties with the papacy and Hungary as an excuse, the Ottomans launched a massive surprise attack against Bosnia. Bosnia's defense was poorly managed and the whole kingdom fell in a matter of weeks; the last king, Stefan Tomašević, was captured and beheaded. At the campaign's end, the Ottomans withdrew part of their conquering forces, which allowed the Hungarians to attack and briefly recover parts of it. However, this recovery did not last, and by the end of 1465 the Ottomans had regained most of Bosnia, although the last fortress in Hercegovina did not fall until 1481, and in Bosnia a Hungarian garrison in Jajce actually held out until 1527. A major reason for the Hungarians' failure was the long-standing hostility of many leading Bosnians toward Hungary, owing to its frequent attempts over the years to eliminate Bosnian independence and to force Catholicism upon the Bosnians of other faiths. This animosity is illustrated by the fact that after Bosnia initially fell in 1463, a group of Bosnian nobles visited Venice, seeking Venetian aid. They expressed their willingness to submit to Venetian overlordship; however, they added that under no circumstances would they consider submitting to Hungary. In fact, rather than do that, they — all of whom were Christians — preferred to remain under the Ottomans.

3

Religious Change and Bosnia's Distinct Situation under the Ottomans

·

THE OTTOMAN CONQUEST ushered Bosnia into a period of large-scale religious changes, the most significant one being the large number of conversions to Islam. The old scholarly explanation of how this occurred, which was a great oversimplification, has unfortunately become widely accepted by many Bosnians to-day; in particular, it has become the popular Muslim view of that community's own past. This view has three main ingredients: (1) The Bosnian Church was Bogomil. We have already shown that this was almost certainly not the case, though probably a majority of Yugoslav scholars still hold to it. (2) The majority of Bosnians were members of the Bosnian Church (or, as they would put it, were Bogomils). This statement on the size of Bosnian Church membership is surely a great exaggeration. (3) At the time of the conquest the Bogomils, frustrated by Catholicism and in particular by the persecutions from king and Catholic Church in the final years of the kingdom, passed over immediately and en masse to Islam. We shall now examine this final point, and show that it too is wrong. First, no conversions occurred en masse at the time of the conquest; conversions were a long drawn-out, gradual process. Secondly, Bosnian Churchmen converted not only to Islam but also to the two other Christian faiths. Finally, many Catholics and Ortho-dox also became Muslims. But this three-point theory was useful to modern Muslims, and, by making them descendants of members of medieval Bosnia's alleged dominant religion, it showed they were not new-comers and gave their community greater legitimacy.   This idea was also encouraged by the Austrians after they occupied Bosnia in 1878, for they too wanted to build up the authority of the Muslim community and, by leaning on local Muslims, reduce the influence of the local Serbs — at the time, both the largest and the most articulate, nationally-aware ethnic community in Bosnia.

Now let us examine the various religious communities in Bosnia under the Ottomans.   Since religious changes in the Ottoman period emerged from the medieval situation, I must recapitulate certain key items from the Middle Ages.   Bosnia had three faiths, and each existed only in particular geographical areas: Catholics to the north, west, and from the 1340s the center (especially in towns); the Orthodox in the south and east; and the Bosnian Church in the center, extending east to the Drina and south along the Neretva River into Hum.   The Catholic and Bosnian Churches were almost entirely based in monasteries, and for all practical purposes had no secular clergy in Bosnia.   Both Catholics and Bosnian Churchmen had few churches, and the ones they had were small.   They had very few clerics and, because those they had were concentrated in monasteries, these few clerics were clustered into a limited number of places.   By 1400 there were only twenty to thirty Franciscans in the whole state (this was basically the sum total of Catholic clergy), divided among four monasteries.   By the time of the conquest (1463), there were about twelve monasteries, but it is doubtful that they had more than a total of seventy-five or eighty Franciscans spread among them.   Thus large areas existed with no clergy at all.   Neither Catholics nor Bosnian Churchmen had a territorial organization, e.g., a figure like a bishop responsible for a province or diocese. The Bosnian Church had no bishops in a territorial sense. The Catholics did in theory, but the Bishop of Bosnia lived outside of Bosnia in Slavonia and had no role in Bosnia proper. Thus many peasants probably rarely or never saw a priest, and peasants tend to be indifferent to formal religion if it is not pressed on them. The Orthodox, though they had bishops and some secular priests, also had a fairly limited number of churches and clerics in their areas. Thus no faith had a strong organization to bind its flock to the Church, either through faith/beliefs or a sense of community.

RELIGIOUS CHANGE UNDER THE OTTOMANS

The Ottoman conquest brought changes in population and religion. First it is important to note that the Ottomans did not categorize people by ethnicity. They did not speak of Serbs, Croats, Bosnians, et al., but of religious groups; thus we find people recorded only under religious labels. From the start we see signs of Islamization in Bosnia, but the Muslim presence appeared on the scene gradually, slowly but steadily increasing through the late fifteenth and sixteenth centuries. Islamization in the first stages came both from migration and settlement of Muslims from elsewhere and from conversion. In the long run, conversion of locals was by far the major source of Bosnia's Muslims, the great majority of whom are thus descended from local Serbo-Croatian-speaking converts. At the time of the conquest there was a large-scale out-migration of Catholics who fled to the still unconquered Catholic regions of Croatia and Dalmatia. They vacated lands that were subsequently settled partly by newcomer Muslims, but also by Orthodox Serbs. These Serbs had started fleeing into Bosnia in the decades of

Ottoman pressure on Serbia (which fell before Bosnia). Further Orthodox/Serb migration into Bosnia was encouraged by the Turks after their conquest, for they wanted vacated lands to be settled. Some of these Orthodox or Serb migrants came not from Serbia but from Hercegovina, whose soil was poorer than Bosnia's. These migrations carried some Serbs beyond the borders of Bosnia, up into Croatia. In the seventeenth and eighteenth centuries, Habsburg authorities settled some of these Serbs' descendants as colonists in the Krajina by offering them — in exchange for military service along the frontier with the Ottomans — land, limited self-rule, and free exercise of the Orthodox faith. For many years these Serbs played a major role as mainstays of the Croatian Military Frontier, defending Christendom against the expansion of Islam. The Serbs in the Krajina — who are today in revolt against the new separatist state of Croatia and who seek secession from, or autonomy within, what has turned out to be a chauvinist polity, defining itself as a state of Croats rather than a territorial state of Croatia — are descended from these migrants.

The most noticeable religious change in Bosnia was from Christianity to Islam. But on closer examination we find that Bosnia was marked by religious change in general. If we look at Bosnia and Hercegovina in about 1550, we see not only many Muslims but also many Orthodox, and the Orthodox are found all across Bosnia and in many places where they were not found earlier, for, as we recall, in medieval Bosnia, the Orthodox were found only in the Drina region and in Hum. The spread of the Orthodox was partly from the migrations noted, but the Orthodox also gained from large numbers of conversions of Bosnian Church members and Catholics to Orthodoxy, for Orthodoxy was the Christian group favored by the Ottomans.

One can easily see why the Ottomans preferred the Orthodox to the Catholics. The Orthodox head, the Patriarch of
Constantinople, lived in the Ottoman capital, where he was
easily controlled. His whole hierarchy lived within the empire.
The Pope lived in Rome, outside the empire, and was the main
sponsor of crusades against the Ottomans. The papacy had
launched a crusade in 1443-44 and Pope Pius II (1458-64) was
trying, though unsuccessfully, to get a new one launched at the
time of the Ottoman conquest of Bosnia. The Franciscans were
seen as a potential fifth column. Evidence of the Ottomans
favoring the Orthodox may be found in contemporary court
records. Certain towns had one church building from the
Middle Ages, a Catholic one. Newly arriving Orthodox would
take over the building. The Catholics, wanting to keep it,
would complain to the Turkish judge (the *kadi*). The kadi
regularly decided for the Orthodox. The Orthodox Church
received Ottoman permission to collect Church taxes from
Christians. Their collectors demanded taxes from the Catholics
too. Faced with double taxation, their own tithes as well as the
Orthodox taxes, the Catholics would appeal to the kadi. The
kadi would then order them to pay the Orthodox clerics the
sums those clerics demanded. Ottoman law allowed no new
churches to be built and required special permission from the
government to repair dilapidated ones. We find in the sixteenth
century the Orthodox in Bosnia and Hercegovina building
many new churches, whereas Catholics with the greatest diffi-
culty — and only sometimes — received permission to repair
dilapidated ones. A noted example of such an Orthodox church
being erected is the Old Orthodox Church in Sarajevo, completed in 1530. Thus there were many reasons for Catholics (or
for members of the small and declining Bosnian Church) who

FIG. 3.1 — THE OLD ORTHODOX CHURCH IN SARAJEVO,
COMPLETED IN 1530

wanted to stay Christian to become Orthodox. They could pay a single Church tax and could attend services in the now Orthodox local church building — which in many cases for the Catholics was the building they were accustomed to attending.

But in any case conversion was a large-scale and multi-directional phenomenon. We find Bosnian Church members converting to Islam, Orthodoxy, and Catholicism and, as a result, disappearing from the scene entirely. We find Catholics greatly declining in numbers, with many migrating out but also with some converting to Islam and others to Orthodoxy. We find Orthodoxy gaining in numbers, but still losing some of its members, particularly to Islam, but even a few to Catholicism. Thus religious change was a general multi-directional phenomenon; Islam certainly won the most new converts, but Orthodoxy won many. Islam had various advantages, of course: it was the religion of the conquering state, and there were worldly advantages in lining up with the new rulers' faith, first and foremost lower taxes. Moreover, the worldly success of Islam would have seemed to be a sign of God's favor.

However, it is worth noting in this context that the theory as to the motivation for the conversions that was long popular with scholars — namely that many of Bosnia's medieval land-holders converted to Islam to retain their lands and positions — has not stood the test of time. For there is no evidence in the sources of any continuity in families between Bosnia's medieval and its post-conquest Muslim landed aristocracy. The two most prominent converts, a son of the last king and a son of Herceg Stefan, both received high Ottoman administrative posts, but not in Bosnia. The king's son became a governor in Anatolia and Herceg Stefan's son, after holding various non-Bosnian posts, rose to the top of the central administration as Grand Vizier under Sultan Selim I.

We also note that changing religion occurred at a gradual rate, and the speed of it varied from place to place. The *defters* (Turkish cadasters or tax registers) show both the gradualness of and variation in this process. First, let us take the Bosnian town of Lepenica over time as an example of the gradualness of Islamization; the defters, it should be noted, do not distinguish between Orthodox and Catholics. (See TABLE 3.1).

The variation in the balance between Christians and Muslims can be seen in the 1485 survey. (See TABLE 3.2). The defters of 1528/29 illustrate the gains Islam had made by that time. However, Christians were still in the majority. (See TABLE 3.3). Islam was to acquire a majority, and then it was to be a small one, only in the seventeenth century. By the time the Austrians occupied Bosnia in 1878, the Muslims had lost their majority position.

TABLE 3.1 — GRADUAL NATURE OF ISLAMIZATION IN LEPENICA

Date of survey	Christian householders	Muslim householders
1468	279	0
1485	329	18
1489	165	65
1509	160	393

TABLE 3.2 — VARIATION IN CHRISTIAN AND MUSLIM NUMBERS,
SARAJEVO-AREA VILLAGES IN 1485

Town	Christian householders	Muslim householders
Dolac	84	13
Hodidjed	35	9
Glavogodina	3	29
Doljani	19	16
Butmir	21	14
Otes	3	17
Presjenica	38	39

The estimates from official Catholic Visitation reports also provide information on religious change. They give estimated numbers of individuals rather than households. (See TABLE 3.4). Again and again Catholic Visitors, to explain Catholic losses, stress the shortage of priests, the ignorance of the existing ones, and the indifference of local bishops.

Why did so many changes in religious confession occur in Bosnia and Hercegovina and not elsewhere in the Balkans (except for Albania)? The reason I suggest is not hard to find and has nothing to do with the content of beliefs of the former Bosnian Church, even though such a view is commonly ad-

TABLE 3.3 — DEFTERS OF 1528/29 FOR WHOLE AREA (IN HOUSEHOLDS)

Region	Christian households	Muslim households
Sandžak of Bosnia	19,619	16,935
Sandžak of Zvornik	13,112	2,654
Sandžak of Hercegovina	9,588	7,077

TABLE 3.4 — FOREIGN OFFICIALS' IMPRESSIONS OF CHRISTIAN AND MUSLIM NUMBERS IN BOSNIA , 17TH - 19TH CENTURIES

Date	Name	Muslims	Catholics	Orthodox
1624	Masarecci*	900,000	300,000	150,000
1626	Georgijevich	(less than Christians combined)	250,000	(more than Catholics)
1655	Maravich	(majority)	73,000	(no figure)
1809	French consul	600,000	120,000	500,000

His estimate: just Bosnia, minus Hercegovina

vanced. The fact is that by and large the Bosnians had never been strong Christians. If one looks at Serbia, Croatia, Bulgaria, and Greece, one finds well-organized state Churches, with large and thriving monasteries, and an active episcopal structure, commanding considerable loyalty. One also finds that in each of these areas one Church organization existed without rivals, linked closely to the state and/or the nobility. In Bosnia, instead of there being a single well-organized Church as elsewhere in the Balkans, there existed three rival organizations, all of which were weak. No Church in Bosnia or Hercegovina had ever had a strong territorial organization, and all three were very short of priests. Moreover, all the discovered church buildings from medieval Bosnia were too small to accommodate congregations of any size. This suggests that the nobles, who presumably erected them, built them as family chapels and did not expect the local peasant population to attend. Thus even those who lived near a church building may rarely or possibly never have attended it. As a result, few Christians were deeply attached to any Christian Church or religious community, be it through belief or through sense of community.

After 1463 Islam appeared on the scene. It was a dynamic, well-preached new religion, having the advantage of being the religion of the conquering state. So, it is hardly surprising in such a region, where Christianity had been poorly organized and generally ineffectively preached, to find that people lacking strong religious attachments would have been open to accepting a new faith. And, since the Bosnians had long been shaky Christians, who had dealt with the Turks for half a century before the conquest, they had no strong prejudices against Muslims. Moreover, in many cases, religious motives may not have been predominant in causing people to accept the new faith. And, finally, *acceptance* is a better word than *conversion* to describe what occurred in Bosnia. Probably few Bosnians in accepting Islam underwent any deep changes in patterns of thought or way of life. Most of those who became Muslims probably continued to live as they always had, retaining most of their domestic customs and many Christian practices. They adopted with conversion a few Islamic practices, which quickly would have acquired great symbolic value and would soon have come to be viewed as the essentials of Islam.

BOSNIAN MUSLIMS' ROLE IN THE OTTOMAN STATE

The political history of Bosnia during the Ottoman period, from 1463 to 1878, can be covered relatively briefly, since Bosnians, as provincials in a large empire, were part of a larger-scale enterprise whose major decisions were reached elsewhere. And even though Muslim Bosnians, as we shall see, had a major role in internal matters, they still had to share power with the Sultan's officials, who usually, when push came to shove, forced upon them what the Sultan wanted. Other Bosnians rose to high positions in the central government and religious institutions of the empire and had great impact there. But in these roles they acted not as Bosnians but as Ottomans and thus were not figures of local history.

CAREER AND ACHIEVEMENTS OF MEHMET SOKULLU

However, such people could have major effects on the local level, most commonly through endowing mosques, schools, and baths in their home towns. A fine case in point, that was to benefit the Christians in particular, is seen in the actions of Mehmet Sokullu (Sokolović). Mehmet was an Orthodox Christian child from Višegrad on the Bosnian side of the Drina. He was rounded up in the child levy, an Ottoman institution by which Christian children were taken from their families, converted to Islam, and assigned, according to their qualifications, to particular military units or to the palace service. Demonstrating ability, he went through the palace school in Istanbul and was placed in the Ottoman administration. Through talent, patronage, and luck he was eventually appointed *Grand Vizier,* the highest administrative office below the Sultan. (A Grand Vizier is roughly equivalent to a prime minister, though one must keep in mind that such a prime minister served only as

FIG. 3.2 — THE BRIDGE ON THE DRINA

long as he kept the favor of an autocratic Sultan.) In any case, Mehmet remembered his hometown, Višegrad, which he honored by ordering and carrying out the building there of the magnificent bridge over the Drina, linking the province of Bosnia with that of Serbia. (This bridge is the center-piece of the Nobel Prize winner Ivo Andrić's magnificent novel, *The Bridge on the Drina*.)

He also remembered his former co-religionists. In the Middle Ages the Serbian Church had been autocephalous. It had had its own patriarch who resided in the city of Peć, in present-day Kosovo. (An autocephalous Church, as noted above, while remaining in communion with the other Orthodox Churches, had jurisdictional independence, but lacked the right to alter doctrine, the protection of which remained with the Patriarch of Constantinople.) Owing to the piecemeal nature of the Ottoman conquest, the territory that had been under the medieval Serbian Church became divided between different superior bishops. In the last quarter of the fifteenth century the southern Serbian lands, which had fallen to the Ottomans earlier, were under the Archbishop of Ohrid in Macedonia. Ohrid's territory included the see of Peć, whose patriarch had been reduced to the rank of bishop and placed under Ohrid. The later conquests (northern Serbia, Bosnia, Hercegovina, and Montenegro) were placed in a separate diocese. In the 1520s, a power struggle ensued between the two bishoprics, which came to involve the Patriarch of Constantinople and various local Ottoman officials. In 1557 Grand Vizier Mehmet Sokullu intervened and resolved the situation by restoring Peć and Ohrid to their preconquest positions. Providing them with the territory of their medieval dioceses, he recreated, with autocephaly, the Archbishopric of Ohrid (over the Slavs of Macedonia) and the Serbian Patriarchate of Peć. The latter held not only its former dioceses in what had been Serbia but also all the Orthodox dioceses in Bosnia and Hercegovina.

Mehmet clearly obtained patronage over the newly restored Patriarchate of Peć. The first three patriarchs were drawn from his own family, first his brother (Makarije) and then in turn two nephews (Antonije and Gerasim). Other family members were to acquire bishoprics in Hercegovina at this time. Thus,

FIGS. 3.3 AND 3.4 — THE BROTHERS SOKOLOVIĆ, MEHMET (OTTOMAN GRAND VIZIER) AND MAKARIJE (PATRIARCH OF THE RESTORED SERBIAN CHURCH)

this Muslim convert from Bosnia still remembered his childhood community (and especially his own family) and promulgated a reform that was greatly to improve the conditions under which its members could practice their Orthodox religion.

BOSNIA AS AN OTTOMAN PROVINCE

After the conquest, Bosnia and Hercegovina were divided into three separate districts (or *sandžaks*) that were included within the greater province (or *beglerbeglik*) of Rumeli under the *beglerbeg* in Sofia. The three Bosnian *sandžaks*, each under a *sandžak-beg*, were: Bosnia (whose headquarters were at first in Sarajevo, which had been conquered in 1451, a decade before the main conquest of Bosnia); Zvornik (which included the eastern part of present-day Serbia); and Hercegovina (whose headquarters were established in Foča in 1470 but were moved to Plevlja in 1572 where they remained until 1833). The sandžak-begs were appointed by the Sultan (as were all Ottoman governors, in-

MAP 3.1 — THE THREE LONG-STANDING *SANDŽAKS* OF THE
BOSNIAN *VILAYET* (c. 1560): BOSNIA, ZVORNIK, AND HERCEGOVINA

cluding the higher beglerbegs) and sent out from Istanbul to the
Balkans for relatively short terms with no set tenure.

Around 1554 the Ottomans reorganized their provincial
administrative structure. Bosnia was upgraded to a
beglerbeglik. Its governor became a beglerbeg; he was soon to be
regularly called a *vizier* or *vali*. Although historians frequently
refer to the holder of this position as a *pasha* and to Bosnia as a
pashalik, "pasha" was a court or state rank (like "general") and

not the title attached to the governorship of Bosnia. The word "pashalik" simply refers to the possessions of a man bearing the title "pasha;" it would include not only the territory he governed, but also his private estates, wherever they might lie. Thus we shall refer to the governor after 1554 as the "vizier." The sandžaks of Hercegovina and Zvornik remained sandžaks under sandžak-begs after the administrative reorganization. But they were removed from the jurisdiction of the Rumeli beglerbeg and placed in the new super-province of Bosnia, whose vizier oversaw the activities of the sandžak-begs. Also placed in the Bosnian beglerbeglik at the time was the Ottoman territory to Bosnia's west, consisting of the three sandžaks of Bihać, Lika, and Klis. Sandžak status for the first two was brief; only that of Klis, with variable borders, still existed in 1700. The beglerbeg (and on a smaller scale the sandžak-beg) came to his post with a large entourage of state officials (e.g., a treasurer) appointed by the Sultan; whatever troops the Sultan assigned him; and his personal retainers, including an armed bodyguard, personal servants, and secretaries. Together, the beglerbeg and the officials comprised the local governing council (or *divan*); they were responsible for the defense of the province, for local law and order, for tax collection, and for the recruitment of Muslims for the army in the numbers the central government required.

GROWTH OF SARAJEVO

After the conquest Bosnia found itself a frontier province, and its governor (then a sandžak-beg) made Vrhbosna his main residence. His residential quarters were called his *saraj*, and by the end of the fifteenth century the whole town was coming to be called Sarajevo. Under the Ottomans Sarajevo grew from a small town with a fort into not only the largest city in Bosnia,

FIG. 3.5 — THE GAZI-HUSREFBEG MOSQUE IN SARAJEVO

but also one of the largest and most important cities in Ottoman Europe. It ranked alongside Thessaloniki and Edirne in
size and importance, eclipsed only by Istanbul itself. Sarajevo

soon acquired all the features of an Ottoman urban center. Its most splendid buildings, including the magnificent *Begova Džamija* (the Beg's Mosque), were built under Gazi-Husref Beg, a dashing and brilliant general who served on three occasions as Bosnia's sandžak-beg between 1521 and 1541. Islamic religious and educational institutions were established. Unsurprisingly, considering the city's glamour and vital Islamic institutions, many Christians in the region converted to Islam. Many other Christians in and around the city, however, did not, and between 1515 and 1530 the Orthodox were allowed to build their own church in town. Both of these impressive sixteenth-century religious buildings were still standing and active until 1992.

As the Ottoman empire expanded up through Croatia into Hungary (conquering Budapest in 1541), the seat of the governor moved to Banja Luka, closer to the action. The Beg, whose title had been upgraded to beglerbeg/vizier or vali in about 1554, was to have his headquarters there from 1583 to 1640. Sarajevo, however, remained the most important city for religious, including educational, institutions; its kadi was upgraded to the rank of *mulla* in 1578, a promotion which placed him over the other religious judges of Bosnia. By 1750 Bosnia was divided into nineteen *kadiliks* (religious court districts under kadis). Sarajevo, by far the largest city in Bosnia, was also the center for both commerce and crafts. An elaborate guild organization was established. The guild leaders were local notables and, along with the local landed elite, were active in city affairs until the guilds (which had become bases of local resistance) were abolished by the central government in 1850. Sarajevo was unlike most other Bosnian towns in that its local urban elite (mer-

chants and guild leaders) participated in functions usually monopolized by the landed elite.

ROLE OF THE LANDED ELITE IN BOSNIA

Many of the families of the landed elite were descended from
members of the Ottoman military class who received their lands
in exchange for military service. As relatively wealthy Muslim
warriors, often with retainers, they were from the start in a
position to influence local affairs. Over time, members of this
class of military estate-holders were able by hook or by crook to
convert their conditional estates or fiefs (*timars*) into more or
less free holdings. The successful ones were also able to increase
their estates through grants, seizures, and purchase. Thus, not
surprisingly, the wealthier ones, many of who remained active
in the military, were able to acquire enormous influence in their
own regions and to dominate those local matters about which
the central government did not concern itself. Sarajevo was
unusual because its leading commercial figures succeeded in
acquiring enough clout to share local power with the landed
elite.

THE *KAPETANS*

The most important of the local landed warriors commanded
fortresses scattered around Bosnia and Hercegovina in various
locations, where the Ottomans had not established permanent
garrisons drawn from professional soldiers. With their retainers, they kept local order and defended their territories from
Habsburg raiders and brigands. Thus these local Bosnian
fortress commanders, each usually bearing the title of *kapetan*,
were a major part of the local defense structure, with *berats* (or
charters) of appointment from the Sultan.

Some of the kapetans seem to have made themselves hereditary holders of this position. In the seventeenth century, when
Bosnia again found itself a province bordering the Habsburg
lands, their importance grew.   In 1730 there were thirty
kapetanijes (captainates) in Bosnia and Hercegovina; by 1800
there were thirty-eight. As local strong-men with armed retainers and responsibility for local order, they set up jails and were
able through purchase and sometimes through seizure and
other illegal means to increase their land holdings. Needless to
say they became very powerful in their regions and, when
unsupervised, which was much of the time, were more or less
autonomous "princes." However, since they also had to worry
about maintaining their independence against encroachment
from the state administration, some appreciated the need for
loyal support from their locality, and cultivated good relations
with those whose support seemed valuable (including at times
Christians, who were to be found in some of the kapetans'
armed retinues in the nineteenth century); thus this need limited the local license of some of them. Though some kapetans
were locals holding particular fortresses over several genera-
tions, others were appointees of the Bosnian vizier.   Thus
throughout the eighteenth century, records show the vizier
appointing and removing kapetans, and sometimes transferring
them from one fortress to another. In some cases their tenure at
a particular post was quite short.

ROLE OF LOCAL MUSLIMS IN OTTOMAN BOSNIA

In any case, in the early seventeenth century, with the vizier
based in Banja Luka (though he frequently did visit Sarajevo
and carry out official business from there), and only a deputy for
him in Sarajevo, the local Muslim elite came to play an ever-
increasing role in local affairs.

As the balance of power in Europe shifted, the Habsburgs started to roll back Ottoman gains. In 1699, as a result of the Treaty of Karlowitz, the Habsburgs regained most of Croatia, and the Sava River became the Ottoman-Habsburg border. Several decades before the treaty, in 1640, the vizier had already moved his seat back to Sarajevo. Once again a frontier province, Bosnia became extremely important. Since much of the local population was Muslim, Bosnians played an active role in the defense of Bosnia and also in the regular Ottoman army. As a result, the local Bosnian notables (*ayans*) came to play a greater role in local administration than did the indigenous population in areas where conversions were rarer. Local ayans were regularly consulted by the vizier and from 1735 attended at least once a year an all-Bosnian meeting with his divan. One should not exaggerate the degree of consultation, however, for it is evident that on occasion the vizier convoked them as an efficient means of presenting the commands he expected them to carry out. The viziers and province-wide officials, moreover, remained outsiders, centrally appointed. It is clear, however, that the Ottoman government tried to avoid offending the local Muslims, who zealously defended their province from the Christian Habsburgs on their border. Thus presumably the state officials did not supervise too closely the relations between local Muslim landlords and their Christian peasants. Moreover, local ayans (often in local councils) had considerable roles in town government.

THE JANISSARIES

By the eighteenth century the local elite in several of the larger towns, especially of Sarajevo, included the Janissaries. No longer raised by the child levy, the Janissaries had become a hereditary caste of soldiers. They were also, by then, being

FIG. 3.6 — A JANISSARY COMMANDER, EIGHTEENTH CENTURY

transferred from one army assignment to another less often; as a result, many were becoming more or less permanently attached to a particular garrison. In 1751, 961 of them were manning the fortress of Sarajevo. Though they were locals, their *aga* (or commander) was sent out from Istanbul by the Sultan. He was frequently caught between his armed charges and the instructions he received from the Sultan or Bosnian vizier. The Janissaries were also heavily involved in trade as well as in acquiring lands. Armed and unruly, and usually more interested in their economic activities than in fighting, they were becoming less and less useful to the state as a military force. Acquiring their broad privileges through birth, there were in the mid-eighteenth century some 78,000 of them in Bosnia, of whom only 16,000 were registered and receiving salaries (which

FIG. 3.7 — COMMANDER OF THE BOSNIAN VIZIER'S GUARD, c. 1730

were often years in arrears) and hence in theory owing service; they resisted training, and when they went on campaign, they were undisciplined and lived off the land, a serious problem when campaigning against Austrians within Bosnia.

THE VIZIERS MOVE TO TRAVNIK

In 1698 the vizier moved to the small town of Travnik. Most Yugoslav scholars interpret this as a triumph of the local Bosnian Muslims (particularly those of Sarajevo) over the vizier and central administration. Seeing this move as an exile of the vizier, they argue that the local *Sarajlije* (as the people of Sarajevo refer to themselves) ran their city and its region themselves with the vizier's deputy having only a minimal role. We do not know why the vizier changed his residence, though his action followed a major Austrian raid in 1697 that burned down

FIG. 3.8 — A NINETEENTH-CENTURY SKETCH OF TRAVNIK, SEAT OF THE
BOSNIAN VIZIERS FROM 1698 TO 1850

much of Sarajevo. Presumably, the need for a new residence
prompted the move, but one might have expected it to have
been temporary until his quarters in Sarajevo could be rebuilt.
Against the idea that the local Sarajevo elite decided to assert
itself and prevent the vizier from reestablishing his residence in
town is the fact that the viziers throughout the eighteenth
century tended to be capable figures who fulfilled their main
task of collecting taxes and recruiting soldiers effectively. Thus
they obtained what the state wanted. Presumably, if they had
wanted to return to Sarajevo, they would have done so. And
since, during most of the eighteenth century, things worked out
well with the vizier residing in Travnik, there was no particular
reason for him to live in Sarajevo. And what is important to
stress, on the main issues of bolstering Islam and defending the

province against its Christian enemies, vizier and ayans shared similar interests. Thus it is possibly appropriate to regard cooperation between the vizier and the Sarajevo ayans, rather than rivalry and conflict, as the norm for the eighteenth century.

TENSIONS BETWEEN LOCAL MUSLIMS AND THE OTTOMAN STATE

In the nineteenth century things were to change, and a model of conflict between Bosnians and the central state (represented by the vizier) becomes more apt. At this time the Ottoman state, seeking to reverse its decay and to maintain peace with the Great Powers who were demanding rights for Christians, began a program of reforms. Many of these changes threatened the dominance of Muslims in society, and conservative Ottoman Muslims (including most leading Bosnians) opposed them. They also felt that many of the reforms would weaken rather than strengthen the state, and they resented being pushed around by the Christian Great Powers. Moreover, some of the reforms cut into their local privileges. For among other things, to strengthen his state, the Sultan sought to rationalize and standardize his administration, and in particular to modernize his army. A standardized system run from the center would leave little room for private defense forces like those of some of the kapetans and might also look more closely at landholding titles. Moreover, the Janissaries refused to accept any of the proposed changes in their status and duties. So, the Sultan, after threats and much consideration, finally in 1826 decided to abolish the whole order. The Janissaries in Bosnia refused to accept this edict and, as part of the local elite, elicited considerably sympathy for their cause.

Thus in this period, Bosnians on various occasions (and particularly after the ban on the Janissaries) actively resisted implementing reforms; as a result viziers were sent in with beefed-up armed retinues and orders to enforce the given reforms, and clashes occurred between viziers and locals. Thus in these years, particularly in the second quarter of the nineteenth century, we do find growing tension and an increasing number of clashes between vizier (and the Ottoman state the vizier represented) and the local Bosnians, who saw their customary way of life being threatened by reforms, which they also felt could only weaken the state and the position of Islam within it. Thus the picture of a vizier isolated out in Travnik, while the Sarajlije acted as they chose in their city, until a provoked vizier (or Sultan) lost patience and took military action (sometimes successfully, but when short of troops less so) has considerable truth for this period. In these years the French consuls, also based in Travnik, reported, possibly with some exaggeration, that the Sarajlije obeyed the vizier's orders only if the town council approved; that the city was an oligarchic republic that did what it wanted and what the vizier did not want; and that unless reinforced with additional troops, the power of the vizier was limited to Travnik, where he sat and sulked with his detachment of Albanians.

The Ottoman state had to steer the delicate path of getting its way without completely alienating the Bosnians, whose loyalty to Islam might encourage them to secede as powerful Muslims had done in some other provinces that lay at a distance from the center in this era (e.g., Ali Pasha in Janina, Pasvanoglu in Vidin). Moreover, there were many conservative Muslims in Istanbul, some of them influential at court, who had considerable sympathy for the Bosnians, and thus at times successfully lobbied for them or intrigued at court against the vizier sent to carry out reforms in Bosnia. Thus, unless a major issue was at

FIG. 3.9 — A NINETEENTH-CENTURY SKETCH OF STOLAC IN HERCEGOVINA
SHOWING ALI PASHA RIZVANBEGOVIĆ'S FORTRESS

stake, the state usually could not risk an all-out assault. The
state, however, considered the abolition of the Janissaries a
major issue; it intervened with outside forces and much violence, including large-scale executions, and achieved its policy.
Though a few individual Janissaries survived, the corps was
eliminated as an organized body in Bosnia by the end of 1827.
Of course, each intervention (especially if it employed violence)
left a legacy of alienation and hostility among the local Muslims, making it less likely that they would accept a new reform
or even supply the troops demanded of them.

In fact, after the Janissaries were destroyed, the Ottomans needed to create a new army. When they tried to recruit Bosnians for this force in 1830, Husein Kapetan launched a huge uprising that the Ottomans needed three years to subdue. Indeed, it was put down in the end only because Ali Pasha Rizvanbegović, the powerful Kapetan of Stolac in Hercegovina, threw in his support behind the vizier. His price was the separation of Hercegovina from Bosnia as a *vilayet* in its own right, with himself as hereditary vizier.

Since most of the kapetans had supported Husein's revolt, the Sultan in 1835 sent a new vizier to Bosnia with orders to abolish the kapetanijes and to set up new centrally-controlled administrative districts for the province. This order set off more warfare, which the state won. As a result, the kapetans and their districts were eliminated by 1837; the kapetans who survived were exiled to Anatolia, and their families and friends who stayed behind became even more alienated from the central state and its reform program. After all this warfare and further clashes in the 1840s and in 1850, mixed with attempts at diplomacy, the Ottoman state won out. Or at least it did so on paper, for some of the reforms perceived by conservative Muslims as the most outrageous (particularly those that allowed Christians rights or participation in spheres until then monopolized by Muslims) were never enforced in Bosnia. However, the vizier did reestablish his residence in Sarajevo. In these pre-1850 clashes, the basic line-up was local Muslims (who were also religious conservatives) against a semi-modernizing state, but it was Muslim against Muslim. A few Christians participated, but they did so as members of retinues of local Muslims.

PEASANT UPRISINGS

But after 1850, a combination of reforms (which now demanded from the peasants more regular payments of taxes in cash rather than in kind, which compounded the hardship) and of the state's unwillingness to antagonize further its considerably alienated local landholding ayans (by looking too closely at landlord-peasant relations) led to a worsening of the position of the peasantry. As a result, in the period after 1850, the pattern of disorder in Bosnia changed. Until 1850 disorders had usually pitted the local Muslim elite against the central state authority; in the years after 1850, unrest took the form of peasant uprisings (chiefly Christian) against local landlords and local officials. These uprisings, first in one region and then in another, became ever more frequent and larger in scale until, finally, massive ones broke out in 1875. The 1875 uprising led eventually to Great Power intervention, which placed Bosnia under Austrian occupation in 1878.

POSITION OF BOSNIAN CHRISTIANS UNDER THE OTTOMANS

In terms of the current strife in Bosnia, the most important aspects of the Ottoman period are those concerned with social matters and the position of Christians in Ottoman Bosnia. Most important is the obvious fact that, under the Ottomans, Islam dominated; thus Muslims ruled over Christians. In addition, since there were large numbers of local converts, local Muslims had a much larger role in local administration than was the case in many other Ottoman provinces. Moreover, many of these locals succeeded in building up large estates. Thus many Christians found themselves serfs on Muslim estates. As the Ottoman empire declined, the central government's ability to supervise local conditions diminished.

Relations between landlord and tenant worsened, eventually deteriorating, as noted above, to the extent that Christian peasants staged uprisings, the last and largest of which (1875-78) brought about Great Power intervention and the end of Ottoman rule. Moreover, in other Balkan areas (except Albania) the Muslim landed class (usually and mainly a foreign element) was expelled when Ottoman rule was eliminated. In Bosnia most of these individuals not only remained but also kept their positions in society after Ottoman rule ended because they were natives and because the new Austrian occupiers wanted them to remain influential to counter the influence of the numerous Serbs, whom the Austrians rightly perceived as the group most likely to oppose Austrian rule. In fact, the Austrians recognized the Ottoman landholding system (with serfdom) and much of the previous Turkish legal order.

Under Turkish rule, Christians and Jews (considered by Islam as people of the Book [Old Testament]) were tolerated. The Orthodox and Jews were defined as members of recognized, self-governing religious communities that came to be known as *millets*. The Catholics did not belong to an empire-wide community, but particular local Catholic communities, including the Catholics of Bosnia, received charters legalizing their status. Thus, Christians were classified as Catholic or Orthodox, rather than as members of ethnic groups. The Franciscans in 1463 received a charter from the Sultan, legalizing their mission and the status of their Catholic flock. Though Catholics suffered the general disabilities placed on all non-Muslims (to be described below) and, as noted above, until the nineteenth century (when the Serbian independence movement arose) were at a disadvantage when compared to the Orthodox, Bosnia's Catholics remained a legally recognized community under the administration of the Franciscans. It is worth noting that the Franciscans in Bosnia were chiefly Croats from Croatia or Bosnians educated in Croatia. Nationalist ideas began to appear in nineteenth-century Croatia; as a result, many Franciscans of Croatian origin had become infected by these ideas, and those of Bosnian origin frequently acquired them while studying in Croatia. As a result, Franciscans teaching in Bosnia and Hercegovina, in increasing numbers as the century progressed, had come to possess a strong sense of Croat identity and the hope that Bosnia might one day be united with Croatia. Not surprisingly, their schools in this period began to push Croatian nationalism as much as they did Catholicism. Thus even before the Austrian occupation, some of their pupils were acquiring a consciousness of being Croats as well as Catholics. Strong nationalism (often becoming chauvinism) has remained a feature of Bosnia's Franciscans to the present, as is clearly seen in the close association of many of them with the grisly activities of the Croatian Ustasha regime (both in Croatia itself and in Bosnia) in the Second World War.

The Orthodox were part of the so-called Orthodox millet. The Ottomans allowed the various millets to govern themselves under their own laws and leaders, interfering very little with them as long as they paid taxes and did not cause disorder. The Orthodox millet was headed by the Patriarch of Constantinople who, after the abolition of the autocephalous Patriarchate of Peć in 1766, directly exercised patronage over the Orthodox Church in Bosnia, appointing its bishops and collecting Church taxes from the Bosnians. On the local scale, the bishop and his council (composed of important clerics and usually some lay notables) were responsible for the local community.

The bishop had a court which not only handled religious and religiously-related matters (like marriages and inheritances) but also dealt with civil suits among his flock.

Education for the Orthodox millet was also the responsibility of the local Church leaders. Needless to say, shortage of funds and the frequently low quality of the responsible ecclesiastics meant that education was not available in many places; usually only the episcopal centers could be counted on to provide schools, and their quality depended on the interest of the given bishop. Since few bishops took much interest in education, the few schools that did achieve some standards were rarely able to achieve any continuity, usually declining or even closing after the death or departure of the individual bishop who had taken an interest in them. And, when the Patriarch of Constantinople regained his control over the Slavic dioceses in 1766, he began regularly to appoint Greeks as their bishops. Few of the Greek ecclesiastics whom he appointed knew any Slavic language and even fewer had any interest in sponsoring schools taught in the vernacular. Thus education tended to be available only for children in towns, and even in them it was often provided only at the primary school level. As the bishops became disengaged, schools became dependent on the support of the town's Orthodox lay community. Only those cities, like Sarajevo, which had a successful and moderately wealthy group of Orthodox merchants and guild leaders were able to establish and maintain schools of any quality to educate their children. In the nineteenth century, many of the lay teachers in urban schools, influenced by the newly autonomous Serbian principality across the Drina, were coming to see themselves as Serbs, and were teaching their charges that to be Orthodox meant to be Serb. As the century progressed and the Ottoman state appeared to be declining further, many Orthodox, particularly those in towns with some education, came to hope for liberation from the Ottomans and union with Serbia.

In any case, education and the civil court system were in the hands of the community, run by the local leaders of the millet, the leading clergy and, insofar as they were qualified, the lay notables as well. And since the state maintained no generalized school system, it was the task of the Orthodox hierarchy, the Franciscans, and the local rabbis to provide whatever education and local justice their respective communities were to have. Needless to say, the non-Muslim communities' lack of access to income-producing occupations (other than crafts and commerce, which were open to them) meant that, except in a few major cities like Sarajevo, funds were so short that these needs could not come close to being met.

Only the Muslim religious system of courts and schools, supported by the state and the wealthy Muslim landed-establishment, had the income to provide a school system. Many of the mosques and schools had been built by private benefactors and were maintained through large-scale bequests and endowments made in perpetuity, known as *vakufs*, often supervised by the donor's heirs and overseen by Muslim religious leaders. Though these schools were sometimes fairly well endowed, a modern critic would have found the Muslim school system wanting because its curriculum was so heavily religious and based on rote learning.

At times, Christians could benefit from the Islamic court institutions. For example, the Catholic and Orthodox Churches both refused to carry out mixed marriages (which many Bosnians, then as now, rising above the confines of a narrow community, wanted to contract) or remarriages after a divorce. The kadis had no trouble in obliging in these cases, and thus proved to be of great service to Bosnian Christians, many of whom could not accept the teachings of their respective Churches that marriage was a sacrament. On one occasion in 1618 the Kadi of Foča legalized a marriage in which the groom was a Catholic priest.

When Ottoman authorities wanted to deal with the Orthodox they dealt with the millet leader: the central government, with the Patriarch of Constantinople; a local vizier, with the local bishop; and the Ottoman equivalent of the small town or village constable, with the local priest. In theory, as long as taxes and demanded services were rendered and the flock was orderly, it was left alone. However, Christians still suffered various disabilities. They could not serve in the state administration or army (though they could form or be part of state-approved militias to keep order and put down brigands). Moreover, non-Muslims faced all sorts of annoying prohibitions and restrictions: on dress (and the colors they could wear), on riding horses, on the height of churches in relation to mosques, etc. Furthermore, even if the legal order sounded tolerable, in reality there were many abuses. Landlords had the right to demand a large variety of produce and services from their peasants, and frequently took more than was legally proper. The peasants had no serious means of recourse. Besides the superior clout Muslim notables enjoyed on the basis of their status, Christian testimony was not accepted in Islamic courts unless the judge gave special dispensation to receive it. Over the centuries, state taxes rose, and the state increasingly demanded supplementary levies (e.g., of horses) or services (e.g., bridge and road repairs). Furthermore, Muslims were in a position to lord it over Christians in all sorts of ways. A legal dispute between a Muslim and a Christian had to go before the Muslim court of the kadi, where the Christian, as noted, was at a huge disadvantage. Moreover, even the Orthodox millet was full of abuses, particularly after 1766 when the Patriarch of Constantinople regained his patronage in appointing bishops in Bosnia. Thereafter, the bishops were regularly Greeks (often knowing no Slavic) who had purchased their office and hoped to recoup their investment as rapidly and profitably as possible.

THE LEGACY OF OTTOMAN RULE

All of this left a negative legacy. For 400 years the Christian population had little or no role in directing its affairs; thus many Yugoslavs refer to the Ottoman period as 400 years without a history. And the second-class position and the disadvantages (usually depicted as oppression, as they sometimes were) have led to the depiction of this period as centuries under the Turkish yoke. In Bosnia, of course, it was not simply a matter of foreign rule, since local Muslims also participated in running the province. Thus Ottoman rule left among Balkan Christians a dislike of Turks and Islam. Though this feeling had greatly decreased over the past century, recent demagogues and media propaganda have made use of colored descriptions of these years, linking the various abuses of that time with Islam. Propagandists can use these themes successfully, because fear of Islam (encouraged by the way the Turkish period is depicted in school books and folklore) lies just below the surface in many semieducated Christians' minds, despite the cordial relations and experiences these Christians have had with Muslim neighbors. This legacy is not a retained centuries-old hatred, but something that can be played upon and greatly distorted by publicists. Thus it is not history itself but the use made of it, by

leaders with ulterior motives, that is at present poisoning relations among people who were accustomed to living in peace and
tolerating their neighbors of other nationalities and faiths.

There were no significant clashes along ethnic lines in
Ottoman Bosnia, just as there were none in the Middle Ages.
When domestic warfare occurred, local Muslims fought against
the central Ottoman government. On the rare occasions when
Christians were involved, they fought on the side of the local
Muslims. In the years between 1850 and 1878, there were for the
first time large uprisings by Christians; they started as peasant
revolts against social conditions and grew into a revolt for
independence from Ottoman rule. Even though the landlords
were Muslims and most of the peasants Christians, this should
not be seen as a case of religious war. Since the causes that drove
them to revolt were the conditions of serfdom under which they
suffered, it makes sense to see the main underlying causes as
being social or class-based. When the revolts spread and
Orthodox Serb townsmen became involved, these urbanites
began stressing Serbianism and the need to make the war into
one of liberation, a liberation which both urban Bosnian Serbs
and Serbian Serbs (and in a short time many of the Bosnian Serb
peasants also) came to hope would mean union with Serbia.
The Great Powers thwarted them and turned the province over
to Austrian occupation, something neither the Serbs nor the
Muslims of Bosnia wanted. To show how little the previous
uprising had been an ethnic or religious war, we find Bosnian
Serbs and Muslims, each for their own and different reasons,
allied in trying to resist the Austrian forces when they came to
occupy Bosnia. Their resistance was impressive, and it took
268,000 modernized Austrian troops four months to defeat the
effort put up by Bosnia's Muslim and Serb resistance forces.

4

The Pre-Modern Legacy and
Contemporary Identity in Bosnia

———— • ————

THE GREAT MAJORITY of the population of present-day Bosnia are descendants of the initial Slavic migrants of the sixth and seventh centuries. These Slavs came from a single Slavic group, the Slaveni. The names "Serb" and "Croat" were drawn from a second group of migrants, two probably Iranian tribes which bore those names, which later in the seventh century appeared in the northern part of what was much later to become Yugoslavia. They asserted themselves over the Slavs of much of northern and central Yugoslavia, but it is not known to what degree they asserted themselves over the Slavs living in Bosnia. In any case, it does not much matter, for their numbers were limited and they were soon assimilated and slavicized, merely providing the names ("Serb" and "Croat") of the peoples who lived to the northwest and east of Bosnia. But people in Bosnia in the Middle Ages did not take up these names or consider themselves Serbs or Croats, except for a few who lived in border areas or had immigrated into Bosnia.

In the Middle Ages the Bosnians called themselves "Bosnians" or used even more local (county, regional) names. When they called themselves "Bosnians," it most probably reflected either a shared geographical identity or participation in a state or regional enterprise (i.e., subjects of the Bosnian king) and not something akin to modern ethnicity. But lest this seem to be only a halfway identity, not to be taken seriously by modern nationalists, it must be pointed out that the same non-ethnic connotations would have been true of the "national" labels of medieval Croats of Croatia and medieval Serbs of Serbia. In medieval Bosnia these identifying names, whether "Bosnian" or more narrowly regional like "Hum-ite," cut across religious communities: a local Catholic was as much a Bosnian as a member of the Bosnian Church was. And, owing to the Bosnian environment, those calling themselves Bosnians, regardless of religious denomination, came to share many specific values and characteristics that distinguished them from the Slavs in Dalmatia and those beyond the Sava and Drina rivers.

Throughout the later Middle Ages, the Bosnians maintained a relatively developed state tradition attached to a relatively stable territory. The larger states which were subsequently to incorporate Bosnia into their midst — the Ottoman empire, Austria-Hungary, and Yugoslavia — respected and reinforced that tradition by recognizing Bosnia as an administrative unit. Thus Bosnia has retained its territorial integrity, except for brief periods, for over 500 years since the passing of the medieval Bosnian kingdom. Despite claims of Serb and Croat nationalists that Bosnia is an artificial entity which lacks traditions, the historical record demonstrates that by having consistency in its approximate borders from the thirteenth century to the present, Bosnia has shown more durability than any territorial state or unit assembled by the Serbs or Croats.

The Ottomans conquered Bosnia and Hercegovina in the fifteenth century. In their administrative structure, they recognized Bosnia as a coherent unit, and for the greater part of their rule, from 1554 to 1878, Bosnia was a beglerbeglik or vilayet in its own right (consisting of at least three sandžaks: Bosnia, Zvornik, and Hercegovina). The Ottomans categorized people not by ethnic labels but by religious ones: Muslims, Orthodox, Catholics, and Jews. In the Ottoman period there also occurred large-scale migrations and multi-directional conversions. Then, finally, in the nineteenth century, and particularly under the Austrian occupation which began in 1878, promoters of nationalism began spreading their ideas. According to their teaching, which gradually but increasingly found a responsive audience, if one was a Catholic, one was a Croat; and if one was Orthodox, then one was a Serb. But in terms of the actual origins of these Bosnian Catholics and Orthodox, this conclusion was nonsense. The population was greatly mixed as a result of the various migrations and many conversions. Thus it was not possible to determine with any accuracy, for example, if a modern Orthodox Christian was descended from a medieval Orthodox believer, a medieval Catholic, or a Bosnian Churchman. Moreover, the translation of one's religious denomination to Serb or Croat nationality also had no relevance to the area's population, since Bosnians before the nineteenth century had not described themselves as either Serbs or Croats.

A Bosnian's identity as a Bosnian — even if it originally referred to his geographical homeland or state membership — has roots going back many centuries, whereas the classification of any Christian Bosnian as a Serb or a Croat goes back barely a century. The idea of being a Bosnian Muslim in a "national" (as opposed to a religious) sense is even more recent. This is not meant to imply that one should discount the "national" feelings of a Bosnian who identifies as a Serb, Croat, or Muslim today; it simply means that the term "Bosnian" is not artificial and should be taken seriously too. And if a nationalist argues that many who adopt the identifying label "Bosnian" even today do not use it ethnically, but only to refer to state membership or citizenship, it still does not diminish the term. Ethnicity need not be the main criterion for having a voice in state affairs. The population of America is not "ethnically" American, but functions in a pluralistic state made up of a mixture of people, some of whom feel an ethnic identity but many of whom do not worry about ethnicity at all. Such a model might seem appropriate for an area of mixed ethnicity like Bosnia.

The fact that Bosnia's traditions from the medieval and Ottoman periods still are relevant to the 1990s means that these pre-modern traditions were maintained, if not even strengthened, during the period of Austrian rule (1878-1918) and the years Bosnia participated as an active and very positive component of Yugoslavia. How these traditions continued after 1878, as the religion-based communities of Ottoman times became increasingly secularized and ethnicity-based, is taken up in the chapters that follow.

5

Bosnia on the Eve
of the Modern Era

ECONOMY

IN THE MID-1870s, Bosnia was one of the most backward areas in Europe. Its cities had declined in population and lost their vitality and prominence. The country was overwhelmingly agricultural, and most peasants were mired in poverty and illiteracy. Members of the dominant class, the Muslim landowners, were largely uneducated in the Western sense and preoccupied with preserving their privileged position in society. Production was done principally by the age-old methods of craftsmen and artisans; industrialization was virtually unknown.

Economically Bosnians were less well off than their neighbors in any direction. To the east in Serbia, a flourishing trade in commercial agriculture had brought downright prosperity to many peasants. In the Croat-inhabited lands of the Habsburg empire to the north and west, industrialization was beginning and agricultural practices were being modernized to produce better yields. Some Bosnians, mainly Orthodox Christians, earned a living through trade and commerce within Bosnia and with foreign lands, but in general the economy was in deep stagnation.

SOCIETY

Bosnia in the late nineteenth century was an overwhelmingly agrarian society; according to the 1895 census, 88% of the

FIG. 5.1 — A MUSLIM *BEG* (LANDLORD) FROM EASTERN HERCEGOVINA

population was engaged principally in agricultural production. The upper stratum of Bosnian rural society consisted of a quite small number of Muslim *begs*, or landlords. Their numbers relative to the rest of the population can be seen in the 1910 census, the most extensive and reliable of the censuses taken before World War I. The 12,560 Muslim landlords (heads of households) made up only 2% of the 612, 137 Muslims, and only 0.7% of the total Bosnian population of 1,898,044. Although their political influence was dramatically reduced by the Ottomans in 1851, the Bosnian Muslim landlords continued to dominate the country economically and socially through the nineteenth and early twentieth centuries. Many of them lived on the lands they owned and administered, but some lived in

FIG. 5.2 — BOSNIAN *KMETS*

towns and cities, leaving to others the task of collecting the burdensome dues paid by the Christian peasants.

Peasants, who made up the majority of the population, were divided by belief and practice into three religious communities: Catholic, Orthodox, and Muslim. Most Christian peasants in the first and second categories were *kmets*, typically rendering over one-third or more of their annual crop to a Muslim landlord and another tenth in levies to the state. The term *kmet* has commonly been rendered as "serf" in English, although one specialist has suggested that "sharecropper" or "customary tenant" would be more accurate.[1] The status of Bosnia's kmets under Ottoman law differed from that of serfs in classical European feudalism in that the kmet was not personally tied to

1 Ivo Banac, *The National Question in Yugoslavia; Origins, History, Politics* (Ithaca: Cornell University Press, 1984), p. 367.

TABLE 5.1 — AGRICULTURAL OCCUPATIONAL CATEGORIES BY
RELIGION, 1910 (HEADS OF HOUSEHOLD)

Occupation	Muslim	Serbian Orthodox	Catholic	Total*
Landholders with kmets	9,537	633	267	10,430
Landholders without kmets	3,023	760	458	4,281
Free peasants	77,518	35,414	22,916	136,854
Kmets	3,653	58,895	17,116	79,667

Total includes an *Other* category not shown

SOURCE: *Die Ergebnisse der Volkszählung in Bosnien und der Hercegovina vom 10. Oktober 1910* (Sarajevo: Landesdruckerei, 1912), Table VII, pp. 68-9.

the landlord, enjoyed freedom of movement, and was granted legal protection against landlord abuses in Ottoman courts. The daily reality was often different from the legal code, however. Many peasants were unaware of their legal rights, and courts regularly sided with the Muslim landlord even if a kmet presented a justified complaint to the Ottoman authorities. Despite decades of Ottoman reforms and a legal code that granted them many rights, Catholic and Orthodox peasants were subject to many abuses at the hands of Muslim landlords in the late Ottoman years.

TABLE 5.1 shows the relative numerical strengths of these groups in 1910, using "head of household" figures. The vast majority of "landholders with kmets" were Muslim; however, there were many more Muslim "free peasants" than Muslim "landholders." Free peasants were not burdened by obligatory payments to a landlord as were the kmets. There were more free peasants than kmets, but over half the free peasants were Muslim. Of the kmets, on the other hand, 74% were Serbian Orthodox, 21% Catholic, and only 5% Muslim.

The continuation of these archaic peasant obligations into the late nineteenth and early twentieth centuries became the chief source of political contention in Bosnian politics and society. Politicians and diplomats referred to it as the "Agrarian Question." As early as the 1850s the practice had become an anachronism in Europe as a whole and in neighboring South Slav lands with the exception of Dalmatia; peasant dues had been effectively eliminated in Serbia in 1817 and in Croatia and Slavonia by 1848. To the Christian peasants of Bosnia and their advocates, the Agrarian Question became a burning issue of social injustice; they advanced the proposition that the land should belong to those who tilled it. The Muslim landlords, on the other hand, fiercely opposed changes that cut into their privileges and defended their practice of collecting peasant dues for themselves and on behalf of the state.[2]

THE EVOLUTION OF ETHNORELIGIOUS COMMUNITIES

The religious conversions of the first Ottoman centuries further enriched the legacy of religious diversity and tolerance in Bosnia. These conversions were the first step in a four-step process that led to the multinational composition of Bosnian society that prevailed until 1992. The second step involved the gradual transformation of religious differences into enduring distinctions among ethnoreligious communities. In contrast to the

2   For a summary of agrarian relations in Bosnia under the Ottomans and Austrians, see Jozo Tomasevich, *Peasants, Politics, and Economic Change in Yugoslavia* (Stanford University Press, 1955), pp. 96-111.

FIGS. 5.3 AND 5.4 — CATHOLIC YOUNG WOMEN

fluid and flexible religious affiliations in the early decades of
Ottoman rule, the lines separating religious communities had
stabilized and hardened by the mid-nineteenth century. Catholics, Serbian Orthodox, Muslims, and Jews developed differing
world views that, over time, became deeply entrenched. Each
religious community developed its own practices and gradually
elaborated distinctive cultural traits. Passage from one religious
community to another became difficult and unlikely; on the
rare occasions when it happened, it was attended by complica-
tions and controversy.

   The third step of this process was the growth of ethnic
consciousness among members of each religious community.

FIGS. 5.5 AND 5.6 — AN ORTHODOX WOMAN AND A MUSLIM YOUTH

Encouraged by similar developments in neighboring lands, Bosnia's Catholics gradually came to think of themselves as Croats, and Orthodox Bosnians came to regard themselves as Serbs. This process accelerated in the late decades of Ottoman rule and was well advanced — particularly in urban areas — by the time Austrian rule began in 1878. Only Bosnia's Muslims did not follow this path, instead defining themselves principally as members of a religious community, rather than a nationality, well into the twentieth century. For other Bosnians, by the end of the nineteenth century, to be a Catholic made it increasingly likely that one accepted the ethnic designation of Croat, and to be Orthodox probably meant that one defined oneself as a Serb.

Thus religious communities gradually evolved into ethnoreligious groups, their members highly aware of the distinctions among them.

The growth of ethnic identities was closely followed and reinforced by the fourth step in the process: the rise of political nationalism which, in the nineteenth and twentieth centuries, mobilized members of these communities in support of specific political programs and encouraged the growth of national identities.

The heightened significance of religious affiliation as a "marker" of group identity was encouraged by Ottoman state policies and practices. The Ottoman rulers set great store by the political significance of religion. Because they classified their subjects according to *millet*, or religious community, religious institutions acquired important political functions in Bosnia under Ottoman rule. Education was virtually the exclusive preserve of religious officials, and the local religious authority for each group was often the de facto leader of the community. Religion, or more accurately religious affiliation, became the principal determinant of group membership in Bosnian society.

In the rural villages of Bosnia, religion became the basis for a variety of cultural practices that were specific to a single religious community. In his perceptive study of Bosnian peasant villagers in the 1960s, the anthropologist William Lockwood noted: "Each religious grouping is also set off by a distinct subculture unrelated to its religious activities."[3] Thus religious affiliation became the source of a host of minor but highly

---

3 William G. Lockwood, *European Moslems: Economy and Ethnicity in Western Bosnia* (New York: Academic Press, 1975), p. 49. Lockwood explains the role of costume, cuisine, and language as ethnic markers and notes that the differences are "small in scale" but "most significant and much appreciated within the region."

significant differences in dress, cuisine, dialect, oral tradition, folk music, housing style, furnishings, and many other everyday cultural practices. Lockwood describes the nuances of traditional men's costume in the area he studied: "[It is] nearly identical for all three groups. It differs only in the color of the sash (red for Christians and green for Moslems), the color of a narrow embroidered trim at the pants cuff (red for Croats, white for Serbs, and none for Moslems) and the style of headgear."[4]

These cultural characteristics and practices evolved from religious allegiance but had no religious significance *per se*. They became distinctive markers of group differentiation, a sort of "code" to assert one's allegiance and identity that carried great significance for the individuals who displayed them, whether or not those individuals held to the tenets of a faith or engaged in religious practices. Historical sources provide few opportunities for us to see how these distinctive cultural traits took root, but the sources clearly affirm that such distinctions were a part of everyday life in rural Bosnia by the middle of the nineteenth century. Western travelers to Bosnia in the latter half of the nineteenth century were very conscious of the markers that rural Bosnians used to express visually their place of origin and affiliation with a particular ethnoreligious community. Foreign visitors typically found these cultural practices quaint and exotic; they were prone to describe and, on occasion, to illustrate them in some detail.

By the mid-nineteenth century, therefore, Bosnians' differing religious affiliations had resulted in the elaboration of cultural, economic, and political distinctions that were gradually transforming the major religious communities into recog-

4 Lockwood, p. 49.

nizable ethnic groups. While ethnicity among Bosnians in the nineteenth century was still very much rooted in religious tradition and practice, "identity" was a complex blend of religious affiliation and conviction, cultural practices, socioeconomic status, and loyalty to one's place of birth or hometown. Ethnic differences were not yet politicized in the sense that they led to the formation of mass parties or the articulation of elaborate nationalist programs, but by 1875 Bosnia was without doubt a highly differentiated multiethnic society.

To note these differences, however, is a far cry from characterizing them as tribal hatreds engendering periodic mutual slaughter. Relations among the ethnic groups were marked by mutual tolerance and frequent intermingling in everyday life. Catholics, Orthodox, Muslims, Jews, and others shared the same marketplaces and, particularly in urban areas, were often acquainted with one another and prone to render mutual assistance and cooperation in times of need. They often joined in celebrating one another's holidays. As we have noted, occasional conflicts occurred after 1850 between landlords and the peasants who were expected to give up a portion of their crop, but one cannot reasonably treat such socioeconomic conflicts as continual ethnic strife.

While many outsiders cling to the insupportable generalization that tribal hatreds and ethnic warfare have characterized Bosnia for centuries, those familiar with Bosnian history and culture more typically have the opposite perception. They ask how Bosnians, who lived together in relative tranquility and mutual tolerance for many centuries, can suddenly turn on neighbors and friends and commit the vicious and murderous acts that have become commonplace in the current Bosnian conflict. As we shall see, these developments of the past few years are inconceivable without an understanding of the external forces that have deepened ethnic cleavages and polarized Bosnian society more than ever before.

To many Westerners, the notion of religion as a source of hatred and war between neighbors is a particularly vexing issue, raising the specter of primeval, irrational impulses taking over people's lives. In Bosnia, where for many, twentieth-century secularization has left religious practice as little more than historical memory, religion as personal conviction has generally been superseded by ethnic affiliation based on a distinct culture and ideology. As with secular Jews in America, the ethnic labels remain religious in form (at least for the Bosnian Muslims), but the cultural content and historical foundations of personal identity are far removed from their purely religious origins.

DEMOGRAPHY

On the eve of the modern era Bosnia was a society of just over one million people. TABLE 5.2 shows the overall population growth, a fourfold increase from 1851 to 1991. (Censuses were of varying reliability; those of 1851 and 1879 in particular should be treated cautiously.)

The numerical strengths of the ethnic groups in Bosnia are shown in TABLE 5.3. (The table shows self-declared religion from 1879 to 1948, but the categories shift to nationality from 1953 to 1991.) Despite some vexing statistical and interpretive problems, the table shows that Bosnia, from 1879 to 1991, was a genuinely multiethnic or multinational society, with no single group commanding an outright numerical majority. This remained the case through two world wars and several episodes of substantial emigration and resettlement.

TABLE 5.2 — TOTAL POPULATION OF BOSNIA AND HERCEGOVINA, 1851-1991

1851	930,000	1948	2,563,767
1879	1,158,164	1953	2,847,459
1885	1,336,091	1961	3,277,948
1895	1,568,092	1971	3,746,111
1910	1,898,044	1981	4,124,256
1921	1,890,440	1991	4,354,911
1931	2,323,555		

SOURCES: 1851 — Djordje Pejanović, *Stanovništvo Bosne i Hercegovine* (Belgrade: Srpska Akademija Nauka, 1955), Table III. This is an estimate after certain border adjustments. 1879-1910 — Austrian census of 1910, Table 30, p. LIII. 1921-81 — *Statistički Godišnjak,* Table 3-6, p. 40. These figures correspond to the 1981 borders of Bosnia and Hercegovina. 1991 — Yugoslav census report.

The numbers for the total territory of Bosnia and Hercegovina are indicative of the complex population blend that existed in almost every region of the land. By the latter half of the nineteenth century, Bosnia was a complex ethnic tapestry whose threads were sharply distinguishable from one another but intermixed and blended in a way that would defy even the most devoted mapmaker. Conversion, migration, and historical happenstance combined to leave major concentrations of a single community in unlikely areas and on occasion to leave some expanses of territory without members of one of the three major groups. Not only did no single group command a numerical majority in all of Bosnia and Hercegovina, but it was impossible to identify sizeable contiguous geographical areas where a single ethnic group was locally dominant. Bosnia's complex demography allowed for no division into "ethnic enclaves."

TABLE 3 — ETHNORELIGIOUS MAKEUP OF BOSNIA AND
HERCEGOVINA, 1879-1991

Year	Orthodox	Muslims	Catholics	Jews		Others
1879	496,485	448,613	209,391	3,426		249
1885	571,250	492,710	265,788	5,805		538
1895	673,246	548,632	334,142	8,213		3,859
1910	825,418	612,137	434,061	11,868		14,560
1921	829,162	588,247	443,914	n/a		28,606
1948	1,136,116	890,094*	614,123	n/a		26,635

Year	Serbs	Muslims	Croats	Jews	Yugoslavs	Others
1953	1,264,372	n/a	654,229	310	891,800	37,079
1961	1,406,057	842,248	711,665	381	275,883	41,714
1971	1,393,148	1,482,430	772,491	708	43,796	53,538
1981	1,320,738	1,630,033	758,140	343	326,316	88,686
1991	1,369,258	1,905,829	755,895	n/a	239,945	93,747

*Includes 71,125 Muslims who declared themselves Serbs by nationality and 24,914 Muslims who declared themselves Croats by nationality.

NOTE: Religious and national categories are not entirely congruent, but are offered for the sake of comparison. The vast majority of the Catholic population has identified itself as Croatian and the Orthodox population as Serbian. Most Muslims have selected a single category in each census, but the categories have changed over time as follows: "Muslim, undetermined" (1948); "Yugoslav, undetermined" (1953); "Muslim in the ethnic sense" (1961); "Muslim in the sense of nationality" (1971); and "Muslim" (1981 and 1991).

SOURCES: 1879-1910 — Austrian census of 1910, Table 39. 1921-81 — *Statistički Godišnjak,* Table 3-10, p. 45. 1991 — Yugoslav census report.

Many residences were spatially segregated by ethnic community, even as all major groups were dispersed geographically and intermingled throughout Bosnia and Hercegovina. In rural areas, the vast majority of villages were inhabited by members of a single ethnoreligious community: Orthodox, Catholic, or

Muslim. Some villages were mixed, but they were the exception. The towns were partly segregated; each religious community typically had its own residential neighborhood (*mahala* in Turkish), where a church, mosque or synagogue often served as a focal point for community activities. (In larger towns, places of worship in the center were also major repositories of the cultural heritage for their particular ethnoreligious community.) In many towns, homes belonging to members of each ethnic group were scattered throughout, so the pattern of neighborhood concentrations often coexisted with a more general residential intermingling. Visitors were able to note the ethnoreligious identity of a home's owner by sight, so the intermingling did not mean that residences were indistinguishable.

The preeminent position of Muslims in Bosnian society was reflected in the makeup of the cities and towns, where Bosnian Muslims typically made up a substantial majority. They dominated economic, political, and cultural life as the primary property owners and allies of the Ottoman (and, after 1878, the Austro-Hungarian) regime. Although the forces of modernization have led to a greater diversification in the makeup of Bosnia's cities over the past century, in the minds of many Bosnians the cities are still the strongholds of the Bosnian Muslim elites, especially the city centers with their impressive mosques, *medressahs* (schools), and other institutions of Islamic architecture and learning.

POLITICAL GEOGRAPHY

Bosnia's economic backwardness was matched by its geopolitical isolation. By the mid-nineteenth century, Bosnia was the westernmost remnant of Ottoman conquests, almost completely surrounded by younger or more powerful states eagerly awaiting the demise of Ottoman rule.[5]

To the west and north was the Habsburg monarchy, which after 1867 was divided into Austrian and Hungarian portions, often referred to as the "Dual Monarchy." The Hungarian crown ruled Croatia and Slavonia, both of which bordered Bosnia. In an arrangement that defied logic, the crownland of Dalmatia was part of the Austrian half of the realm and was governed separately from the other two lands. Croatia and Slavonia, while they enjoyed a certain degree of theoretical autonomy after 1868, were in fact ruled with a relatively firm hand by the Hungarians who appointed the *ban* (governor). Despite Hungarian efforts to discourage it, the national consciousness of the Catholics in Croatia and Slavonia continued to grow in the latter half of the nineteenth century.

Dalmatia, the Austrian crownland, was a relatively impoverished land with sun-washed coastal cities of mixed Italian-Slavic population but an almost exclusively Slavic (Croatian and Serbian) hinterland.

On the map and in the imperial drawing rooms, Bosnia loomed as the great obstacle to Habsburg dreams of conquest and greater influence in the Balkan peninsula. As the Ottomans were driven from Europe, Bosnia appeared, in the eyes of many Europeans, as the westernmost outpost of an empire that had seen better days.

To the east of Bosnia lay Serbia, where independent-minded livestock farmers led a successful revolt in the first part of the nineteenth century that led to an autonomous Serbian principality. The inhabitants of Serbia, proud of their own success in

5 For a survey of these lands and their history, see Barbara Jelavich, *History of the Balkans: Eighteenth and Nineteenth Centuries,* vol. 1 (Cambridge University Press, 1983).

driving out the Ottomans, coveted Bosnian territory, aware that Bosnians of the Serbian Orthodox faith might someday be persuaded to help them annex some or all of Bosnia and create a Greater Serbia.

To the southeast was the principality of Montenegro, a ministate situated on the rugged mountains of the Dinaric range. Its inhabitants, many of whom were shepherds, nurtured a tradition of fierce independence. Adherents of the Serbian Orthodox faith, most Montenegrins sympathized with Serbia and held strong feelings of affinity for their Serbian brethren, but for most their tribal loyalties were the most significant component of their identity. Having vigorously resisted Ottoman overlordship for several centuries, the Montenegrins often encouraged and supported Christian brigands in the border areas of eastern Hercegovina and Bosnia in their struggles against the Ottomans and the Bosnian Muslim landowners.

Separating Serbia and Montenegro was a narrow corridor of land with the exotic name of the Sandžak of Novi Pazar (*Novi Pazar* means "new bazaar"). This region, the only direct link between Bosnia and the rest of the Ottoman empire, was strategically vital to Ottoman control.

In this dangerous environment, any major disruption in Bosnia was bound to draw the attention of neighbors and the rest of Europe. Thus began the Bosnian crisis of 1875-8.

YEARS OF TURMOIL, 1875-8

In the history of Bosnia, 1875 was a watershed year, comparable to 1776 in America, 1789 in France, or 1917 in Russia. For Bosnians, it marked the beginning of the end of the Ottoman empire; only three years later in 1878 the Ottoman empire was replaced by Austria-Hungary.

MAP 5.1 — POLITICAL BOUNDARIES IN THE BALKANS FOLLOWING THE
CONGRESS OF BERLIN (1878)

In 1875, a peasant uprising in Hercegovina against the abuses
of Muslim landlords quickly became a revolt of Christian
peasants throughout Bosnia and Hercegovina. Although the
uprising began as a social protest directed against Ottoman and
Muslim landlord abuses, some of its leaders soon expressed a
desire for political union with Serbia, marking the growth of
Serbian political nationalism within the Orthodox ethnoreligious
community and the spread of Serbian nationalist ideals in
Bosnia and Hercegovina. The rebelling peasants found support
and encouragement from Serbia and among Pan-Slav activists
in Russia who hoped to exploit the occasion to expand Russian
influence in the Balkans. The Great Powers failed through
diplomacy to force the Ottomans to implement reforms, and

Serbia and Montenegro declared war on the Ottoman empire in the summer of 1876. When the Ottomans readily defeated the Serbs on the battlefield, Russia entered the fray on the side of Serbia and Montenegro, declaring war on the Ottoman empire in 1877. By the spring of 1878, Russian troops had advanced to the outskirts of Istanbul. Soon Britain and France became alarmed at the prospect of vast Russian gains at Ottoman expense, particularly after the Russians dictated the peace of San Stefano in March 1878 that created a huge Bulgaria, universally presumed to be a Russian puppet state, to the east and south of Serbia.

To diminish Russian gains and reestablish the European balance of power, the Great Powers convened a meeting in Berlin in June 1878. The Berlin Congress led to an agreement that recast the map of southeastern Europe. The Treaty of Berlin reduced Bulgaria in size and restored much of its territory to the Ottomans. To protect Austro-Hungarian interests in the Balkans, the Treaty of Berlin awarded Bosnia and Hercegovina to the Habsburg monarchy to "occupy and administer," delivering a bitter disappointment to Serbs who had hoped that the peasant rebellion of 1875 would result in Bosnia's being annexed to Serbia.

6

Austro-Hungarian Rule
1878-1918

———— • ————

Ottoman rule in Bosnia lasted more than 400 years, but since the end of the Ottoman era in 1878, the country has been governed by five different polities: Austria-Hungary (1878-1918), royal Yugoslavia (1918-41), the fascist "Independent State of Croatia" (1941-5), socialist Yugoslavia (1945-91) and the nearly-stillborn republic of Bosnia and Hercegovina (1992-?). The two longest periods, those of Austria-Hungary and socialist Yugoslavia, have had the most enduring consequences for the current situation in Bosnia.

AUSTRO-HUNGARIAN MILITARY OCCUPATION, 1878

From the time the Treaty of Berlin was signed on July 13, 1878, officials of the Austro-Hungarian empire treated Bosnia as a territory of the monarchy and moved quickly to take over their newly-won Balkan provinces. Four imperial divisions, consisting of 72,000 troops, crossed into Bosnia and Hercegovina on July 31, 1878. The monarchy's diplomats and military commanders anticipated that the army would encounter little or no resistance in its march through the mountainous terrain.

Word of impending Austro-Hungarian occupation was welcomed by most Bosnian Catholics but received with dismay by many Bosnian Muslims. The Muslims of Sarajevo overthrew the enfeebled Ottoman authorities, seized munitions and arms from the Ottoman garrisons, and organized guerrilla resistance to the entry of Austria-Hungary's troops. Of forty-one Ottoman battalions stationed in Bosnia in the summer of 1878, thirty consisted of Bosnian Muslim conscripts who were prepared to fight for their homeland against the "Christian" occupier; these units, with their arms and munitions, made up the core of the resistance forces. Ottoman units were joined by Muslim irregulars defending local areas and in many places by sympathetic Serbs, including bands of brigands in eastern Hercegovina.[1]

The Austro-Hungarian troops were confronted with the classic guerrilla tactics favored by indigenous forces against a foreign occupier. The Bosnians attacked Austro-Hungarian convoys from the hills that rose above the primitive roads leading into the province's interior. Snipers harassed the monarchy's troops and forced them to deploy large flanking units to provide security for the main columns. Even after imperial troops conquered Sarajevo through house-to-house fighting on August 19, 1878, resistance in the countryside continued to grow. Determined to prevail before the arrival of winter, the Austro-Hungarian army reached a peak strength of 268,000 troops before defeating the Bosnian forces in the fall of 1878. Although a major uprising again challenged Austro-Hungarian military control in 1881-2 and Serbian brigandage remained an incessant problem in eastern Hercegovina into the 1890s, by November 1878 the major resistance forces had been defeated by the superior arms and tactics of the Austro-Hungarian imperial army.

---

[1]   For an account of the Austrian army's victory over the resistance movement, see Robert Donia, "The Battle for Bosnia: Habsburg Military Strategy in 1878," *Akademija nauka i umjetnosti Bosne i Hercegovine*, Posebna Izdanja, XLIII (Sarajevo, 1979), pp. 109-21. The article is in English.

FIG. 6.1 — BOSNIAN TROOPS OF THE AUSTRO-HUNGARIAN IMPERIAL ARMY

In contrast to the German failure in World War II to secure Bosnia militarily, the Austrians were also able to conquer and ultimately pacify the area. The cost was substantial: The monarchy committed over one-third of its fully mobilized combat capability to the Bosnian campaign and suffered over 5,000 casualties. There were, of course, major differences between the situations, including over sixty years of development in the art of warfare and, in World War II, a resistance movement that drew highly-motivated recruits from all three major Bosnian national groups. For those observers who see nothing but despair in the prospects for foreign military intervention in the current Bosnian situation, the Austrian success in 1878 is an instructive case of a successful invasion and conquest by a determined foreign force.

AUSTRO-HUNGARIAN ADMINISTRATION

The Habsburg Emperor Franz Josef assigned responsibility for Bosnia's occupation and administration to the Joint Ministry of Finance, one of three ministries that owed allegiance only to the crown. By placing the newly acquired territory under the Joint Ministry of Finance, the Emperor avoided a constitutional struggle over which half of Austria-Hungary would gain territory at the expense of the other and ensured that policies in Bosnia would reflect principally the interests of the crown rather than those of the empire's competing nationalities.

Once in power, the Austrian administration surprised many European observers and disappointed Bosnian Christians by retaining the existing social structure with few changes. Fearful of the massive social upheaval that might be unleashed if they undermined the leading position of the Bosnian Muslim landowning class, the new authorities kept in place the onerous obligations of Christian peasants to their Muslim landlords. The Austrians undertook limited reforms to codify and regulate the nature of peasant obligations, establish an orderly land-registry system, and provide court procedures that gave the peasants some protection against abuses by Muslim landowners. In 1911 a law was passed, based on an Ottoman reform measure of 1876, that encouraged peasants to purchase the land they tilled; the peasant, however, had to provide full compensation to the landlord, a burden few could afford. These modest measures did little to resolve the underlying problem; the peculiar Bosnian form of peasant dependence was prolonged into the early twentieth century. The Agrarian Question continued to fester and remained a central source of contention and conflict under Austrian rule.

Despite their social conservatism, the monarchy's authorities were relatively successful in developing Bosnia's communication and transport infrastructure and in promoting industrialization.[2] Railroads were built, albeit under the heavy-handed nationalist influence of politicians from the monarchy who sought routes that would benefit their constituencies. The steel industry in Zenica, in central Bosnia northwest of Sarajevo, dates from Austrian times. Many towns and cities achieved new economic and demographic vitality: Sarajevo tripled in population during the first thirty years of Austrian rule. An influx of Catholics from the monarchy, most of them Slavs, diluted the Muslims' dominance in Sarajevo and other cities and towns.

Austrian policies toward the principal ethnonational groups in Bosnia went through three phases. During the first phase (1878-1903), the Austrian authorities encouraged the revival of religious hierarchies and the growth of religious education in Bosnia. They subsidized the religious organizations of the Serbian Orthodox, Catholics, and Muslims in the hope of discouraging political activism. At the same time, officials under the leadership of Benjámin von Kállay, Austro-Hungarian Finance Minister from 1882 to 1903, promoted the notion of *bošnjaštvo* (Bosnianism). This concept encouraged patriotic loyalty to Bosnia itself as an alternative to separate Croatian, Serbian, or Muslim identities. Hoping to discourage Serbian and Croatian nationalism from taking root in Bosnia, and to gain the loyalty of Bosnia's Orthodox and Catholic residents, they encouraged the exploration of Bosnia's unique history and romanticized its cultural traditions. Among other institutions, they established the Provincial Museum in Sarajevo to preserve

2 Peter Sugar, *Industrialization of Bosnia-Hercegovina, 1878-1914* (Seattle: University of Washington Press, 1963).

MAP 6.1 — BOSNIA AND HERCEGOVINA UNDER
AUSTRO-HUNGARIAN RULE (1878-1918)

large medieval tombstones and other cultural artifacts from
Bosnia's past.

Although Austrian efforts produced important tangible results in the form of cultural and educational institutions in
Bosnia, Bosnianism found no significant echo in the popula-

tion. Identification with ethnoreligious communities was already too advanced for an appreciable number of Bosnians to renounce their ethnic identity in favor of regional patriotism. Rather than serving as a counterweight to Serbian and Croatian nationalist influences, the traditional religious hierarchies were frequently a catalyst for ethnically-based political movements that challenged Austrian government policies. Kállay's efforts to discourage dissent did little to curb the growth of political movements; by the time of his death in 1903, ethnically-based groups were stronger than ever and were demanding autonomy for their constituents and a stronger voice in government.

The second phase of Austrian policies toward Bosnian groups began in 1903 with the death of Kállay and the appointment of his replacement, István von Burián, as Joint Minister of Finance; it lasted until the outbreak of war in 1914. Under Burián's rule, the authorities gradually liberalized their policies and tolerated political activities and expression within broad limits. Bosnians were permitted to form political parties, to publish a variety of newspapers, and to use publicly the names of their respective nationalities. The government negotiated with representatives of all major parties and granted substantial religious and cultural autonomy to both the Bosnian Serbs and the Bosnian Muslims.

In 1908, after maintaining for thirty years the legal fiction that the monarchy was merely occupying the territories on behalf of the European Powers, Austria-Hungary proclaimed the formal annexation of Bosnia and Hercegovina. Although this touched off a storm of diplomatic protests by the Great Powers and aroused antagonism from Bosnians domestically, the crisis gradually passed without armed conflict. In the next two years the Great Powers, the Ottoman empire, and all major

Bosnian political parties formally recognized the annexation, paving the way for a brief constitutional era in Bosnia from 1910 to 1914. In 1910 Austrian officials promulgated a constitution, convened a parliament, and allowed elections based on a narrow franchise and a complex "curia" system that assured representation to ethnically-based political parties and guaranteed a leading role for middle- and upper-class candidates. With these provisions, the Austrians hoped to cultivate moderate, manageable parties sympathetic to the monarchy's interests.

In the third phase, the Austrian authorities repressed a single group, the Bosnian Serbs, from 1914 until the monarchy's collapse in 1918 (see further discussion at the end of this chapter). This radical change in direction was rooted in the suspicion of the authorities that the Bosnian Serbs were seeking to undermine the Austrian state in wartime.

The first two phases of Austria-Hungary's nationality policies anticipated in many ways the approaches of Tito and the Communists to Yugoslav and Bosnian nationality issues in the era of socialist Yugoslavia (1945-91). Just as Kállay hoped for the emergence of a Bosnian nationality, Tito hoped for the growth of a "Yugoslav" loyalty rather than the reemergence of particularist nationalism. When those hopes proved futile, each regime shifted to tolerating national political activities within broad limits of acceptability, although the two regimes defined these limits differently.

The third phase of Austro-Hungarian policy, that of repressing a single group, was never practiced in the era of socialism. Nor did repression in the Austro-Hungarian period approach in scope the genocidal campaigns of the Ustashe in World War II or the ethnic cleansing practices that became part of wartime Bosnia in 1992 and after.

MODERN POLITICAL MOVEMENTS IN BOSNIA

Bosnia's relative economic and social backwardness in the latter half of the nineteenth century was reflected in public life as well: political parties, formal organizations, newspapers, well-formulated ideologies, and other trappings of present-day political life were more numerous and more advanced in neighboring Croatian and Serbian lands than in Bosnia when Austria-Hungary began its occupation in 1878. Despite strong encouragement from outside activists in the case of the Serbs and Croats, political nationalism — in the sense of organized political movements — developed quite slowly and unevenly in Bosnia around and after the turn of the twentieth century.[3]

THE BOSNIAN SERBS

The Orthodox church and school communes became significant local institutions in the late years of the Ottoman empire. Aided by funds and assistance from Serbia proper, the communes provided education and maintained church facilities as best they could. They also flourished under Austrian rule and became the basis of the first modern political formation in Bosnia, the movement for Serbian church and school autonomy.

Leaders of the Serbian commune in Mostar, protesting a law introducing conscription in Bosnia, presented their first petition to the Austrian authorities in 1881, but the movement did not have widespread support until the late 1890s. Although Mostar Serbs led the way, they were joined by representatives of church and school communes from all major regions of Bosnia and Hercegovina. They circulated petitions, negotiated with

3 For more information regarding Austrian-era political movements, see Robert Donia, *Islam under the Double Eagle: The Muslims of Bosnia and Hercegovina, 1878-1914* (Boulder, Colo.: East European Monographs, 1981).

the government, began publishing the newspaper *Srpska Riječ* (Serbian Word), and held meetings to rally Serbian support in various towns. After much struggle their efforts produced an agreement with the government, and in September 1905 the regime promulgated a statute providing for the autonomy of Serbian church and school communes throughout Bosnia.

The Serbian autonomy movement, besides achieving its stated goal of communal autonomy, provided the Serbian community in Bosnia with political experience, recognized leaders, a newspaper, and its first formal political organization. At the same time, the autonomy movement mobilized many Orthodox Christians to think of themselves as Serbs. In October 1907, encouraged by a liberalized Austrian stance toward political expression, Serbian activists convened and formally created the Serbian National Organization (SNO). This was an umbrella organization encompassing three factions. It remained the strongest Serbian party and won all thirty-one seats allocated to the Serbs in the Parliament that convened in 1910. Echoing the arguments of nationalists in Serbia proper, the SNO boldly asserted in its political program that Bosnia and Hercegovina were Serbian lands and that the Bosnian Muslims were Serbs by nationality who had embraced Islam.

The SNO, like the leading parties of other ethnic groups in the Austrian period, rested on a rather narrow social base. Although most Serbian peasants supported the party, the SNO entered into a coalition with leading Muslim landlords in Parliament and refrained from pressing for agrarian reform to end the onerous obligations of Christian serfs. Still, the party was less compliant than the Austrian authorities had hoped, and continued to prosecute the Serbian cause in Parliament and in the press. The SNO became the foundation of subsequent Bosnian Serb nationalist parties in royal Yugoslavia.

THE BOSNIAN CROATS

Because fewer Catholics than Serbian Orthodox had entered the middle class in Bosnia, the Croatian nationalist movement had a weaker social base than the Serbian movement. Lacking institutions such as the Orthodox church and school communes that bridged the secular and religious interests of the Catholic population, Croatian political movements originated among intellectuals, the small but growing middle class, and the Franciscan Order.

Two factions contended for leadership. The first, which was liberal, middle-class, and secular, espoused a program that was in many respects the Croatian counterpart of the moderate nationalist ideals of the SNO. In February 1908 a small group of Croatian Catholics met near Travnik and created the Croatian National Union (CNU). Their party program claimed that Bosnia and Hercegovina were Croatian lands, declared that the Muslims were Croats, and called for unification with Croats in the other lands of the monarchy. These Croats were thus very much in tune with other liberal groups in Croatia proper in calling for an inclusive South Slav solution to the nationality problems of the monarchy, a viewpoint known as *Trialism*. (Trialism was the notion that the South Slav lands should be united under the aegis of the Habsburg Emperor to create a third, South Slav dimension to the monarchy in addition to the Hungarian and Austrian entities.) Recognizing that the Croats could never achieve a majority in Bosnia, the CNU sought a coalition with the Bosnian Muslim landlord party, and, to promote this coalition, avoided demanding an end to peasant obligations.

The second strain in Croatian politics, represented by Archbishop Josef Stadler, insisted on Catholicism as the basis of personal identity for all Croats. A vigorous promoter of Catholic propaganda and proselytism, Stadler organized the Croatian Catholic Association (CCA) in January 1910. His party's program emphasized clerical ideals and religious exclusivity. Given the CCA's commitment to Catholicism and its efforts to convert Muslims to the Catholic faith, a coalition with Muslim political groups was unlikely.

In elections to the 1910 Bosnian Parliament, the liberal CNU won twelve seats; Stadler's clerical CCA won only four, reflecting a substantial majority of support for the secular nationalist approach of the CNU. At first, the Croatian parties were excluded from the governing coalition between the Bosnian Muslims and Serbs, but in 1911 a new Muslim-Croat coalition was formed and held together until Parliament was dissolved in June 1914.

THE BOSNIAN MUSLIMS

In the platforms of their dominant parties, both Serbian and Croatian nationalists asserted identical but diametrically conflicting claims: each insisted that the Bosnian Muslims were a part of *its* nation. Without including the Muslims, neither Serbs nor Croats could assert a credible claim to a demographic majority in Bosnia. Without the Muslims, each of these groups had to resort (as they still do today) to more tenuous historical or geopolitical arguments to advance their nationalist causes. Each side wanted, in fact needed, the Bosnian Muslims. This was the central reality in post-Ottoman Bosnia until 1992, when extremists in both the Serbian and Croatian camps prevailed; at that point, no one wanted the Muslims. Serbian and

Croatian extremists each decided, to the world's horror, that they would achieve demographic supremacy by driving the Muslims out, creating permanent refugees in Europe.

A second constant in Bosnian political life, which endures to this day, is that the Bosnian Muslims cannot long survive without an alliance or coalition with a major South Slav national partner. Repeatedly throughout the past century, they have been at the fulcrum of political life, supporting the center, whether of the Bosnian polity or of Yugoslavia, against centrifugal forces. While there has certainly been intolerance among the Muslims, and they have sometimes participated in opposition coalitions in parliamentary situations, the dominant theme in Bosnian Muslim politics has been their quest for a durable, stable political alignment and support for multinational entities that would protect their interests. From the Austrian era to the present, the Bosnian Muslims have survived as adept and pragmatic coalition-builders, the "swing" group with the most to lose. Although they have frequently played a vital role in creating workable coalitions, they have also acquired an unfortunate reputation among other South Slavs as cynical opportunists.

The end of Ottoman rule was a shock to many Bosnian Muslims. Although they spoke Serbo-Croatian and sometimes opposed rule from Istanbul, the Muslim landowners viewed themselves as inherently a part of the privileged elite that dominated the Ottoman empire. The prospect of living under a Christian, Western occupier frightened many. In the early years of Austrian occupation, thousands emigrated from Bosnia, moving east to Istanbul and other areas that remained under Ottoman rule. Some émigrés agitated politically against

Austrian policies and maintained ties with Muslims who remained in Bosnia.

Like the Bosnian Serbs, the Muslims became concerned about the vitality of their religious, educational, and cultural institutions and launched a movement for autonomy in the 1890s. Their concerns arose in part because of aggressive efforts by Archbishop Stadler and his Catholic followers to convert Muslims to Christianity. In most instances the conversions were related to potential mixed marriages or other situations of social expediency. Although Stadler's efforts met with only limited success, they nonetheless aroused the Muslims to political action in defense of their faith and the integrity of their ethnoreligious community.

In 1899 a sixteen-year-old Muslim girl, Fata Omanović, disappeared from her village near Mostar, fled to Dalmatia under Church protection, and converted to Catholicism in order to marry a Catholic suitor. When Archbishop Stadler and other Catholic officials refused to disclose her whereabouts, Mostar Muslims demanded that the government intervene and return the girl to her familial home. Under the leadership of Mufti Ali Džabić, the Mostar Muslims prepared petitions and dispatched delegations to Austro-Hungarian authorities, demanding greater control over the educational and cultural institutions in which their children were educated. The stern and pious Mufti thus turned the concerns of the Mostar Muslims into a crusade for religious purity and Islamic orthodoxy.

The movement soon attracted the support of Muslim landowners and Muslims living in Bosnian towns. Consistent with Kállay's policy of repressing political activities of every stripe, the Austrian regime harassed and intimidated the movement's leaders. In 1902 Mufti Džabić emigrated to Istanbul to protest the government's harassment. Thereafter the movement was taken over by Muslim landowners, who demanded that the government respect their rights to collect dues from Christian peasants.

After Kállay's death and the appointment of Burián in 1903, the government's more tolerant approach to political activism led to negotiations with the movement's leaders. The Muslim negotiators asked that separate, autonomous Islamic institutions be established to protect the interests of all Bosnian Muslims. After years of intermittent negotiations, in May 1909 the regime promulgated a statute which met nearly all Muslim demands. The statute created the office of the *Reis-ul-ulema* for Bosnia; the *Reis* was the leader of the Islamic community with responsibility for the preservation of cultural and religious institutions. Additionally, the statute provided that Islamic charitable foundations, known as *vakufs*, be administered by a Vakuf Commission elected by the Muslim population. These institutions became a permanent part of Bosnian Muslim life and have survived, albeit with substantial changes, to the present day.

By defending the principles of Islamic law and protecting Muslim communal integrity, the Muslim elite could successfully claim to represent the interests of all Muslims, even though the landlords made up only a small minority of their number. At the same time, the Muslim landlords who co-opted the autonomy movement argued that Islamic law should prevail in relations between landowners and the peasants who worked their land.

The autonomy statute was more than just a triumph for the religious community of Islam; it also assured the preservation of the Bosnian Muslim landowning class and its privileges. Despite the benefits that they won for the landowning class, the negotiators retained the support of the Muslim peasants and urban lower classes. The Muslim autonomy movement also established the precedent that religious concerns of the community, although often important in initiating political action, were superseded by the secular interests of the Muslims' political leaders. This pattern was to be repeated throughout the twentieth century, and it meant that the Bosnian Muslims became a largely secular community with no inclination to adopt the religious fundamentalism that attracted Muslims elsewhere.

In December 1906 the Bosnian Muslim landowners created a formal political party, the Muslim National Organization (MNO). Just as the SNO was the direct descendant of the Serbian autonomy movement, the MNO was the formal embodiment of the leadership that had controlled the Muslim autonomy movement since 1900. The MNO and its post-1918 successor, the Yugoslav Muslim Organization (YMO), dominated Bosnian Muslim politics until 1941.

MNO leaders were offended and tormented by Austria's decision to annex Bosnia in 1908. In February 1910, after much turmoil, the party became the last of the major ethnically based parties in Bosnia to acknowledge formally the Austrian *fait accompli.* This declaration of loyalty paved the way for Muslim participation in the Bosnian Parliament. In elections for the Parliament that convened in 1910, the MNO won all twenty-four Muslim seats. As in the negotiations for cultural autonomy, the MNO's primary mission was to protect the archaic privileges of the Muslim landlords against the demands of Christian peasants for agrarian reform.

Having secured religious and cultural autonomy, and the government's support for landowner privileges, the Bosnian Muslim leaders became the most loyal supporters of Bosnia's Austrian regime in the brief but increasingly tumultuous constitutional era of the monarchy's rule (1910-14). For the first year the Muslims were allied with the SNO, whose leaders incongruously agreed to keep the issue of agrarian reform off the agenda. The alliance ended in 1911 after a peasant uprising directed at the Muslim landowners; MNO leaders suspected that Serbian nationalists had instigated the revolt. In 1911 the Muslim leadership, true to its historic mission as guardian of coalitions in support of central rule, entered an alliance with the Croatian CNU. In return, the Croats agreed not to oppose the continuation of Muslim landowner privileges. The Serbs went into opposition and remained an opposition party for the rest of the constitutional era, emboldened by the successes of neighboring Serbia in the Balkan wars of 1912 and 1913.

Sessions of the Bosnian Parliament soon became stormy confrontations. Insults, active obstruction, and walkouts became common forms of political dissent. Constitutional life in Bosnia was off to a rocky start.

THE BOSNIAN MUSLIMS AND NATIONAL RECRUITMENT

As Bosnia entered the modern political era, many Serbian and Croatian nationalists courted the Muslims, hoping that some or all would adopt a Serbian or Croatian national identity. These campaigns of national recruitment produced limited successes in both the Austrian and royal Yugoslav periods. On the other hand, the ultimate failure of these efforts speaks eloquently for the depth of Muslim identity in the post-Ottoman period.

FIG. 6.2 — SARAJEVO'S CITY HALL UNDER AUSTRO-HUNGARIAN RULE, LATER
MADE A LIBRARY; THE BUILDING AND ITS CONTENTS BURNED
FOLLOWING SERBIAN SHELLING IN 1992

Some Muslim activists and intellectuals were attracted to the Serbian and Croatian national causes. Most Muslims asserted their own identity as confessional, leaving the issue of their national identity an open question well into the socialist era. Consequently, the Serbs and Croats each extended a kind of open invitation to the Muslims to declare themselves as Serbs or Croats. While relatively few Muslims made such declarations, those who did were commonly high-profile intellectuals or political activists. The gaining nationality often celebrated these declarations publicly as proof of its virility and superiority.

Generally, more Muslims declared themselves Croats before the turn of the century. Many were young intellectuals who had been educated in Zagreb or Vienna, where they were exposed to Croatian nationalist ideals. After 1900, however, the international fortunes of independent Serbia rose, and the Serbian option drew more declarations.

National declarations by the Bosnian Muslims proved both transitory and shallow. Muslims changed from one national identity to another with about the same ease that an American might change political parties. Those who declared themselves as Serbs or Croats nonetheless retained their fundamental identity as Muslims and members of the Islamic confessional community. While they may have become active in Serbian or Croatian organizations for a time, most also continued to be politically active in Muslim groups, playing a tactical dual role. Even at the height of Croat-Muslim cooperation in 1911, the MNO explicitly rejected the Croatian nationalist program that called for Bosnia to become a part of Croatia.

National coloration as a Serb or Croat became an acceptable, even preponderant trait among Muslim politicians and intellectuals from the late Austrian period until the time of socialist Yugoslavia. Of the Muslims elected to the Constituent Assembly in royal Yugoslavia in November 1920, thirteen declared themselves Croats, five Serbs, one a Yugoslav, one a Bosnian, and four were undeclared.[4] By the 1970s, however, few Muslims expressed "coloration" as a Serb or Croat. Some Serbian and Croatian nationalists nevertheless clung to the belief that a Bosnian Muslim intellectual, despite a public denial, secretly harbored a national affinity for either the Serbs or Croats.

---

4 Atif Purivatra, *Jugoslavenska Muslimanska Organizacija u političkom životu kraljevine Srba, Hrvata i Slovenaca* (Sarajevo: Svjetlost, 1967), p. III.

The failure of Serbs and Croats to inspire any significant loyalty to their causes among the Bosnian Muslims, coupled with the Muslims' unmistakable tendency to organize separately in pursuit of their own political interests, demonstrates that a separate Bosnian Muslim identity was too deeply ingrained by 1900 to be subsumed by a Croatian or Serbian national movement. Many Muslims saw no incompatibility between their identity as Bosnian Muslims and a casual acceptance of Serbian or Croatian national "coloration," but such acceptance did little to alter their basic political allegiance and behavior as Bosnian Muslims. Some Muslims were repelled by the nationalist intensity of Serbian and Croatian political leaders, particularly those who insisted that religion (Orthodoxy for the Serbs, Catholicism for the Croats) was an indispensable component of national identity. Yet until the socialist period was well advanced, most Muslims stubbornly resisted proposals to define their own identity in national terms, opting instead for the refuge of a confessional identity based on historical foundations and cultural traditions.

POPULAR UPRISINGS AND REVOLTS

Besides the large-scale political movements that led to the creation of parliamentary parties, sporadic violent events peppered the Bosnian historical landscape in the nineteenth and early twentieth centuries. Most of these violent events were social conflicts, principally peasants rising to oppose the excesses of Bosnian Muslim landlords or to resist the Ottoman or Austrian state. Truly ethnic or national conflicts and violence were unknown until the early twentieth century.

Abuses of peasant rights were commonplace in Bosnia despite Ottoman reform efforts — in the laws and edicts of

1839, 1856, and 1858 — to codify peasant rights and limit the rapacity of the Muslim landlords. The peasants revolted several times in the late Ottoman years. The peasant and sheepherding inhabitants of eastern Hercegovina, adjacent to Montenegro, were particularly restive. They played a leading role in the great revolt of 1875 that led to the Russo-Turkish war and eventually to the demise of Ottoman power in Bosnia.

As noted earlier, the Austrian military occupation of 1878 drew heavy resistance from Muslim-led Bosnian forces. Although the Austrians ultimately prevailed, eastern Hercegovina proved particularly difficult to pacify. In an effort to generate support for its rule, the Austrian regime allowed indigenous forces to retain their own commanders. In 1881 the Austrians announced that military conscription would be extended to the occupied lands, and eastern Hercegovina burst again into rebellion. While the main resistance was subdued by 1882, the battle against bandits and outlaws in eastern Hercegovina went on for more than a decade. Again in 1910 the peasants of Bosnia revolted, having been disappointed by a halfhearted Austrian attempt at agrarian reform in 1906 which "averaged" peasant dues over several years without eliminating them. Muslims in the MNO suspected Serbian nationalists of instigating the revolt.

In the early twentieth century, friction mounted between Austria and independent Serbia, emboldening Bosnia's Serbs and destabilizing their parliamentary coalition with the Bosnian Muslims. In 1906, in an unsuccessful attempt to force Serbia to renounce an economic pact with Bulgaria, the Habsburg monarchy closed its borders to Serbian livestock. The Bosnian annexation crisis of 1908 ended in an Austrian diplomatic victory, but it further heightened tensions between the monarchy and Serbia. In the Balkan wars of 1912 and 1913,

MAP 6.2 — POLITICAL MAP OF THE BALKANS SHOWING SERBIAN GAINS
IN THE BALKAN WARS (1912-13)

Serbia nearly doubled its territory at the expense of the Ottoman empire. When these wars passed without Austrian military involvement, many South Slavs concluded that Austria was
overrated as a military power and developed contempt for the
Habsburg monarchy.

By 1914, international events were reverberating in Bosnia
with more disruptive impact than ever before. The Balkan wars
initiated a period of constant agitation in the border regions of
Bosnia and Hercegovina adjacent to Serbia and Montenegro.
Austrian border guards intercepted infiltrators carrying bombs,
rifles, and propaganda. The police discovered heavily armed

Bosnians with supplies and uniforms from Serbia and Montenegro. Brigands skirmished with Austrian border patrols, fleeing afterwards with impunity into the mountainous havens of the neighboring states. In these rural border regions, unrest on the eve of World War I encompassed a blend of peasant discontent, brigandage, and Serbian nationalist agitation.

STUDENT UNREST AND THE ASSASSINATION OF FRANZ FERDINAND

Unquestionably the most notorious single violent event in Bosnian history was the assassination of the Austrian Archduke Franz Ferdinand in Sarajevo on June 28, 1914.[4] The Archduke was the heir apparent to the Imperial Habsburg throne of Franz Josef, who by that time had reigned for sixty-six years. Serbian nationalists suspected the Archduke of sympathizing with *Trialism.* Since such a program necessarily implied that further territorial acquisitions by independent Serbia would be thwarted, the assassins viewed the Archduke as a menace to Serbian national aspirations.

Of the eight perpetrators, seven were Bosnian Serbs; the eighth was a Bosnian Muslim. All eight were captured; the actual assassin, Gavrilo Princip, died of tuberculosis in the Habsburg prison in Theresienstadt in 1918. Austrian investigations revealed that the assassins were members of *Mlada Bosna* (Young Bosnia), a shadowy student group with ties to the Black Hand, a Serbian secret society, and to a group known as *Narodna Odbrana* (national defense). The Black Hand, whose members included a number of high-ranking Serbian army officers, provided weapons, training, and support to the assassins. Despite their ties to Serbian secret societies, the conspira-

---

5 An engaging account of the assassination and its historical context is found in Vladimir Dedijer, *The Road to Sarajevo* (London: MacGibbon and Kee, 1967).

tors themselves were Bosnians. Many were connected to the growing student movements in Mostar and Sarajevo which condemned Bosnia's conventional parties as timid and compromised by collaboration with the Austrians.

The assassination touched off violent anti-Serbian demonstrations in the marketplace of Sarajevo. Mobs of Bosnian Muslims and Catholic Croats, unhampered at first by police intervention, beat Bosnian Serbs and looted their shops. In the Bosnian Parliament, the major parties passed a resolution condemning the assassination; the government then adjourned the Parliament, never to reconvene it. Thus ended the Austrian attempt to establish a viable political order in Bosnia based on a constitution and limited parliamentary rule.

WAR AND THE DEMISE OF THE HABSBURG MONARCHY

The Archduke's killing did not immediately touch off war between the Habsburg monarchy and Serbia, let alone a world war. The risk of the latter lay in the fact that each antagonist was tightly locked into one of two competing European alliances; a local conflict could thus easily escalate into an all-European conflagration pitting Germany, Austria-Hungary and their allies (the Central Powers) against France, England, and Russia (the Entente Powers). The fuse was lit on July 23, 1914, when Austria-Hungary delivered a ten-point ultimatum with a forty-eight-hour deadline to Serbia, demanding the suppression of anti-Austrian activities in Serbia and the right to participate in an investigation of the assassination on Serbian soil.

The Serbian government's response was both timely and surprisingly conciliatory. It agreed to suppress anti-Austrian groups, muzzle hostile publications, and arrest certain agitators named in the Austrian ultimatum. The Serbs further agreed to keep Austria informed of their investigation of the assassination, but they declined to accept direct Austrian participation on grounds that their sovereignty would be violated. Ignoring both the frenzied efforts of Europe's diplomats to keep the peace and the unmistakable Serbian invitation to negotiate further, the war party in Vienna persuaded the aged Emperor Franz Josef to punish the Serbs. The Austrians declared war on Serbia on July 28. Russia began a general mobilization on August 1, and Germany quickly declared war on Russia and France. A few days later, German troops rolled into Belgium. All belligerents expected a quick resolution and a return to normality; instead, the war became a costly and bitter conflict that lasted more than four years.

In the first strike in the Balkan theater of conflict, Habsburg troops invaded Serbia on August 11, crossing the Drina from Bosnia. Despite initial Austrian successes, the Serbian forces soon drove them back. In a second offensive, the Austrians once more proved unable to defeat the Serbian forces, and by December 1914 the Serbs had again cleared their territory of Austrian forces. Not only did they sustain major losses on the battlefield, but hundreds of thousands of Serbs fell prey to a virulent typhus epidemic in the winter of 1914-15.

In October 1915 the tide turned dramatically against Serbia. A joint German-Austrian-Bulgarian operation conquered Serbia, and the Central Powers occupied the country for the next three years. Under appalling winter conditions, remnants of the Serbian army conducted a heroic march through Montenegro and Albania, withstanding Albanian attacks to reach the Adriatic coast. From there they sailed to the Greek island of Corfu. In the final Allied offensive from Thessaloniki, these troops led the campaign to drive the Central Powers from Serbia for a third time.

Except for brief engagements in eastern Bosnia, the belligerents conducted no major operations on Bosnian soil. Habsburg rule, however, became harsher after the assassination of the Archduke. Bosnian peasants were subject to mandatory crop requisitions to supply the troops and feed the population in the monarchy's cities. Bosnians served in the imperial forces, and some soldiers — principally Bosnian Serbs — fled into exile to join the Serbian army as volunteers.

During the war the Austrian authorities employed extensive repressive measures against the Bosnian Serbs, whom they came to view as a fifth column dedicated to destroying the Habsburg monarchy. Over 5,000 were interned in camps; many were mistreated and some starved to death. To cope with the almost continuous state of rebellion in the border regions in eastern Hercegovina and eastern Bosnia, the authorities resettled or deported thousands of families in one final, futile effort to pacify the area. Austrian military courts condemned and executed 250 persons for treason, espionage, or aiding and abetting the enemy. Political trials against Serbs, begun as early as 1909, continued in the wartime years and resulted in hundreds being sentenced to prison terms. Other Serbs were imprisoned or killed by the military authorities without the benefit of formal legal proceedings.[6] In April 1916, sixteen Serbs were condemned to death after a protracted trial in Banja Luka; their sentences were commuted in March 1917 by the Emperor Karl I, who ascended the throne after the death of Franz Josef in 1916. Thus World War I marked the first time in

---

6 Osman Nuri-Hadžić, "Borba Muslimana za versku i vakufsko-mearifsku autonomiju," in *Bosna i Hercegovina pod austro-ugarskom upravom* (Belgrade: Geca Kon, 1938), pp. 156-9.

Bosnian history that a significant number of people were killed for their national or ethnic affiliation.

The war ended ingloriously for the Habsburg monarchy. On October 16, 1918, the Emperor Karl proclaimed a federation, which to most of his subjects signified defeat and the end of the monarchy. Soldiers left the front and the bureaucrats stayed home. After dominating much of east-central Europe for more than 500 years, the much vaunted Habsburg empire disappeared almost overnight from the face of the earth.

7

Royal Yugoslavia
1918-1941

—————— • ——————

LATE IN THE war, Woodrow Wilson and America's European allies became enamored with the notion of national self-determination and hoped to make it the overarching principle of any peace accord. Most politically conscious South Slavs welcomed this approach, as it coincided with the notions of South Slav unification that were widely popular, at least among Serbian, Croatian, and Slovenian intellectuals. The impending defeat of the Central Powers gave hope to many that a land of the South Slavs, or Yugoslavia, would be created as a free and independent state to embody the national aspirations of the Serbs, Croats, and Slovenes. These hopes were embodied in the Corfu Declaration of July 1917, negotiated between representatives of the Serbian government headed by Nikola Pašić, and the Yugoslav Committee, a group of prominent Croats, Serbs, and Slovenes who had fled Habsburg territory to represent South Slav interests abroad. In the Corfu Declaration, the signatories agreed to create a "constitutional, democratic, and parliamentary monarchy" under the Serbian Karadjordjević dynasty.[1]

---

[1] For a comprehensive treatment of interwar Yugoslavia emphasizing political developments, see Joseph Rothschild, *East Central Europe between the Two World Wars* (Seattle: University of Washington Press, 1974), pp. 200-80.

Yugoslav unity, however, meant one thing to Pašić and the Serbian leadership and something quite different to the Croats and Slovenes of the Yugoslav Committee. These conflicting expectations, aggravated by the very different perceptions that each group had of the other, caused repeated clashes in the years of royal Yugoslavia (1918-41). The Serbs, about to experience triumph in war after several years of suffering and losses, perceived Yugoslavia as the fulfillment of their dream of a Greater Serbia, not unlike the expansion of Serbian territory in the two Balkan wars. In Serbian eyes, Yugoslavia was to be the embodiment of Serbian centralism, ruled by the Serbian dynasty and led by Serbian army officers, bureaucrats, and parliamentarians. The Serbs felt particular affection for Bosnia, which they considered to be rightfully Serbian territory and which would now become an integral part of their state. The Serbs tended to see their Slovene and Croatian cousins as weak-willed compromisers corrupted by decadent Western influences, believing they had acquiesced in constitutional compromises with their Habsburg overlords for centuries.

To the Croats and Slovenes, Yugoslavia was conceived as a partnership of equals that would have a federalist structure and would unite the historic Croatian and Slovenian lands of the defunct Habsburg imperium with the kingdom of Serbia. While admiring Serbia's military prowess, the Croats and Slovenes tended to look down on the Serbs as uncouth country bumpkins who lacked the cultural development that they themselves had achieved in centuries of closer association with the West. Conceding to the Serbs the honor of greater distinction in battle, the Croats and Slovenes saw themselves as accomplished administrators and state-builders, talents they aspired to put to work in the new Yugoslav state.

Many Bosnians viewed their future in the new South Slav state through the prism of the perennially unresolved Agrarian Question. Opinions, of course, followed national fault lines. The Serbian dynasty was firmly committed to ending all feudal relations, having abolished serfdom a century earlier when the Serbs first carved out a tiny principality and achieved autonomy from the Ottomans. In 1914 the Serbian government stated that its war aims included the "liberation and unification of all our subjugated brothers."[2] In February 1917 the Serbian government-in-exile promised five hectares of land to each combatant after liberation. Motivated by these promises and expecting an end to peasant payments to Muslim landlords, some Bosnian Serbs volunteered to fight for Serbia and participated in the final demise of the Central Powers.

Muslim leaders, while they shared in the general enthusiasm for a Yugoslav state, sought to moderate the impact of any agrarian reform or, if possible, to thwart it altogether. The Agrarian Question continued to be the focal point of much political controversy in Bosnia after World War I.

Inspired by further commitments of the Serbian dynasty, many Bosnian Christian peasants withheld their payments to Muslim landlords when the fortunes of war turned decisively in favor of the Serbs and the Entente Powers in 1918. Some Christian peasants seized land from their Muslim landlords, and physical attacks against Muslims increased. Most of the perpetrators were Serbs. Disorder and violence were particularly pronounced in eastern Hercegovina, but the movement soon encompassed much of Bosnia and parts of Croatia. On November 3, 1918, faced with a full-blown peasant revolt, the Bosnian

2   Tomasevich, p. 219.

MAP 7.I — CONSTITUENT PARTS OF THE KINGDOM OF THE SERBS, CROATS, AND SLOVENES (1918-29)

provincial government invited Serbian troops into Bosnia to quell the disorders. On November 6, Serbian troops entering Sarajevo were greeted as liberators. Despite the military response, individual Bosnian Serbs continued to attack Muslims and seize their property, even as Muslims protested to the Belgrade government that Serbian troops and officials failed to act against those responsible.

On December 1, 1918, Prince Regent Alexander (acting on behalf of his aged and infirm father, King Peter I) declared the creation of the Yugoslav state and named it the "Kingdom of the

Serbs, Croats, and Slovenes." The declaration was made in the presence of delegates from the Yugoslav Committee who represented South Slavs from the former Habsburg lands. The new state was to be a democratic parliamentary monarchy along the lines envisaged in the Corfu Declaration, but from the beginning it was in many respects a triumph of Serbian predominance. Called in to quell peasant unrest and to confront land-grabbing Italians in the northwest, the Serbian army occupied many of the former Habsburg territories of the new state. Serbian officials were quick to follow; they also began to replace Bosnian Muslims in key positions in Bosnia.

PARLIAMENTARY POLITICS AND AGRARIAN REFORM

Politically, the royal Yugoslav era may be divided into two periods: royal parliamentarianism (December 1918 - January 6, 1929), and the royal dictatorship (January 6, 1929 - April 1941) declared by King Alexander. The two eras had much in common. During both, periodic elections were held in the new South Slav state, the government was made up of ministers representing shaky and often short-lived parliamentary coalitions, and political life was dominated by constant disputes over the issue of Serbian dominance in the kingdom.

Throughout the era of royal Yugoslavia, the Bosnian Muslims displayed remarkable political cohesion by voting in overwhelming numbers for the Yugoslav Muslim Organization (YMO), as shown in TABLE 7.1. Although three other Muslim parties sought votes in the 1920 election to the Constituent Assembly, together they garnered less than 2% of that vote and soon disappeared from the scene. The number of votes for the YMO from one election to another varied by only 20% over

TABLE 7.1 — CONSISTENCY OF ELECTORAL SUPPORT FOR THE YUGOSLAV
MUSLIM ORGANIZATION (YMO)

Election	Date	YMO Votes	YMO Seats
Constituent Assembly	NOV. 28, 1920	110,895	24
Parliament	MAR. 18, 1923	122,494	18
Parliament	FEB. 8, 1925	132,296	15
Parliament	SEPT. 11, 1927	132,326	18

SOURCE: Joseph Rothschild, *East Central Europe Between the Two World Wars,*
pp. 215, 219, 224, and 229.

seven years, a testimony to the solid foundations of Bosnian
Muslim identity and the stability of Muslim voting patterns.

The YMO was led by middle-class, urban Muslims such as
civil servants, merchants, journalists, and other professionals;
however, the party was also very effective in promoting the
interests of the Muslim landowning class. Led by Dr. Mehmed
Spaho, an able politician who was in and out of governing
coalitions throughout the royal Yugoslav period, the YMO
played out the historic role of the Bosnian Muslims as a swing
group in coalition politics, typically supporting the center against
centrifugal tendencies.

Serbs and Croats displayed no such cohesion in the era of
parliamentary centralism. The Serbs were almost evenly divided in supporting two parties. The Serbian Radicals, led in
the early years by the old war-horse Nikola Pašić, a crafty and
effective proponent of Serbian centralism, found their support
almost exclusively in the former Serbian state. The Serbian
Democrats drew votes from Serbs everywhere but were particularly popular with Serbs living in the former Habsburg lands of
the kingdom. Bosnian Serbs supported both these parties but

voted in large numbers for the Serbian Agrarian Party, a smaller party whose program focused on the Agrarian Question and related issues of land reform.

Most Bosnian Croats supported the Croatian Peasant Party, led by Stjepan Radić. Favoring a radical land reform program to give the land to those who tilled it, the party won widespread support from Croats everywhere except the major cities. Radić and his followers boycotted the Assembly from the beginning and took their seats in Parliament only in 1924, creating for the Serbian parties a need for coalition partners that was eagerly filled by the Muslim YMO and Slovene Populists.

The Communist Party of Yugoslavia (CPY) was the third largest party in the Constituent Assembly with fifty-eight seats. Restricted in its grass-roots activities, the Party nevertheless won widespread popular support among urban workers and peasants. Like the Social Democrats, the Communists withdrew from the Assembly in 1921, and shortly thereafter the Communist Party was banned by the State Security Act of 1921. Its leaders were hounded and imprisoned by the authorities, and the Party was driven underground for the remainder of the royal Yugoslav period. Not until the appointment of Josip Broz (Tito) as general secretary in 1937 did the Party's fortunes begin to revive.

On June 28, 1921, the Vidovdan Constitution passed with 223 votes, although 163 of the 419 members of the Assembly boycotted the vote. All YMO delegates voted for the constitution, having won a major concession from the Serbian Radicals to retain the boundaries of Bosnia and Hercegovina as a distinct administrative unit. Royal Yugoslavia was thus divided administratively to respect the historic boundaries of the former Habsburg territories, even though day-to-day administration of the country was an ongoing exercise in Serbian central control. Despite submitting numerous complaints of Serbian violence against Muslim landowners and protesting government passivity in prosecuting Serbian perpetrators, Spaho and the YMO leadership supported the new constitution. Their votes, in fact, proved an essential component of the assembly majority that approved the document.

Muslim political influence in the new state also figured in the agrarian reforms that were promulgated in the kingdom's early years. In the Interim Decree of February 25, 1919, King Alexander laid out three principles for solving the Agrarian Question: (1) an end to serfdom; (2) division of large estates; and (3) indemnification of former owners by the state. Subsequent legislation defined the scope of land transfers and the amount of compensation to be paid to the Muslim landlords, and YMO delegates negotiated compensation terms that appeared to be liberal in exchange for their support of the Vidovdan Constitution. The reforms were not legally complete until 1931; however, they resulted in over 150,000 peasant families receiving over one million hectares of land. Previous owners of the land received a combination of cash and long-term bonds guaranteed by the Yugoslav government.

The agrarian reforms of 1919-31 ended the institution of serfdom in Bosnia, but other major objectives of these changes remained unrealized. Since most peasants received in ownership only the land they had previously cultivated, the average holding remained small and agricultural productivity did not increase appreciably. Advocates of more radical reform, such as the leaders of the Croatian Peasant Party, continued to argue that the reforms did not go far enough. Compensation paid to the Muslim landlords was often inadequate for them to start anew, and the bonds received in partial payment consistently traded below face value. Those Muslim landlords who had made the transition to the urban professions and other commercial ventures fared the best. Finally, the Great Depression devastated all the agricultural economies of Europe, including those of Bosnia and the rest of Yugoslavia, and impoverished many peasants despite the reforms.

Coalition politics continued until 1929 in the kingdom of the Serbs, Croats, and Slovenes. The YMO was frequently part of the governing coalition in Belgrade; at other times it was excluded from power in the increasingly desperate search for a stable political alignment. Despite protracted efforts to bring together the leading Serbian and Croatian parties of Yugoslavia, relations between them deteriorated, and conduct on the floor of the Parliament descended to new depths.

The leader of the Croatian Peasant Party, Stjepan Radić, spent much of the period obstructing legislative agreement, boycotting Parliament, and seeking support for Croatian separatist positions in London, Moscow, and elsewhere abroad. Heated parliamentary debates erupted into physical violence when Radić and four other Croatian deputies were shot during a heated exchange in Parliament on June 20, 1928. Radić died on August 8. The Croatian delegates again walked out. Soon bitter recriminations by politicians were followed by street demonstrations as public order declined. Finally, on January 6, 1929, the king suspended Parliament, annulled the constitution, and proclaimed himself the sole source of all authority in the kingdom.

ROYAL DICTATORSHIP AND THE RISE OF FASCISM

King Alexander's declaration of a royal dictatorship was followed by several proclamations that made his kingdom a more unitary, centralized, Serbian-ruled state. The "Kingdom of the Serbs, Croats, and Slovenes" was renamed the "Kingdom of Yugoslavia." Alexander outlawed all political parties and associations based on confessional or ethnic grounds and extended the ban (first decreed in August 1921) on the Communist Party of Yugoslavia. On September 3, 1931, he promulgated another constitution that reestablished Parliament, although the king alone retained the authority to designate and dismiss ministers and to appoint mayors and others municipal officials. The 1931 constitution restored coalition-building as a central activity in Yugoslav political life but gave the king authority to intervene at will in political processes and to invoke extraordinary emergency powers.

Under Alexander's dictatorship, Bosnia lost its distinctive status as a provincial unit for the first time in centuries. The king abolished the provincial boundaries that existed before 1929 and divided Yugoslavia into nine *banovinas* (administrative units ruled by *bans*), all but one of which were named after rivers that flowed through them. Boundaries of the banovinas ignored historical precedent and cut across ethnic boundaries, giving Serbs a numerical majority in six of the nine units. The historical territory of Bosnia and Hercegovina was divided among four of the nine banovinas: Vrbas, Drina, Zeta, and Primorska. Royal appointments favored the Serbs. In many Bosnian towns, elected Muslim mayors were replaced by Serb appointees.

On the day the dictatorship was declared, an emissary of the king met with Mehmed Spaho and other YMO leaders in a bid

MAP 7.2 — THE KINGDOM OF YUGOSLAVIA (1929-39), SHOWING DIVISION
INTO BANOVINAS

to win support for the planned changes. Despite their displeasure with the dissolution of Bosnia as a province and their fears
of more centralized Serbian control, the YMO leaders did not
oppose the imposition of royal dictatorship.

On October 9, 1934, King Alexander was assassinated while
visiting the French city of Marseilles. The assassination was
plotted by Croatian fascists, known as *Ustashe* (insurrectionists),

who favored the destruction of Yugoslavia and full independence for Croatia.[3] The Ustashe operated under Benito Mussolini's protection in Italy and as an underground group within Yugoslavia. In World War II their leader, Ante Pavelić, was put in charge of the "Independent State of Croatia" (encompassing Croatia and Bosnia) by the Germans and Italians.

After the king's death, power passed into the hands of Alexander's cousin, Prince Paul, and two other regents who were to rule jointly until Alexander's son Peter, heir to the Karadjordjević crown, reached majority in September 1941. New elections to the Yugoslav Parliament were held in May 1935, and in June 1935 Milan Stojadinović became prime minister in a government supported by the Bosnian Muslims. Mehmed Spaho, leader of the YMO, served as minister of transportation in the Stojadinović government. Thereafter, Spaho and other Bosnian Muslim leaders were represented in each Yugoslav government until World War II reached the country in April 1941.

Stojadinović's government moderated some of the harsher aspects of the royal dictatorship, granted amnesty to political prisoners, and made overtures of reconciliation to the leader of the Croatian Peasant Party, Vladko Maček. Stojadinović retained the foreign minister's portfolio and, at a time when Hitler's power was rising rapidly in Europe, traveled extensively abroad, seeking to strengthen Yugoslavia's ties with Nazi Germany and fascist Italy. In March 1936 he selected the German firm of Krupp over French and Czech competitors to modernize the large steel plant at Zenica in central Bosnia.

---

3   *Ustashe* is a plural form. In this work *Ustasha* is used as the adjectival form of the same word.

Despite his efforts, Stojadinović failed to reach a political compromise with Maček and the Croatian Peasant Party. In February 1939, Prince Paul replaced him with Dragiša Cvetković, hoping that a political compromise could be reached to win broader Croatian support within Yugoslavia. As before, Mehmed Spaho and the YMO leadership supported the Cvetković government; Spaho's resignation from the Stojadinović cabinet had in fact helped Paul to justify the change in prime ministers.

Negotiations for an agreement between the Cvetković government and Maček's Croatian Peasant Party gained urgency as Yugoslavs became more concerned about the growing power of Italy and Germany. The rising threat was underlined by Italy's occupation of Albania in April 1939. On August 20, 1939, Cvetković and Maček agreed to restructure the Yugoslav kingdom, giving autonomy to an enlarged Croatian banovina.

The Cvetković-Maček agreement constituted a genuine powersharing arrangement between Serbs and Croats, but it came at the expense of other Yugoslav groups. Western and central Hercegovina, where Croats were a majority in many rural areas, were added to the Croatian banovina, along with the city of Mostar. (This territory was the object of Croatian nationalist demands in 1971 and again in 1992, when Hercegovinian Croats proclaimed the "Republic of Herceg-Bosna" and received military backing from the regime in Zagreb.) Nevertheless, Mehmed Spaho and the YMO supported the agreement in the belief that it would strengthen the Yugoslav state. As the storm clouds of Nazism gathered in Europe, the agreement was attacked by two groups: Croatian extremists, who wanted full Croatian independence rather than mere autonomy; and Communists, who demonstrated against the "antinational" policies of the government.

ECONOMY AND SOCIETY

Economic growth was essential if parliamentary democracy were to succeed in Yugoslavia and elsewhere in Eastern Europe. Industrialization, initiated in Bosnia during the Austrian period, resumed modestly after World War I. Later in the royal Yugoslav period, much of the industrial development, particularly in heavy manufacturing and mining, was driven by German investment and the German desire to secure access to strategic raw materials.

The Great Depression of the 1930s was a severe setback to royal Yugoslav efforts to encourage economic development. Peasants were caught in a classic "price scissors" that plagued all Eastern European countries. They were squeezed between deeply depressed prices for their agricultural products and the high cost of manufactured goods that they purchased. As noted previously, average landholdings remained small, and agricultural productivity showed little improvement despite postwar agrarian reforms. Bosnia, with the rest of Yugoslavia, remained an overwhelmingly agrarian society whose major cities did not grow appreciably in the royal Yugoslav era.

CONFLICT WITH HITLER: THE ROAD TO WAR

As Hitler's acquisitions increased, so did his Balkan ambitions. Between November 1940 and March 1941, he compelled Hungary, Romania, and Bulgaria to adhere to the Tripartite Pact, effectively making them allies of Germany and Italy. Yugoslavia's central position in Hitler's plans became more critical when the Italian invasion of Greece, launched from Albanian territory in October 1940, was repulsed. Hitler issued an ultimatum to Yugoslavia. On March 25, 1941, Cvetković and Foreign Minister Aleksandar Cincar-Marković capitulated to Hitler and signed the Tripartite Pact in Vienna.

Yugoslavia's adherence to the pact angered many Yugoslavs, including military officers opposed to an alliance with Hitler. On the night of March 26, 1941, officers of the royal Yugoslav air force led a bloodless military coup and replaced Prime Minister Cvetković with General Dušan Simović. Carried out in the name of King Peter (who was still a few months short of his eighteenth birthday), the coup forced Prince Paul to resign and leave the country along with his two co-regents. Large demonstrations in Belgrade greeted the new government, calling for armed resistance rather than peaceful capitulation to the Nazis. The new government won the support of a broad coalition of political forces, including the Bosnian Muslims and Vladko Maček, the leader of the Croatian Peasant Party, who joined the government a few days after the coup.

Hitler was enraged. On learning of the coup he ordered the Wehrmacht to invade Yugoslavia and destroy it as a state. Despite the new Yugoslav government's desperate maneuvers and plaintive appeals in late March and early April 1941 to prevent a German invasion, the mighty Axis war machine prepared to strike Yugoslavia by land and air.

The Nazi destruction of royal Yugoslavia's armed forces was swift and complete. On April 6, 1941, with no formal declaration of war, the German Luftwaffe began a relentless three-day bombardment of Belgrade that took an estimated 20,000 lives. German ground forces simultaneously attacked from Romania and Bulgaria; Yugoslav defenses held out for only a few days. The Germans entered Zagreb on April 10 and took Belgrade on April 13. Italian forces invaded Slovenia and Dalmatia; on April 17 they captured the Bay of Kotor and much of the Yugoslav fleet. The remnants of the royalist General Staff fled to the Bosnian interior, taking refuge first in Pale, a resort outside Sarajevo, and then in Montenegro. King Peter and his ministers were evacuated by the British and taken to London, where they established a Yugoslav government-in-exile. After eleven days of catastrophic military defeats, Yugoslavia's former Foreign Minister and Ambassador to Germany, Aleksandar Cincar-Marković, signed an unconditional surrender to the Axis Powers on April 17, 1941.

8

World War II: The Yugoslav Apocalypse

— • —

IN WESTERN EUROPE and the United States, World War II was experienced principally as a colossal struggle against Nazi Germany and its fascist allies. In the Yugoslav lands, however, the war was multidimensional, involving three distinct conflicts. First, the war was a struggle of the occupied against the occupiers, a battle of Yugoslav resistance movements against the Germans and Italians. Second, it was a civil war involving rival national extremists and the competing domestic resistance movements. Finally, it became a struggle for a revolutionary social transformation, since the Communist Party of Tito and his Partisans espoused an ideology that advocated an end to the old order. These three conflicts were interwoven and at times indistinguishable. They resulted in violence and devastation of unprecedented proportions, but they also led to a radical recasting of Yugoslav society along lines dictated by Tito and his triumphant Partisans.

Bosnia, in the geographic center of Yugoslavia, was at the heart of these epic struggles. Its rough, mountainous terrain and the immediately adjacent areas of Serbia, Montenegro and Croatia became the primary theater of conflict between the Communist-led Partisans and the German and Italian invaders who relentlessly pursued them. During the wartime years, external players intruded in new and unprecedented ways in Bosnian affairs. Not by coincidence, some Bosnian political groups for the first time systematically perpetrated large-scale atrocities against members of other ethnic groups. The wartime conflicts, in other words, redefined the Bosnian political landscape and helped radicalize the perceived alternatives for interethnic relations. The primary contenders of World War II have been emulated in ideology, rhetoric, symbolism, organization, and even disorganization by the groups that emerged in the early 1990s as combatants in the Bosnian conflict.

THE OCCUPATION AND DIVISION OF YUGOSLAVIA

Once they secured the major Balkan cities and lines of communication in April 1941, the Axis Powers implemented Hitler's orders regarding their new possessions. Royal Yugoslavia was carved into several political entities under Axis supervision. Croatia and almost all of Bosnia and Hercegovina were incorporated into a newly created "Independent State of Croatia." This entity, however, was not much of a state, and it was certainly not independent. The Axis Powers subdivided the "Independent State of Croatia" into German and Italian zones of occupation, divided by a southeast to northwest line. Sarajevo and most major Bosnian cities fell within the German zone; Mostar was under Italian occupation.

In Serbia, the Germans eventually created a puppet occupation regime under the command of General Milan Nedić, who had served as Minister of War in royal Yugoslavia before the war. Undistinguished in most respects, the Serbian rump state nonetheless acquired the distinction of being the first country in all of occupied Europe in which the Nazis and their collabora-

MAP 8.1 — THE WARTIME PARTITION OF YUGOSLAVIA (DECEMBER 1941)

tors completed the deportation and extermination of Jews and Gypsies.[1]

Much of Macedonia was occupied by Bulgaria. Hitler permitted Italy to annex or occupy Dalmatia and Montenegro on its own behalf and parts of Macedonia and Kosovo on behalf of its Greater Albanian client. To the northwest, Slovenian lands were divided between Italy and Germany.

---

1   Raul Hilberg, *The Destruction of the European Jews* (Chicago: Quadrangle, 1961), p. 442.

"INDEPENDENT" CROATIA: THE USTASHE AND ETHNIC ATROCITIES

By creating the "Independent State of Croatia," the Nazis followed the practice they had established elsewhere in Eastern Europe of creating puppet states under the titular governance of native fascists. The newly created entity was headed by the Croatian Ustasha leader Ante Pavelić, a longtime extremist and mastermind of the 1934 assassination of King Alexander.

Pavelić's Ustasha regime combined the worst of German Nazism and Croatian fascism. Although the "Independent State of Croatia" was the fulfillment of Croatian dreams of a single, unified Croatian homeland, its population of 6.3 million included about 2 million Serbs, 30,000 Jews, and 750,000 Bosnian Muslims. The Ustashe set out with ruthless determination to eliminate the Jews, Gypsies, and Serbs. On April 30, only a few weeks after the German conquest, the Croatian government published its definition of a "Jew," the first step in the process of identifying Jews, confiscating their property, concentrating them, and ultimately shipping them off to camps for extermination. Acting under careful German tutelage, the Ustashe by 1944 had transported many of the 30,000 Jews living in the "Independent State of Croatia" to Nazi labor or death camps, where almost all perished. Some Jews survived by fleeing to the forests, joining the Partisans, and fighting against the occupying forces. A few Jews remained in Zagreb, Sarajevo, and other towns of the former Ustasha state, but by the end of the war their numbers had been reduced by 90% or more.

The Ustashe adopted a tripartite strategy toward the Serbs living under their rule, aiming to eliminate the Serbian nationality through extermination, deportation, and conversion to Catholicism. The Ustashe brutally killed many Serbs in their churches, streets, and villages in front of other inhabitants.

UPI/Bettmann

FIG. 8.1 — ANTE PAVELIĆ, SECOND FROM RIGHT, CONFERS WITH NAZI
LEADERS AT HITLER'S HEADQUARTERS IN JULY 1941

Estimates of deaths from Ustasha genocide vary widely, from
about 185,000 to 700,000 and even higher. Serbian polemicists
regularly claim (in an estimate that is probably exaggerated) that
one million Serbs perished at Ustasha hands. Croatian nationalists, on the other hand, argue that the Tito government over-
stated the number of deaths for political purposes.[2]

Ustasha atrocities aroused great antagonism and encited the
desire for revenge by Serbs. In retaliation, Serbian Chetnik
units slaughtered Croats, Muslims, and others suspected of
Ustasha sympathies. Thousands fled the Ustashe and joined

2   For a summary of the debate, albeit from a distinctly Croatian viewpoint,
see Vladimir Žerjavić, *Yugoslavia — Manipulations with the Number of
Second World War Victims* (Zagreb: Croatian Information Center, 1993).
A well-reasoned evaluation is found in Aleksa Djilas, *The Contested
Country: Yugoslav Unity and Communist Revolution, 1919-1953* (Cam-
bridge: Harvard University Press, 1991), pp. 125-7.

resistance forces; Partisan numbers in particular swelled as the brutality mounted.

The Ustashe killed Serbs, Jews, Gypsies, and others with chilling efficiency at the large concentration camp at Jasenovac. Although almost all observers agree that the majority of those killed were Serbs, the number of deaths at Jasenovac has become a matter of heated dispute. Franjo Tudjman, a historian by training who became president of Croatia in 1990, has claimed that only 70,000 Serbs died at Jasenovac, very probably a low number. One Serbian estimate, on the other hand, has put the number of Serbian victims at an unlikely high 1.1 million.[3] In the Serbian nationalist lexicon, *Jasenovac* is an instantly identifiable symbol of Croatian genocide.

Ustasha efforts to convert Serbs to Catholicism were aided by some members of the Catholic clergy, who either equivocated or openly endorsed these activities. The Catholic Archbishop of Zagreb, Alojzie Stepinac, periodically visited the regime's leaders; even though he spoke out publicly against forced conversions, his visits gave the conversion campaign the stamp of legitimacy from the Catholic hierarchy. Bosnian Franciscans were in the forefront of these conversion efforts, and wartime Sarajevo became a center of the Croatian Catholic campaign to convert Serbs. Archbishop Šarić of Sarajevo openly endorsed the conversion efforts. Over 200,000 Serbs converted to Catholicism, although most of these conversions were clearly tactical and temporary.

The Muslims held a more ambivalent position in the Ustasha scheme of things. As Croatian nationalists, the Ustashe held that the Muslims were Croats who had strayed from the Catho-

3   Mack Thompson, *A Paper House: The End of Yugoslavia* (New York: Pantheon Books, 1992), pp. 267-8. See also Stan Markotich, "Ethnic Serbs in Tudjman's Croatia," *RFE/RL Research Report*, Sept. 24, 1993, p. 29.

lic fold and converted to Islam, but the Ustashe made no significant attempt to convert Muslims to Catholicism as a precondition for acceptance as Croats. The regime's Education Minister even proclaimed that "Independent Croatia" was a state of two religions, Catholicism and Islam. A mosque was established in Zagreb for Bosnian Muslims.

The Ustashe attracted many Bosnian Muslims who declared themselves Croats or acknowledged Croatian coloration. To encourage Muslim participation, the Ustashe organized a special Muslim SS division to collaborate with them in persecuting Serbs and in fighting the war. Pavelić successfully wooed several YMO leaders to serve in the Ustasha government. Muslim collaboration was particularly common among upper-class Muslims and in eastern Hercegovina, where Muslims accepted many local government appointments. In eastern Hercegovina and southeastern Bosnia, many Ustasha atrocities against Serbs were conducted by Muslim collaborators, provoking Serbian retaliatory atrocities against Muslims on several occasions.[4] On the other hand, many Croats and Muslims joined the Partisans, particularly in 1943 and thereafter.

In a war noted for cruelty on all sides, the Ustashe stood out for their relentless brutality and senseless violence. They hounded and executed political opponents from every ethnic group, including the Croats. Their brutality cost the Ustashe much public support and drove thousands into the ranks of the Partisans and Chetniks. Ustasha rule left a legacy of bitterness and brutality that was brought to life again by participants in the strife that erupted in 1991 and 1992.

4   Jozo Tomasevich, *The Chetniks: War and Revolution in Yugoslavia, 1941-1945* (Stanford University Press, 1975), pp. 258-9. For another excellent treatment of wartime conflicts, see Matteo J. Milazzo, *The Chetnik Movement and the Yugoslav Resistance* (Baltimore: Johns Hopkins University Press, 1975).

MIHAILOVIĆ AND THE CHETNIKS

Most political leaders and members of the royal family fled into exile after the Yugoslav government collapsed in April 1941. A small group of officers and men of the former Yugoslav army, under the leadership of Colonel Draža Mihailović, gathered in the hills near Doboj in northern Bosnia, moved to Ravna Gora in western Serbia shortly thereafter, and declared themselves to be Chetniks, the nucleus of resistance to German and Italian occupation.

The Chetniks took their name from the armed bands of Serbs who, as bandits, had challenged Ottoman rule in Serbia, Bosnia, and Macedonia. Mihailović and his followers reverted to peasant garb and grew long hair and beards, cultivating the appearance of primitive Serbian brigands. Reflecting their loyalties as army officers of royal Yugoslavia, the Chetnik leaders espoused a Greater Serbian ideology and hoped to restore the Serbian royal family as rulers of a reconstituted Yugoslavia. This meant that their appeal was largely limited to the Serbian population of the various Yugoslav lands, a large constituency but far from the only Yugoslavs prepared to fight the Axis Powers. Mihailović was strongly supported by the London-based Yugoslav government-in-exile, and in January 1942 he was appointed its minister of war.

From May until November 1941, Mihailović and his forces fought the Germans, at times in alliance with the Partisans. However, the Chetniks viewed the resistance very differently from the Partisans. First, to the degree that they followed the lead of the London government-in-exile, the Chetniks were committed to a strategy of delaying active resistance until the Allies invaded the Balkans; then they were to rise and harass Axis communications lines in support of the broader Allied effort.

Furthermore, Mihailović was deterred from active resistance by Hitler's cruel directive of September 1941, that 100 Serbs should die for every German soldier killed by resistance forces. This raised for Mihailović the specter of a repetition of Serbia's massive losses in World War I. Mihailović soon turned on the Partisans, whom he saw as the worse of two evils, and began to tolerate and eventually collaborate with the German and Italian occupiers.

TITO AND THE PARTISANS

The Communist Party of Yugoslavia, despite its success in elections to the Constituent Assembly in 1920, was hounded and repressed by the royal Yugoslav government after it was outlawed in August 1921. The Party's leadership was further decimated by Stalin's purges, by participation of key leaders in the Spanish Civil War, and by internal factional disputes. By 1937 the Party was reduced to a few thousand demoralized members, and it had been seriously discredited by slavishly adhering to the shifting whims of Soviet foreign policy in the Balkans. But the Party's fortunes began to rebound after a seasoned underground organizer, Josip Broz, was sent by Moscow to lead the Party's organizational work.

Josip Broz was born in 1892 at Kumrovec, a village on the Croatian-Slovenian border, of a Croatian father and a Slovenian mother. He became a metalworker and machinist and was active before World War I in the Social Democratic Party. He was drafted into the Austro-Hungarian army and captured on the Russian front, but he escaped in 1917 and went to Petrograd, then in the throes of revolutionary upheaval. As a witness and participant, he saw the Russian Revolution at first hand, and when he returned to Yugoslavia in 1920 he took employment as

FIG. 8.2 — KUMROVEC: BIRTHPLACE OF JOSIP BROZ TITO

a metalworker, becoming over time a leader in the Communist Party in Zagreb. He was imprisoned briefly in 1927 and began a five-year prison term in 1929 for illegal organizing activities. His prison time proved to be a blessing in disguise, for it kept him insulated from the Party's bitter factional feuds. Emerging from prison in 1934, he was known by several code names, including "Tito." After extensive organizing activities and travel, including a stint in Moscow, Josip Broz Tito was designated as first secretary of the Communist Party of Yugoslavia in September 1937.

By the time of the German invasion in 1941, the Party under Tito's leadership had become an effective revolutionary underground force with a membership of 12,000. When the Germans attacked, the Party urged Yugoslavia's soldiers to keep their weapons and prepare for resistance; in contrast, the royal government called upon all those under arms to lay down their weapons and submit to the occupiers. The Party began all-out resistance after Hitler's attack on Russia in June 1941. On July 4, the Party issued a call to all Yugoslavs to resist the fascist invaders using all possible means.

Thus began the four-year struggle between Goliath and David, between the German juggernaut and a small band of Yugoslav Communist-led guerrillas with little combat experience (except for some Spanish Civil War veterans) and, at the outset, a very modest following. Few observers in 1941 could have imagined that Tito and his Partisans, with little aid from the Western Allies and the Soviet army until late in the conflict, would expel the German invaders from much of Yugoslavia.

THE SOURCES OF PARTISAN SUCCESS

Like other successful popular resistance movements of the twentieth century, the Partisans succeeded only insofar as their leaders were able to reach out and mobilize a broad base of popular support on which they depended for recruitment, provisions, and daily assistance. Their success can be attributed to the leadership's resolute commitment to active resistance, firm discipline, and the pursuit of clear, consistent goals that were articulated by Tito and his lieutenants. The Partisans appealed for national liberation, which meant a revolutionary uprising of all Yugoslav nationalities to defeat the occupying powers and their domestic collaborators. Tito personally maintained a firm hand in directing these strategies through political and military leadership and by maintaining extensive correspondence with subordinates throughout the country. He instigated and led actions against enemy forces, orchestrated policy changes, and reined in excesses. At least twice he narrowly escaped death or capture.

At the core of the Partisans' appeal was the nationality policy of the Communist Party, embodied in the slogan *Bratstvo i jedinstvo* (brotherhood and unity). Unlike the discredited assumption of royal Yugoslavia that the South Slav peoples would homogenize into a single Yugoslav nationality, the Communist-led Partisans asserted that the nations of Yugoslavia were distinct and should be treated equally. The principle of national equality stood in contrast both to the royal Yugoslav government's practices of Greater Serbian centralism, endorsed and continued by Mihailović and his Chetniks, and to the extreme Croatian nationalism of the Ustashe, who aimed by one means or another to create an all-Croatian state.

Before the German invasion of 1941, the Party went through many wrenching debates, factional disputes, and esoteric changes in its approach to the national question. In wartime, Tito spelled out the key principles of national relations that were to guide the Partisans during the war and Party policies after the German defeat.[5]

Borrowing heavily from Stalin and the Soviet nationality model, Tito elaborated the twin ideas of full national self-determination for Yugoslavia's nationalities and, simultaneously, a strong, centralized Party organization that would be the sole political expression of each nation's will. The constitutional and legal mechanisms of government would respect national rights and, as in the Soviet case, even extend to recognized nationalities the theoretical right to secede from the state. At the same time the Communist Party, as the sole legitimate

---

5 The Party's approach to nationality issues is ably presented in Paul Shoup, *Communism and the Yugoslav National Question* (New York: Columbia University Press, 1968), and in Djilas, *The Contested Country.*

agency of the popular will, would maintain a discipline imposed from the center and assure that no nationality would exercise that right. This apparent sleight of hand would, of course, lead to fragmentation of the state if the Communist Party were to collapse or lose its monopolistic role, as happened in both the Soviet Union and Yugoslavia in the early 1990s. In wartime Yugoslavia, however, with its raging conflicts among national extremists and its unhappy recent experience of Greater Serbian hegemony, the Partisan policy was a refreshing blend of national liberation and a centrally-imposed discipline that could preclude nationalist excesses.

For Bosnians and other Yugoslavs, two critical questions naturally arose: What nationalities would be recognized in this scheme, and how would territorial boundaries be drawn in areas where nationalities were geographically intermingled? Tito and the Party leadership answered the first question with sweeping statements intended to include all possible claimants while specifically identifying five key nationalities: the Serbs, Croats, Slovenes, Macedonians, and Montenegrins. The Bosnian Muslims were not included in this core group of nationalities, being viewed by the Party at that time as a distinct community with no separate national status. However, since mainline Partisan operations were centered in Bosnia, Muslim support was critical, and Tito was careful to recognize their distinct status in numerous declarations and appeals.

The Bosnian Muslims also found comfort in the Party's promises of a separate status for Bosnia and Hercegovina. Since the most intense struggles between the Partisans and their adversaries were carried out largely in Bosnia and Hercegovina and the immediately adjacent mountainous regions, Bosnia became the crucible in which the Partisan commitment to national equality was forged in the wartime years. Tito proposed to create a federal structure made up of separate republics for each of the five key nationalities, with Bosnia and Hercegovina constituting a sixth federal unit. The principles of federalism were soon implemented in the liberated territories, which expanded (although not without some setbacks) as the war progressed.

STRUGGLES OF THE RESISTANCE MOVEMENTS

Almost immediately after the German invasion in April 1941, spontaneous resistance to the Axis began in the traditional epicenters of brigandage and revolt in eastern Hercegovina. Soon the Partisans and Chetniks were conducting sporadic harassment actions. With the Partisan call to arms on July 4, 1941, organized resistance began on a large scale, and by September the Partisans were able to establish a liberated territory in western Serbia and eastern Bosnia centered in Užice.

In the first months of the war, Partisans and Chetniks cooperated in various operations, but tensions soon developed between the two groups concerning their ultimate goals and the extent to which they should offer armed resistance to the occupiers. In October 1941, in the Serbian towns of Kragujevac and Kraljevo, German soldiers rounded up thousands of innocent civilians, including schoolchildren, and slaughtered them in retaliation for guerrilla attacks against German soldiers many miles away. Appalled by such wanton brutality and fearful that a Partisan victory would mean a Communist revolution that would sweep away all vestiges of the old order, Mihailović's resolve wilted, and he came to view the Partisans as his primary enemy. The last meaningful efforts at Chetnik-Partisan cooperation collapsed in November 1941. In the subsequent months

FIG. 8.3 — MONUMENT TO THE VICTIMS OF GERMAN KILLINGS IN
OCTOBER 1941 AT THE SERBIAN TOWN OF KRAGUJEVAC

and years Mihailović allowed some of his forces to be disarmed
by the Germans and arranged for others to become "legalized,"
that is, to pass under the titular command of the Nedić puppet
regime. Both under Chetnik command and as "legalized" units,
Mihailović's men fought beside the Germans and Italians in
battles against the Partisans.

Faced with surprisingly successful resistance movements in
the hills of Serbia and Bosnia, the Germans launched a total of
seven offensives between November 1941 and May 1944 in an
increasingly frustrated and futile attempt to crush the Partisan
movement.[6] Accounts of the seven German offensives, and of

6   An excellent, balanced account of these conflicts is found in Walter R.
    Roberts, *Tito, Mihailović, and the Allies, 1941-1945* (New Brunswick, N.J.:
    Rutgers University Press, 1973).

incredible Partisan survival and heroism in the midst of these assaults, assumed the dimensions of biblical lore in postwar Yugoslavia. The German failure has also contributed to US and European reluctance in the 1990s to consider military involvement in these same territories.

Each offensive forced Tito and the Partisan main command to flee to another refuge with their main units. These struggles reached epic proportions. Driven from eastern Bosnia in the spring of 1942, the Partisans crossed the rugged mountain terrain to capture Bihać in northwest Bosnia, where in November 1942 they convened the Anti-Fascist Council for the National Liberation of Yugoslavia (known by its Serbo-Croatian initials AVNOJ). In 1943 the Germans forced them from Bihać; again they marched the length and breadth of Bosnia to seek refuge in southeastern Bosnia and eastern Hercegovina. The fifth German offensive in the spring of 1943 sent them back to the northwest, where a second AVNOJ congress met on liberated territory at Jajce in November 1943. The seventh German offensive was an airborne assault on a Partisan headquarters at Drvar from which Tito narrowly escaped in May 1944. Nevertheless, the number of Partisan fighters grew and the size of liberated territories increased even as these offensives took an enormous toll in Partisans killed and wounded.

In the early phases of the war, a disproportionate number of Serbs joined the resistance movements relative to the other Yugoslav nationalities. Steeped in a tradition of armed resistance to foreign rule, Serbs were more inclined to join either the Chetniks or the Partisans early in the conflict. Since the Partisans experienced their first successes in western Serbia and in adjacent eastern Bosnia with its large Serbian peasant population, more Serbs joined the Partisan ranks in these areas. In territories of the "Independent State of Croatia" (that is, historical Croatia, Bosnia, and Hercegovina), Ustasha atrocities drove many Serbs into Partisan ranks. Members of other nationalities joined in large numbers later in the war, some drawn by the Partisan commitment to "brotherhood and unity" and others by conscription to the Partisan forces. In 1944 Tito recorded that 44% of the Partisans were Serbs, a percentage that probably understated the extent of their participation, for it reflected the swelling numbers of other Yugoslavs who joined the Partisans later in the war.

The preponderance of Serbs in Partisan ranks posed serious challenges to Tito's commitment to national equality. The Partisans of the historical "Military Frontier" region in Croatia proclaimed a separate republic. Partisan documents suggest that its Serbian leaders, rather than aggressively challenging the Germans and Ustashe militarily, were more interested in establishing and protecting an autonomous Serbian territory at the expense of Croats. (Serbs from the same communities, aided by some units of the Yugoslav People's Army, asserted autonomy from Croatia in 1991 and declared themselves part of the "Serbian Autonomous Region of Krajina.") Partisan leaders addressed these problems in 1942, urging all Partisan formations to fight the Germans and their fascist allies rather than reverting to nationalist squabbling.

The Partisan quest for popular support was particularly successful in Bosnia, the critical center of safe havens and military operations against the Germans. Croats and Muslims initially feared Partisan reprisals for the actions of the Ustashe, and many Muslims were haunted by the legacy of Serbian outbursts against Muslims, particularly in eastern Hercegovina. The Partisan command sought to allay these fears and proved willing to discipline errant Serbs and others in their ranks. The Partisans imposed elaborate rules for entering Muslim and Croatian villages. When Muslims fled their villages in fear, Partisan units secured their homes against reprisals and looting. Although imposition of this discipline was difficult and at times erratic in wartime conditions, the Partisans succeeded in dampening interethnic conflict and in winning widespread support in Bosnia through effective implementation of their patriotic slogans.

British and Allied support for Mihailović was strong in the early months of the war, but this support waned when Allied military missions learned that the Chetniks were avoiding resistance and collaborating with the Axis forces. The British, who sent missions to Tito as well as to Mihailović, became convinced by mid-1943 that the Partisans were deserving of support and parachuted supplies that had previously been bestowed on the Chetniks. In February 1944 the British ordered their liaison officers to withdraw from the Chetniks, and thereafter the Allies gave sole backing to Tito's military endeavors.

Stalin and the Soviets, although in an ideal position to claim credit for Tito's successes, nevertheless had rocky relations with the Partisans and the Yugoslav Communist Party during the war. Anxious to hide his revolutionary intentions from his American and British allies, Stalin grew uneasy with Tito's public pronouncements of "liberated" territories and claims that the Party was the sole legitimate political force in the Yugoslav lands. When the first AVNOJ congress (Bihać, November 1942) declared a Yugoslav "state" in liberated territory, Stalin reprimanded Tito and reminded him of the need to maintain a "united front" with non-Communist resistance forces. Such admonitions seemed to spur Tito on to more independent, Yugoslav-oriented objectives and to turn away from the goals of the international Communist movement. This led to the ironic situation in which Stalin was urging his presumed Yugoslav lackeys to moderate their actions while the Western Allies were encouraging a more aggressive course of resistance.

THE PARTISAN TRIUMPH

Although the Partisans succeeded largely on account of their own policies and actions, they benefited in growing measure from Allied victories as the war progressed. The Soviets repelled the German invasion of Russia in the bitter winter fighting of 1942-3, and the British and Americans were freer to pursue their Balkan aims after their triumphs in the North African campaign in May 1943. After the Italian surrender on September 8, 1943, the Germans, Chetniks, and Partisans scrambled to take over the Yugoslav territories previously occupied by Italian forces. The Germans took over the Italian zone of the "Independent State of Croatia," but the Partisans were able to liberate large swaths of territory in Montenegro, the Sandžak of Novi Pazar, and Hercegovina. The Chetniks, increasingly starved of popular support, were effectively eliminated in western Yugoslavia.

In August 1944 the Partisans began a push into Serbia as the Soviet Red Army approached from the east. Tito visited the Soviet Union in September 1944 (his absence carefully hidden from the British) and secured from Stalin a commitment that the Red Army would leave Yugoslav soil as soon as Belgrade was liberated. The Partisans and the Red Army, in a joint operation, subsequently expelled the Germans from Belgrade on October 20, 1944. Three weeks later the Red Army left Yugoslav soil in accordance with the promise Tito had secured in September.

From then until May 1945, Partisan military efforts focused on expanding the liberated territories and driving the Germans out of all Yugoslav lands. On April 6, 1945 (exactly four years after the German attack on Yugoslavia), the Partisans entered Sarajevo. They liberated Zagreb on May 8, 1945. On May 15, the last German and Ustasha troops surrendered to the Partisans.

To the Ustashe, Chetniks, and their collaborators and sympathizers, the Partisan victories were triumphs of Communists committed to a revolutionary destruction of the old order. Many fled to the West, hoping that the Allies would give them refuge so they could live to fight another day. The Western Allies, demanding that all Axis supporters surrender to troops in their native lands, turned away many fleeing Yugoslavs and forced them back into the arms of the Partisans. In their quest to eliminate opposition and to wipe out all armed formations the Partisans killed thousands. Some with records of collaboration made their way to the United States, Canada, Australia, Austria, and other refugee havens, making those countries centers of émigré anti-Communist agitation for the next several decades. Many faced execution at the hands of the Partisans after they were captured. Mihailović evaded capture for almost a year. He was arrested in March 1946, tried for collaboration, and executed four months later.

Besides the radical changes that the Partisan victory would bring to Yugoslav society, World War II had three consequences of great import for later events. First, the ascendancy of Serbs in the Partisan command structure would resurface in subsequent years in various forms. Tito combatted this tendency in many ways, but the Yugoslav army never completely eliminated the preponderant Serbian influence in its officer corps. Secondly, the legacy of Bosnia as a refuge of last resort against foreign invasion, compared to the vulnerability of Zagreb and Belgrade, influenced Yugoslav military policy thereafter. Bosnia became the focal point of Yugoslav defense theory and the center of Yugoslav munitions production in the postwar years.

Finally, the Partisan victories marked the rebirth of the Yugoslav ideal in a new form. The royal Yugoslav era ended in mutual recriminations when Yugoslavia rapidly collapsed before the German onslaught. Many Serbian nationalists blamed the collapse of royal Yugoslavia on a Croatian "fifth column" that stood to gain from a German and Italian occupation. Many Croats, on the other hand, blamed the collapse on the cowardice of Belgrade politicians and inadequacy of the Serb-dominated Yugoslav army. The new, postwar Yugoslavia gave its citizens the chance to create a forward-looking enterprise, one in which national "brotherhood and unity" was enlisted in the campaign to build a revolutionary new society.

9

Socialist Yugoslavia: The Tito Era, 1945-1980

THE WAR RAVAGED all areas of Yugoslavia, killed over a million people, and left millions more wounded or maimed. Unlike World War I, in which Serbia had suffered the heaviest losses, Bosnians were killed in disproportionate numbers in the conflict. All Bosnian groups experienced heavy losses in the war, but Bosnia's Serbs accounted for the greatest number of deaths and experienced a higher percentage of losses than the Croats or Muslims. The causes of death were not limited to the battlefield; many died because of the Ustasha campaigns of genocide and the ensuing fratricidal warfare. Bosnia's Jews and Gypsies were nearly exterminated; their communities were almost wiped out by deportations and killings.

Of the East European lands, Yugoslavia stood alone with Albania in having largely liberated itself from Axis occupation by a widely popular indigenous resistance movement. This achievement was comparable to that of the Chinese and Vietnamese Communists in their successful battles against Japanese occupiers. Foreign support was limited to supplies, diplomatic encouragement, and the Red Army's participation in the liberation of Belgrade. Most Yugoslavs and foreign observers accepted Tito's claim that he and his Partisans fought the Axis enemy and their South Slav collaborators with conviction, consistency, and great bravery. Most of those who held a different view fled Yugoslavia or were silenced or killed in the fierce repression that accompanied Tito's consolidation of power in 1945 and after.

The nature of Yugoslav socialism was radically altered after Stalin's decision in 1948 to expel the Communist Party of Yugoslavia (CPY) from the Cominform. The expulsion caused Tito and his associates to set off on a different path, one that eventually led to innovative domestic and foreign policies with profound consequences for the Yugoslavs, especially the people of Bosnia and Hercegovina. Abandoning earlier policies of control and repression, Tito presided over a liberalization that later led to unrestrained competition among republics and open ethnic rivalry.

THE MAKING OF SOCIALIST YUGOSLAVIA

At the heart of the Yugoslav Communist ethos was a profound desire to follow the example of the Soviet Union. This drive coexisted, paradoxically, with Tito's strong sense of personal independence and instinctive urge to mold the Communist movement to satisfy the particular needs of the Yugoslav situation. In other words, Tito wanted to emulate Lenin and Stalin rather than obey Stalin's every whim. The course of events in the immediate postwar years is a study in the interplay of two contradictory impulses, the flattery of imitation and the quest for an independent course.

In their eagerness to emulate the Soviet model, Tito and his Communists promulgated their social revolution with a zeal and speed unrivaled elsewhere in Eastern Europe. As one observer noted, "Outwardly the Yugoslavs between 1945 and 1948 appeared to be the most apt pupils and loyal allies of the

Soviet Union."[1] Thus the first years of Communist rule were harsh by any standard as the CPY moved quickly to consolidate its power, establish the foundations of the new order, and begin the social revolution it had proclaimed during the war.

Partly in recognition of the revolutionary zeal displayed by Tito and his comrades, and partly in hopes of controlling that zeal, Stalin chose Belgrade as the headquarters of the Communist Information Bureau (Cominform). Anxious to obscure his long-term revolutionary intentions from his Western Allies, Stalin had openly disbanded the Communist International in 1943. In September 1947 it was reborn under the more benign title of the Communist Information Bureau, charged with the same dual functions of promulgating world revolution and imposing Soviet policy priorities on the international Communist movement. The Cominform's official publication was given an ungainly moniker, *For a Lasting Peace, for a People's Democracy*, and trumpeted the party line to Communist Party faithful everywhere in the world.

1946 CONSTITUTION: THE STRUCTURE OF SOCIALIST YUGOSLAVIA

To mollify the Allied Powers, Tito entered into a coalition government in March 1945 with non-Communist politicians led by Ivan Subašić, a prewar governor of Croatia who spent the wartime years in the United States. While the Tito-Subašić government won much-needed international recognition for the socialist regime, the liberating Partisan forces played the leading role in setting the new political course. The "Democratic Federative Yugoslavia" that was proclaimed in 1945 had

---

1   Fred Singleton, *A Short History of the Yugoslav Peoples* (Cambridge University Press, 1985), p. 212.

MAP 9.1 — THE REPUBLICS AND AUTONOMOUS REGIONS OF
SOCIALIST YUGOSLAVIA (1945-91)

only a few non-Communists in its executive council, by way of
window dressing. Elections were held on November 11, 1945, for
a Constituent Assembly, and a single slate of candidates, principally Communists, was offered to the voters. The slate garnered
over 90% of the votes. A few weeks later, on January 31, 1946,
a new constitution was proclaimed by the Communist-dominated Constituent Assembly.

The 1946 Constitution, closely modelled on Stalin's Soviet
Constitution of 1936, established the basic political system of

socialist Yugoslavia. Fulfilling Tito's wartime commitments, the constitution specifically recognized five Yugoslav nationalities: Serbs, Croats, Slovenes, Macedonians, and Montenegrins. The Bosnian Muslims were not included, for the official party line held that the Muslims were a separate group without a national identity.

Six republics were established, closely corresponding to the historic units that were brought together in 1918 to form the kingdom of the Serbs, Croats, and Slovenes. The constitution, following Soviet precedent, recognized certain national minorities, the most important being the Hungarians and Albanians. Vojvodina, a region with a large Hungarian population, was established as an autonomous province; Kosovo-Metohija, an area with a large Albanian population, was created as an autonomous region. Both were attached to the republic of Serbia.

Bosnia and Hercegovina, the sixth republic, was the only one with no majority nationality and no national name. Its boundaries closely followed prior borders that dated back several centuries and were reestablished by the Austrians in 1878. One specialist has concluded that "these borders, also in large part an Ottoman legacy, are ... among the oldest and most continuous in Europe."[2] Thus Tito and the CPY, despite their commitment to radical change, preserved the distinctiveness of Bosnia and Hercegovina in establishing their political system.

The Constitution reaffirmed the two fundamental principles, outlined at the AVNOJ wartime congresses, of national self-determination and the Party's domination in public life. Republics were granted the right to secede. The constitution also granted the right of secession to the "peoples" of Yugoslavia,

[2] Dennison Rusinow, "The Ottoman Legacy in Yugoslavia's Disintegration and Civil War," in L. Carl Brown (ed.), *The Ottoman Legacy,* forthcoming.

but it suggested that they had exercised that right, once and for all, in choosing to become a part of the Yugoslav federation.[3] Later constitutions, including the last one of 1974, also guaranteed the right of Yugoslavia's peoples to secede from the federation. However, power was concentrated in the federal organs and the CPY in the early years of socialist Yugoslavia. Although the republics initially exercised little real political power, their creation and the drawing of boundaries between them would profoundly influence events in later decades.

THE CPY CONSOLIDATION OF POWER

The Communist Party took a two-pronged approach to the consolidation of power, ruthlessly pursuing those who had actively collaborated with their foes and at the same time seeking the support of the Serbian Orthodox, Catholic, and Muslim religious communities.

The Partisan forces, as noted above, hotly pursued all rival armed formations as the war ended, killing thousands of Germans, Ustashe, and Chetniks in the waning days of the conflict. Isolated units of Chetniks and Ustashe took to the same mountains that had sheltered the Partisans and continued small-scale guerrilla actions for years after the war ended. Yugoslav police reported that the last unit was captured in 1955.

Partisan policies against their enemies inspired fear in many prewar and wartime leaders who had collaborated or tolerated atrocities against other South Slavs. Catholic Archbishop Šarić of Sarajevo and the Bishop of Banja Luka fled from their flocks. Many intellectuals, particularly Croats and Muslims, fled to Vienna, Canada, the United States, or any place that would take them, leading to a bumper crop of anti-Communist émigré academics at Western universities in the postwar years. Com-

3   Djilas, p. 167.

pared to the broader Yugoslav picture, however, the exodus from Bosnia was modest.

Like the Austrians seventy years earlier, the Communist regime sought a working relationship with leaders of the major religious communities. The Serbian Orthodox Church had a centuries-long tradition of coexistence with very different regimes, including those of the Ottomans, Austrians, and royal Yugoslavs. After the war, Patriarch Gavrilo returned to Belgrade from German imprisonment. Despite the Church's generally avid support for Mihailović and the Chetniks, Tito and Gavrilo met personally and ended the major causes of animosity. The regime subsequently tolerated the Orthodox faith in Bosnia, Serbia, and elsewhere without, however, providing any special support.

The Party also avoided any overt attacks on the Muslims, despite the pattern of collaboration with the Ustashe, since many Muslims had also belatedly joined the Partisans and made important contributions in the fierce warfare in Bosnia. The Muslims of Sarajevo split between support for and opposition to the Communist Party. In 1945 elections to the Vakuf Assembly (the body established by the Austrians in 1909 to govern Islamic charitable foundations), religiously conservative anti-Communist candidates won key posts, and the prospect of a confrontation increased. The government cut off funding for Islamic cultural institutions, forcing Muslims to collect voluntary contributions at mosques. In August 1946 the Vakuf Assembly changed course and pledged to support the government. Thereafter the Communist regime allowed the continuation of key Islamic institutions that had been established in the Muslim-Austrian agreement of 1909, including the *Reis-ul-ulema*, the Vakuf Commission, and the Vakuf Assembly. Despite some confiscations and reforms, the vakuf system remained largely intact, and vakufs continued to support major Islamic cultural institutions in Bosnia throughout the socialist period.

Government relations with the Catholic Church were more stormy. The controversy centered on Archbishop Stepinac of Zagreb, who had openly endorsed some Ustasha actions even though he protested (more discreetly) other excesses. Stepinac stubbornly refused to leave his post despite encouragement from the regime to go into exile. Although he gave his lesser clergy permission to leave, most remained in place, posing a continuing challenge to the Communist regime. Tito at first encouraged Catholics to declare a "national" church that would be independent of the Vatican, but Stepinac did not respond to Tito's proposals. Stepinac and other church officials were publicly tried, along with leading Ustasha collaborators, in September 1946, a few months after Mihailović's execution. The Archbishop was sentenced to sixteen years' hard labor, but he served only five years in relatively comfortable confinement. Upon his release in December 1951 he was allowed to reside in his native Croatian village of Krasić, where he died in February 1960. Thousands of mourners attended his funeral, and his tomb in Zagreb Cathedral — surmounted by a simple, white marble memorial by the eminent Croatian sculptor Ivan Meštrović — became a shrine to Croatian nationalism in the late socialist years.

When the Vatican made Stepinac a Cardinal in 1952, Yugoslavia broke off diplomatic relations with the Vatican. In a compromise arranged several years later, relations were restored and a new Archbishop-Coadjunctor was appointed for Zagreb. The Catholic Church pursued an independent course in socialist Yugoslavia much as it did in Poland, at times supporting, but more frequently frustrating, the government.

THE ECONOMIC TRANSFORMATION

A key part of the CPY program was the socialization of the Yugoslav economy, intended to strengthen the working class and improve the lot of the average worker. The Party was also committed to rewarding the peasants, who had been the backbone of support for the Partisan liberation efforts in the war, with a radical agrarian reform intended, at last, to give the land to those who tilled it. Both of these changes profoundly altered the character of Bosnian society.

The CPY, following the Soviet example, was committed to the rapid industrialization of the Yugoslav economy. In the first instance this meant rebuilding the shattered economic infrastructure, an undertaking supported financially by the United Nations and aided by enthusiastic volunteer youth brigades organized by the CPY. Despite widespread devastation, these efforts succeeded by the end of 1946 in bringing productivity back to prewar levels. Roads, bridges, and railway lines were repaired and rebuilt, factories were restored to working order, and power facilities were reconstructed.

In 1947, under the direction of Slovene Communist Boris Kidrić, a Five-Year Plan was instituted to accelerate the industrial development of the country. Like its Soviet counterparts, the plan was accompanied by elaborate central planning techniques and a vast bureaucracy to mandate and monitor production and prices. The plan quickly proved unworkable in the highly diversified Yugoslav environment, but the CPY pursued it with diligence despite setbacks in the next few years. Bosnia, one of several less developed regions, received a disproportionate share of central support for industrial development.

The CPY introduced comprehensive agrarian reform in August 1945. The new law stated that no parcel larger than thirty-five hectares could be owned by a single producer, bringing an end to large holdings by individual landholders. Over 1.5 million hectares throughout Yugoslavia were confiscated and allotted to ex-Partisans, landless peasants, and peasant smallholders. While participation in collective farming was encouraged, the law did not touch off any significant drive for forced collectivization. After decades of discussion and promises, 1946 was the year in which a Yugoslav government finally turned over agricultural land to those who tilled it. The reforms aroused protests from the Catholic Church, which owned substantial tracts of land under monastic cultivation or administration. And, of course, opposition to agrarian reform was a major factor in the anti-Communist stance of some Bosnian Muslims in the early postwar years.

The reforms ended the Agrarian Question in Bosnia. The last vestiges of Muslim landlord privilege were eradicated. In most instances, the former great families were allowed to retain their homes but were limited to the same amount of arable land as everyone else. Many affluent Muslims had already relocated to the towns and cities, driven from the countryside by war or drawn by the professional and social benefits of city life. In some instances they lived in urban residences of distinction, located in or near the city centers. One such residence was a stately two-story home built by a Muslim member of the Austrian-era Parliament in 1910 on a small hill just outside Sarajevo. After the agricultural reforms, all that remained of the family's traditional lifestyle was the dwelling, which was subdivided into four apartments, each owned by a different family member. A nearby hut, once the servant quarters, had passed to separate ownership, but its inhabitants remained loyal to the family and kept an eye on the house. In a typical transition, the oldest son became a manufacturer's representative in the 1960s and, with his family, took an apartment in the center of Sarajevo.

EXPULSION FROM THE COMINFORM: THE TITO-STALIN DISPUTE

As the Yugoslav Communists rushed to make up for lost time in their drive to socialize the country, frictions developed between Stalin and his overachieving emulators. The dissensions ostensibly centered on trade policy, foreign policy, the organization of the Yugoslav army, and interparty relations, but fundamentally the strains developed because the CPY refused to follow obediently the perverse twists and turns that Soviet foreign policy demanded of the international Communist movement. These disagreements went back to the early phases of the war, when Stalin reprimanded Tito after the 1942 AVNOJ congress for exposing the CPY's revolutionary zealotry when all Communist parties were under instructions not to offend non-Communist elements in the resistance movement.

In February 1948 Tito was summoned to Moscow to discuss the growing interparty tensions with Stalin and Soviet Foreign Minister Vyacheslav Molotov. He declined the invitation but sent Croatian Party Chairman Vladimir Bakarić and the Slovene Edvard Kardelj in his place. After their disputatious visit, the Yugoslav and Soviet parties exchanged a series of letters, subsequently published by the Yugoslavs, in which the Soviets criticized the CPY with growing animosity. In May the Yugoslavs arrested two prominent CPY members as Soviet agents. The dispute became a crisis on June 28, 1948, when members of the

Cominform, meeting in Bucharest without Yugoslav representatives in attendance, expelled the CPY from their organization. Following this unprecedented expression of Stalin's displeasure, pro-Soviet elements in the CPY called for Tito's overthrow. For the next several years the press and radio in all Soviet bloc countries attacked the CPY in the bitterest possible terms and demanded that the traitorous Yugoslavs be punished for their unorthodoxy.

Expulsion from the Cominform, tantamount to the excommunication of a devout Church member, deeply shocked Tito and other leaders of the CPY. Their initial response was to insist upon their Communist orthodoxy and, briefly, to intensify their arduous efforts to make Yugoslavia a Soviet clone. The principal outcome of this response was a hurried effort to collectivize Yugoslav agriculture from 1949 to 1951. At the height of this campaign, some 2.5 million hectares were put under collective cultivation. A serious drought in 1950 stalled the drive, and soon Party leaders recognized that the campaign had yielded few benefits and incurred enormous social and economic costs. In 1951 the Party changed course. Over the next ten years over 90% of collectivized land reverted to private hands.

Coming as it did on June 28, the date on which the Ottomans fought the Serbs at Kosovo in 1389 and Franz Ferdinand was assassinated in Sarajevo in 1914, the Cominform's expulsion of Yugoslavia provoked a surge of Yugoslav patriotism that encouraged the CPY leadership to resist the Soviet-inspired humiliation. Some Party members responded sympathetically to the Soviet-inspired attack on Tito, causing Tito loyalists to conduct purges and reeducation campaigns to root out disloyal elements. Some dissidents were arrested, tried, and imprisoned

FIG. 9.1 — JOSIP BROZ TITO

or shot. Indeed, the specter of "Cominformists" in the Party was an issue, particularly in Montenegro and Bosnia, for the duration of the socialist period. But the vast majority of Party members and Yugoslavs rallied in support of Tito, who had, in an eight-year span, defeated Hitler and defied Stalin.

THE YUGOSLAV NEW COURSE

The Cominform dispute caused the CPY leaders to search for a new course to define their mission differently from that of Stalin and the Soviets. Tito and his associates became aware that their passionate pursuit of revolutionary goals had cost them popular support. The Tito-Stalin dispute, however, meant that Stalin was now competing with Tito and the CPY for the loyalty of Yugoslavs, particularly Party members. The CPY leaders turned to Marx's original writings in search of policy alternatives that would fit the Yugoslav situation and have broad popular appeal. Over the course of several years after 1948, the Yugoslav Communist new course was spelled out. Western scholars often refer to these changes and the resulting social and political system as Titoism. At the heart of Titoism were two concepts: self-management in the domestic economy and nonalignment in foreign affairs.

Self-management was a theoretically inspired response to Marx's complaint that workers in a capitalist society are alienated from the means of production. As opposed to the Soviet solution to this problem, rife with statist central direction, the Yugoslavs proposed to create workers' councils for each factory and enterprise. The workers would then hire managers of their choice and have direct responsibility for the policies, and the success or failure, of their enterprise. Marx had argued that the modern state is a by-product of bourgeois capitalism, and that under true Communism the state would become superfluous and wither away once workers learned how to govern themselves. Workers' self-management, in Yugoslav ideology, was to make unnecessary many central state functions and contribute to the "withering away of the state." The concept clearly implied a radical devolution of power from central planners to workers on the factory floor. By the mid-1950s workers' councils had been established in most factories and enterprises, and were gradually given more authority. The state, however, stubbornly refused to wither as predicted.

The notion of self-management also implied profound changes in the role of government and the CPY in Yugoslav society. In a series of changes implemented in the 1950s, the strong grip of the federal government and the CPY was loosened in favor of the republics and their parallel party organs. These changes were gradual at first and involved shifts in assigned functions and nomenclature. The Party, instead of being a vehicle for social control, was to be a leading force that set the tone and pace of social change through example and persuasion. Reflecting this change, the Communist Party of Yugoslavia (CPY) was renamed the League of Communists of Yugoslavia (LCY) at the Sixth Party Congress in 1952. It retained that designation until its demise at the Fourteenth Party Congress in 1990.

As part of the greater sensitivity to local sentiments, separate Party organizations were created for the republics of Bosnia and Montenegro, where the Serbian Communist Party had jurisdiction before that time. Because of wartime recruitment patterns, Serbs predominated in the Bosnian Party organization. At the First Bosnian Party Congress in 1949, Party leaders particularly lamented the slow growth of Party participation in the heavily Croatian and Muslim areas of western Hercegovina, where Ustasha influence had been strong. By creating a separate Bosnian Communist Party, the CPY set the stage for moving toward greater ethnonational balance in later years and completed a process of making the Party organization correspond to the organization of republics in socialist Yugoslavia. However, the issue of Serbian domination in the Bosnian Party persisted for years. Although they responded to Stalin's challenge with considerable confidence, the Party's leaders gradually loosened the grip of the Party and government on everyday life.

Nonalignment was the engine that drove Yugoslav foreign policy for four decades. Elected as a nonpermanent member of the Security Council in 1949, Yugoslavia advanced a nonaligned agenda and cooperated with India and Egypt on several issues. At the Bandung Conference in 1955, Tito emerged with Nehru of India and Nasser of Egypt as leaders of the nonaligned countries, and by September 1961 Tito was hailed as the "Father of Non-Alignment" at the Non-Aligned Conference in Belgrade. Tito's ceaseless travels brought him into contact with every Third World leader, and the Yugoslavs used the notion of opposing blocs as a slogan of convenience whenever they were unhappy with either the Soviet bloc or the Western Allies.

The Bosnian Muslims contributed to and benefited from the Yugoslav commitment to nonalignment. Since many of the nonaligned nations were Islamic or had substantial Muslim populations, the Bosnian and Kosovo Albanian Muslims were touted as trophies by Tito and other Yugoslavs, who boasted of their treatment as a distinct religious community. Džemal Bijedić, a Muslim from Mostar with impeccable credentials as a prewar Party member and wartime Partisan, served as prime minister from July 1971 until his death in January 1977. His ceaseless smile and easygoing manner made him an excellent emissary to the Third World and an effective spokesman for Yugoslav causes. The Bosnian Muslims themselves cultivated support abroad. However, their representatives found little to admire in Islamic fundamentalism, a movement incompatible with the secular spirit that prevailed among the Bosnian Muslims in the twentieth century. Yugoslav leadership in the non-aligned movement unquestionably made it easier for the Party, in 1968, to recognize the Bosnian Muslims as a distinct nationally in the pantheon of Yugoslav nations.

THE POSTWAR ECONOMIC BOOM AND BOSNIAN PROSPERITY

The government's commitment to investment and economic development, coupled with the liberalization that slowly took hold after the Cominform dispute, led to an economic boom in Yugoslavia from the 1950s through the mid-1970s. Although successive reforms altered somewhat the methods for achieving their goals, the Party, the Yugoslav federal government, and the Bosnian republican government shared the objective of making Bosnia a center of heavy industry. Critics, who often focus on the inequalities that continued to exist among Yugoslavia's regions, have tended to overlook or understate the extent of this economic transformation. But for Bosnians the changes were highly visible and rapid. In the first three decades under socialism, Bosnia was transformed into a thriving center of heavy industry, and its inhabitants experienced both the positive and negative consequences of industrialization.

Physical geography aided in these changes. Bosnia's rich mineral resources and an abundance of water made it an ideal location for heavy manufacturing. At the end of the war, transportion and communications links were inadequate, but the building of normal-gauge railroads and better roads increased access to other Yugoslav regions and to the growing Adriatic port of Ploče. Bosnia saw rapid development in its mining, steel, aluminum, and hydroelectric power industries and in the growing and packaging of agricultural products. By the 1980s many of these plants and their technologies were antiquated relics of socialist inefficiency, but in earlier decades they were the very essence of modernity in a traditionally underdeveloped land. In the decade of the 1950s Yugoslavia as a whole experienced the fastest economic growth of any country in the world. Growth suffered a setback in 1961-2, but more conventional growth rates resumed thereafter.

Unique to Bosnians was the experience of having been the military refuge of last resort for the Partisans. The Yugoslav army continued to believe that Bosnia was its safest haven in the event of foreign invasion, fears of which were stoked by the Soviet actions against Hungary and Poland in 1956 and especially by those against Czechoslovakia in 1968. Bosnia increasingly became the center of weapons and munitions production for the Yugoslav army. By 1990, much of the production for the Yugoslav military was done in Bosnia and many of the army's weapons and munitions were stockpiled there, making the republic indispensable to its future.

Industrialization brought with it the concomitant evils of pollution and congestion, particularly in the valley where Sarajevo is located. Industrial smoke, auto exhaust, and residues from coal-fired home heating units combined to make Sarajevo in the 1960s and 1970s one of the most polluted cities in the world. The unabashed enthusiasm for industrialization was manifest in ideology and symbols. In the ornate National Theater in Sarajevo, the beautiful gilt decorations installed by the Austrians early in the century were painted grey by the enthusiasts of socialized industrialization. The Habsburg double eagle emblem was replaced by the symbol of socialist Bosnia: a huge factory with a chimney belching a plume of dark, sooty smoke.

NATIONALITY POLICIES: THE RISE OF THE BOSNIAN MUSLIMS

Titoism involved three different approaches to the nationalities of Yugoslavia. Common to all three approaches were two overriding general principles: national equality, embodied in the slogan "brotherhood and unity" that began in the war but was also widely employed in peacetime; and federalism, with the six republics as the constituent parts of the Yugoslav federation. It is nearly impossible to identify particular points in time when policy changes were adopted. More accurately, changes from one approach to another were gradual and progressive, since the national question was constantly debated and policies frequently modified by LCY leaders throughout the Titoist period.

The first approach, reflecting Stalinist nationality policies, lasted from the 1942 AVNOJ congress through the immediate aftermath of the Cominform's expulsion of the CPY in June 1948. During this time the Party vigorously promoted the notion of national equality and championed the right of self-determination of each of the five recognized nationalities: Serbs, Croats, Slovenes, Macedonians, and Montenegrins. At the same time, a highly centralized Party structure and strong federal government apparatus made unlikely the rise of any nationalist movement that would threaten the Yugoslav socialist order. The 1948 census reflected the Party's view that Bosnia's Muslims made up a separate community but that they, unlike Serbs and Croats, had no separate *national* identity. In that census, respondents could identify their religion as Orthodox, Catholic, or Muslim. They could designate their nationality as Serb, Croat, or "undetermined" but were not given the option of specifying that they were Muslim by nationality. Of the 890,094 respondents in Bosnia and Hercegovina who said they

TABLE 9.1 — RELIGION AND NATIONALITY IN BOSNIA AND HERCEGOVINA IN
THE CENSUSES OF 1948 AND 1953

1948	Religion:	*Orthodox*	*Catholic*	*Muslim*
		1,067,728	580,970	890,094
	Nationality:			*"Muslim, undetermined"*
		Serb	*Croat*	
		1,136,116*	614,142†	788,384
1953	Nationality:			*"Yugoslav, undetermined"*
		Serb	*Croat*	
		1,264,372‡	654,229‡	891,800

*Includes 71,125 of Muslim religion
†Includes 24,914 of Muslim religion
‡Includes some of Muslim religion; exact number is unknown

were Muslims, 89% elected to identify their nationality as "undetermined," 8% as Serb, and 3% as Croat. The 1948 census results confirm that the national identities of the Serbs and Croats were firmly fixed in Bosnia but that most Muslims viewed themselves as part of a third group and were reluctant to adopt a Serbian or Croatian national identity.

The second approach began with the Party's decision to liberalize and seek wider popular support in the wake of the Cominform's expulsion in June 1948. Gently prodded by the complex theoretical writings of Slovene Party leader Edvard Kardelj, the Party cautiously encouraged Yugoslav nationality as a more advanced form of loyalty than the nationalism of the Serbs, Croats, and other constituent nations. Aware that Yugoslavism had been a shabby cover for Greater Serbian chauvinism in royal Yugoslavia, the Party took pains to assure the sensitive Croats, Slovenes, and Macedonians that Yugoslavism

would not be forced on anyone. Kardelj argued that nationalism had a positive role in socialist society and that, in the natural
course of socialist development, the constituent nations would
join in a broad Yugoslav vision.

To many, the Bosnian Muslims, who were viewed as resis-
tant to the nationalist appeals of others, were logically the core
of such a strategy. In the 1953 census the "undeclared" option
was withdrawn, and respondents could declare themselves nationally as Serb, Croat, or "Yugoslav, undetermined," but still
not as Muslim. In Bosnia, 891,800 declared themselves Yugoslavs,
far more than in any other republic, making it apparent that
most Muslims had chosen the Yugoslav designation but that few
Serbs and Croats had joined them. 1,264,372 respondents identified themselves as Serbs and 654,229 as Croats. The result of
the two censuses, shown in TABLE 9.1, are broadly congruent
with census results from previous and from later years.

The hope that a Yugoslav identity might emerge around a
Bosnian Muslim core is reminiscent of Benjámin von Kállay's
aim, in his tenure as Austro-Hungarian Joint Finance Minister
from 1882 to 1903, to create a supranational loyalty to Bosnia.
Tito and Kardelj, however, did not use Yugoslavism to contain
or repress the nationalism of individual groups, although the
Party in general was careful to keep nationalist political behavior
within broadly acceptable limits. During his rule, however,
Kállay sought to repress all contending political expression. The
LCY's campaign was neither as overt nor sustained as Kállay's
efforts. Like their Austrian precursor, however, the Party leaders
quietly abandoned their efforts without renouncing them. By
the early 1960s, the campaign for Yugoslavism in the LCY was
forgotten if not entirely gone, a victim of recurrent opposition

from the republics which most feared a revival of central (or Serbian) control and consolidation.

The third approach to nationalism, which lasted until the end of socialist Yugoslavia, coincided with the LCY's broader effort to liberalize and decentralize authority in the Party and the state. While committed to avoiding excesses of nationalism, Tito and his lieutenants openly encouraged the flowering of national expression by all legitimate contenders while trying to achieve compromise and reconciliation at the all-Yugoslav level.

For Bosnia, this policy resulted in the recognition of the Bosnian Muslims as a distinct nationality. The 1961 census stopped short of recognizing them as a nationality, but it included a category for "Ethnic Muslim," a status claimed by 972,954. In the 1960s various Bosnian Muslim spokesmen developed the case for Bosnian Muslims as a secular nation rather than as a religious community. In 1968 the LCY completed the process by formally recognizing these claims. In the census of 1971, Bosnians could identify themselves as Bosnian Muslim in the sense of nationality. In 1981 and 1991, they could state that they were Muslims, Serbs, or Croats. According to the 1991 census, the number of Muslims exceeded 1.9 million, and their status as a nationality distinct from Bosnia's Croats and Serbs seemed secure.

TESTING THE BOUNDARIES: THE DRIVE TO CURB EXCESSES

Writing in 1978, onetime *Washington Post* Belgrade correspondent Dusko Doder suggested that the Yugoslav government approach to political expression was "like that of a choke collar on a dog," setting broad limits within which activity was tolerated, used rarely but forcefully to rein in excesses. "The leash is very long indeed … [but] when you step too far out of line, you realize that the leash is held carefully."[4] The image captures Titoist Yugoslavia's approach to nationalist dissidents during much of the postwar period. The Party became reluctant to pull the choke chain as Tito became increasingly removed from day-to-day involvement in Party affairs. The Bosnian Party and government, the most committed in Yugoslavia to orthodoxy and discipline, proved willing on several occasions to prosecute nationalist agitators perceived as threats to the constitutional order. An examination of those incidents is instructive in explaining the boundary between behavior that the Party found acceptable and unacceptable.

Tito and his allies had avidly prosecuted their enemies in the immediate postwar years, including the trials of the Chetnik leader Mihailović and Catholic Archbishop Stepinac of Zagreb. After the Cominform expulsion in 1948, numerous Party members were tried for subversive activities in support of the Soviet bloc; some were jailed and a few executed. Once the Yugoslav Communists had survived these initial challenges to their power, subsequent actions more typically took the form of firings, expulsion from the Party, and/or prison sentences.

In the early 1950s, in the heyday of the experimental thought that produced the basic principles of Titoism, Tito's close wartime associate Milovan Djilas published a series of articles advocating a pluralist approach and endorsing an end to the monopoly on power exercised by the LCY. For this he was expelled from the Party and imprisoned. Djilas later published other works critical of the Party's behavior: most damaging was *The New Class.* For this he was jailed again. When released he

4   Dusko Doder, *The Yugoslavs* (New York: Random House, 1978), p. 108.

settled in Belgrade, where he lives, at the time of this writing, as the sole survivor among the close Partisan colleagues of Tito. His apartment is a routine stop for news correspondents seeking a colorful link with the past.

Aleksandar Ranković, another close associate of Tito, became a high Party official and Yugoslav Minister of the Interior. In the early 1960s he argued against economic reforms promoted by others in the leadership. After an extensive investigation by republican and security organs, his resignation from all Party posts was accepted at the Fourth Party Plenum held at Brioni in July 1966. As former head of the Yugoslav Security Services (UDBA), he was held responsible for excesses committed against Albanians in the autonomous province of Kosovo. He lived in seclusion until his death in 1983. Just as Archbishop (Cardinal) Stepinac became a Croatian national hero whose death was mourned by thousands, Ranković's funeral in 1983, attended by an estimated 100,000 mourners, became a public demonstration of Serbian national sentiment.

NATIONALISM IN THE STRUGGLE FOR ECONOMIC RESOURCES

The greatest source of inter-republican contention, both within the LCY and in public debate, was the issue of the distribution of economic resources, principally the investment funds awarded to the various republics by the federal government. Since all republics except Bosnia were dominated by a single nationality, the distribution of federal funds was also a national issue, and the national leadership of each republic demanded more than its share. The least developed republics of Montenegro and Macedonia and the autonomous region of Kosovo, often joined by Serbia, demanded disproportionate shares, arguing that they needed industrial development to raise the standard of living of their citizens. Leaders of Croatia and Slovenia, noting that funds invested in their republics typically yielded better returns and that the tourist business on the Dalmatian Coast produced large sums of foreign currency, argued that monies earned in their republics ought to stay there. In the increasingly free-wheeling environment of the late 1960s and 1970s, the specifics of these policy questions were debated daily in Party circles, in government bodies, and in the press. Journalists thrived on reporting instances of corruption, misuse of investment funds, and wasteful projects that yielded little benefit to the working class.

The increasingly vociferous inter-republican polemics regarding investment funds obscured a fundamental incongruity in interethnic relations: Each of the republics had an ethnic or nationality problem of its own. The problem was to become acute in the late 1980s in Serbia, which had jurisdiction over the autonomous areas of Kosovo and Vojvodina, and in 1991 in Croatia with its large Serbian minority concentrated in the former Military Frontier area.

Bosnia, with no single dominant ethnonational group, nonetheless had to compete with the other republics for investment funds and other resources. While national differences were certainly not alien to Bosnia, the leaders of the Bosnian Party organization were remarkably effective at representing Bosnian republican interests within the federal and Party structures. Emboldened by their newfound recognition as a nationality and their leading role in Yugoslavia's diplomacy of non-alignment, the Bosnian Muslims made common cause with Bosnian Serbs and Bosnian Croats on many issues even as the republics of Serbia and Croatia took different positions. The Party organization of Bosnia in the later Tito years, and after his death, acquired a reputation as being the most conservative and orthodox of any republic, with the possible exception of Montenegro. The Bosnian LCY consistently aligned with other forces that favored recentralization of political authority, firm Party discipline, and closely regulated relations among the nationalities.

RESURGENT CROATIAN NATIONALISM

After Ranković's removal in 1966, the victory of liberal reformers in Yugoslavia seemed assured, and significant structural changes in the economy led to renewed growth and prosperity in the late years of that decade. But the northern republics of Slovenia and Croatia found themselves receiving fewer foreign currency reserves than they generated, leading to widespread complaints of economic discrimination and unfair treatment. In the flourishing liberalization of the late 1960s, Croatian nationalists generated a growing list of grievances concerning the position of Croats in the Yugoslav federal state. Croats complained of being treated as linguistically second-class in the preparation of a Serbo-Croatian dictionary; of demographic plots by Serbs to encourage Croats to work abroad; and of Serbian plans to encourage a separate autonomous status for the tourist-rich area of Dalmatia.[5]

Significantly for developments in Bosnia, one component of resurgent Croatian nationalism in 1971 was the claim by members of *Matica Hrvatska*, the Croatian literary society, that Croats in Bosnia were being denied basic rights. In November 1971, Croatian publications cited statistics demonstrating that

---

5   For a description of the Croatian nationalist movement and its aftermath, with special attention to the intra-Party debates, see Dennison Rusinow, *The Yugoslav Experiment, 1948-74* (London: Hurst, 1977), pp. 287-318.

Croats were underrepresented in the Bosnian Party organization and in all major political, economic, and social bodies in the Bosnian republic.[6] Based on these allegations, some Croatian nationalists proposed that Croat-dominated territories be detached from the republic of Bosnia and Hercegovina and annexed to Croatia. This demand for Bosnia's dismemberment led the Bosnian Party to join Communist Party organizations of other republics in condemning Croatian nationalist excesses.

Tito intervened personally and forcefully in early December 1971 to repress the rapidly escalating Croatian nationalist movement. On December 12, the three leading Croatian Party members resigned, and more than 1,000 Party members were subsequently purged for involvement in Croatian nationalist excesses. When students demonstrated in Zagreb to protest the crackdown, riot police took to the streets. Thousands of Croats were imprisoned, mostly for brief periods of time, and offending publications were shut down. Tito thus pulled the "choke chain" after many months of hoping that moderate elements would prevail in the Party. The episode nonetheless left many Croats feeling that their national aspirations could not be realized within the Yugoslav federal structure; Croatian nationalism was effectively driven underground rather than eliminated.

ALBANIAN NATIONALISM AND THE QUESTION OF KOSOVO

Of the many nationality problems facing Yugoslavia in the socialist era, the issue of Kosovo's Albanian population was viewed by foreign observers and many Yugoslavs as most likely to lead to large-scale violence. For Serbs, the evolution of events

---

6 Sabrina P. Ramet, *Nationalism and Federalism in Yugoslavia, 1962-1991,* 2nd edn. (Bloomington: Indiana University Press, 1992), pp. 124-5.

in Kosovo was ominous. They viewed with alarm the decline in the number of Serbs and the growth of the Albanian population in Kosovo, contending that Serbs had been driven out by Albanian intimidation. In 1953, Serbs and Montenegrins accounted for 27.9% of the population; by 1987, they made up only 10%.

In March and April 1981, widespread student-led Albanian protests turned violent, and Yugoslav federal troops were ordered into Kosovo to establish order. Serbian fears of being overwhelmed in Kosovo were skillfully exploited by Serbian President Slobodan Milošević in his climb to power in 1987. Upon achieving it, he replaced the Party leadership of Kosovo with pro-Serbian officials to administer the province.

In February and March 1989, a series of strikes resulted in thirty-one deaths, and the federal army was deployed in the area for the fourth time since World War II (1945, 1968, 1981, and 1989). Serbian paramilitary forces thereafter came to control Kosovo's Albanians through a combination of brute force, prohibition of public demonstrations, harassment of potential political organizers, and repression of the press, media, and educational institutions. At the time of this writing in April 1994, war on the scale of the Croatian and Bosnian conflicts has not been visited upon Kosovo, but the situation remains volatile, and Serbian forces have consistently practiced human rights abuses on a large scale.

URBANIZATION AND THE EROSION OF ETHNIC EXCLUSIVITY

The growth of Bosnian industry led to rapid expansion of its urban areas. Sarajevo, the republic's capital and long its largest city, was the epicenter of development and growth; but other cities such as Mostar, Travnik, Banja Luka, and Tuzla also expanded exponentially in population and physical size. Sarajevo lay at the heart of the central mountainous region of industrial development, with the huge Zenica steel complex to its north and numerous factories located to its south and west. Its airport grew up and handled a rising volume of passenger traffic, although federal policies prevented it from becoming a true center of international travel.

High-rise apartment buildings were constructed to house the influx of new urbanites. In the early postwar years these buildings were the bleak, nondescript concrete structures that arose in every city of Stalinist Eastern Europe, but in later decades they became increasingly attractive in style and amenities. Many longtime urban dwellers preferred the new apartments to older, more traditional homes and left their family residences to live in high-rise units. These planned neighborhoods were given names such as "New Sarajevo" and "New Travnik," leaving the older city centers as the home of markets, shops, entertainment, and cultural activities. The main street of most large Bosnian cities was the center of the evening *korso*, the traditional stroll when friends walked together and met others or repaired to a local coffee shop for gossip.

Before socialism, common practice dictated that given names reflect ethnic background, often by adopting the masculine or feminine form of the name of a Christian saint or Islamic holy person. After the war, names often became more generic, lionizing a Partisan hero or concept such as "Dolan" or "Goran," roughly translated as "Valley Man" and "Mountain Man." Thus it became much more difficult for Bosnians to determine the ethnic identification of a new acquaintance by name.

These changes tended to obscure the differences among traditional ethnonational communities. Whereas older town centers were often divided into ethnic neighborhoods, the new high-rises were ethnonational conglomerates. Mixed marriages, the inevitable consequence of greater intermingling in schools and workplaces, became not only acceptable but commonplace in Bosnian cities and towns. By 1990 some 40% of Bosnian urban couples were ethnically mixed. In many instances, the children of mixed marriages thought of themselves as Yugoslavs or Bosnians without ethnic allegiances.

For the vast majority of Bosnian urbanites, loyalty to Bosnia overrode ethnocentric sentiments. Bosnians ardently rooted for local sports teams, republic teams, or Yugoslav national teams, generating far more passion and enthusiasm for their athletic heroes than for any nationality or ethnic group. Humor among Bosnians, as among all Yugoslavs, tends to be self-effacing and often borders on cruelty. The most common humor featured "Mujo and Sujo," two quintessentially Bosnian village idiots. The stories typically made fun of Bosnians for their provincialism and laziness, contrasting them to the more sophisticated peoples of Croatia and Slovenia.

While urbanization moved Bosnian cities and towns in the direction of becoming melting pots, peasants and village dwellers retained much of their previous character, despite the universal availability of many modern amenities and greater participation in the market economy. Thus the historical distinctions between peasants and urbanites remained and, in some ways, were reinforced during the socialist era, even as the number and relative demographic strength of urban dwellers increased vastly. Most villages remained ethnically segregated, and mixed marriages were much less common in rural areas than in the cities. When affluent urbanites began building weekend retreats (known appropriately as *vikendicas* — pronounced Veek-end-eetsas) in the 1960s and 1970s, the traditional peasants viewed them as strange interlopers and were perplexed that anyone would abandon the amenities of city life for the rustic countryside.

The continued dichotomy between rural and urban attitudes contributed to the spread of the Bosnian conflict in 1992 and 1993, for peasants were drawn to the ethnic militias more readily than long-term urbanites. Many urban dwellers of all national allegiances perceive the conflict as one in which primitive peasants are seeking to destroy urban civilization in Bosnia.

THE POST-INDUSTRIAL ECONOMY

Blessed with balmy beaches and some of the world's most beautiful historic port cities, the Adriatic Coast became a magnet that drew tourists to Yugoslavia by the millions from the 1960s through the 1980s. Bosnia's leaders, although preoccupied with developing industry and promoting commercial agriculture, were eager to get their share of the hard currency that tourism could bring. Those areas on and closest to the Adriatic Coast benefited the most, particularly the town of Neum, Bosnia's one "outlet to the sea." A visitor to Dubrovnik could arrange a daytrip by coach up the harrowing, winding road to Mostar, view the Ottoman-era bridge, and proceed on to Sarajevo to see the central marketplace before returning to the hotel by late evening. In the drive to attract tourists, the Muslim town of Počitelj, between Mostar and the Adriatic, was restored and made an artist colony, and the historic sections of Mostar and Sarajevo were restored or rebuilt.

The International Olympic Committee's selection of Sarajevo as the site of the 1984 Winter Olympics was a landmark, not only in terms of international recognition but also for its economic benefits. The republic received extensive federal funds to assist in preparation for the games, and the drive to construct athletic facilities and housing for Olympic contenders and guests changed the face of Sarajevo and its environs. Drab buildings, long neglected and discolored by pollution, received facelifts and fresh paint. Construction boomed. Within the city, the Holiday Inn (at the time of this writing the city's only function-ing hotel) was built, a monument to modernity and bold architectural style with a brown and yellow color scheme that offended just about everyone. (Some *Sarajlije* even hoped, perversely, that the Holiday Inn might become an early and complete casualty of Serbian shelling.)

Once the Tito-era reforms took hold, Yugoslavia became a country of open borders and free movement of peoples unlike any other Eastern European Communist-led state. The eco-nomic disparity between Yugoslavia and the countries of West-ern Europe led many younger workers to seek temporary work in Europe, primarily in West Germany, Austria, and Switzer-land. These workers numbered about two million by the early 1970s. A disproportionate number of Yugoslavs abroad came from Bosnia; a Yugoslav government source reported that 9.2% of the Bosnian work force was employed abroad in 1971.[7]

By sending hard-currency savings to their families and returning with Western goods, the workers abroad substantially enhanced Yugoslav living standards in the 1970s. The workers also brought back to their villages an awareness of better eco-nomic conditions in the West and contributed to the overall cynicism regarding the Yugoslav economic system. As recessionary pressures led host countries to limit or expel guest

7   Ramet, p. 104.

workers in the mid-1970s and thereafter, the value of this safety valve declined rapidly.

At the level of governmental organization, successive reforms resulted in a weakened and fragmented federal structure that relied heavily upon consensus and cooperation among republican power contenders. The structure reflected certain inclinations and preferences of Tito himself, the need to accommodate various constituencies while maintaining the principles of national equality, and incessant jockeying for power in the Party and government.

The political history of Yugoslavia in the years between 1949 and 1990 is, in large measure, a succession of changes undertaken within two parallel organizations, the Party and the government, to resolve the multifaceted controversy concerning the fundamental nature of Yugoslav society. The changes occurred slowly and irregularly, by fits and with false starts, and in many different forums and documents. The principal changes in the governmental structure were embodied in the four postwar constitutions of 1946 (already discussed), 1952, 1963, and 1974, and in various amendments and laws passed by the Yugoslav Assembly. The Party's reform efforts can be traced in the various Party congresses, from the Sixth Congress in 1952 through the Fourteenth Extraordinary Congress in 1990.

Tito grew more averse to the notion of a single strong successor as he grew older, and he sought instead to ensure the fragmentation of political power after his death. He initiated or sanctioned the removal from power of several close associates and potential successors: Milovan Djilas (1954); Vladimir Dedijer (1954); Aleksandar Ranković (1966); and even his third wife,

Jovanka. He advocated, and saw written into Yugoslav constitutional law, the principles of collective leadership, separation of power between the Party and government, and frequent rotation of high governmental offices.

In 1971 Tito proposed to amend the Constitution to create a collective federal Presidency made up of fifteen persons: two representatives from each of the six republics, one from each of the two autonomous provinces, and Tito himself as president of the LCY. The proposed amendments were modified, at the urging of Bosnian representatives, to provide for *three* representatives per republic, to ensure that each of the three major nationalities in Bosnia would be represented. (The autonomous provinces were then each given two representatives.) Tito was to function as the president (yes, the president of the Presidency) over this hopelessly unwieldy body of twenty-three.

The 1974 Constitution modified and simplified this arrangement and provided for a federal Presidency made up of only nine persons: one representative from each of the six republics; one from each of the two autonomous provinces of Vojvodina and Kosovo; and, as the ninth representative, Tito himself, who (as head of the LCY) was to hold the position of president for life. Tito's death would thus result in an eight-member Presidency, and the 1974 Constitution provided that the post-Tito president of that body would rotate annually on May 15. The Presidency arrangement thoroughly fragmented political authority in post-Tito Yugoslavia and precluded effective leadership by any one person.

Taken as a whole, these changes amounted to the radical decentralization and fragmentation of political power in Yugoslavia. The central Party organs and the Yugoslav federal government lost power to the republics, the Party organizations of the republics, economic enterprises, and even local governments. As authority devolved to the republican level, each of the republics started behaving like a ministate; competition among republics and shifting alliances between them became the key realities of everyday Yugoslav political life. In a perceptive and telling analysis of Yugoslavia after 1960, one scholar has argued that the Yugoslav republics and autonomous provinces behaved very much like sovereign states that would be found in a "balance of power" system of international relations.[8]

After Tito's death in 1980, prospective constitutional changes were discussed incessantly. Party leaders recognized, however, that reformulating the constitution without Tito's guiding presence could unleash uncontrollable forces and potentially lead to complete disintegration, so the 1974 document remained the operative — if often disregarded — constitution until the collapse of Yugoslavia.

TITO AND HIS LEGACY

In an environment of national rivalry aggravated by economic decline, retaining popularity is a remarkable achievement for any leader. Even as he withdrew from the day-to-day operations of the Party and the state, Tito retained a stature and popularity among most Yugoslavs as a leader above politics and nationality. He was, for many, the One True Yugoslav, the single source of unity and cohesion to whom members of all nationalities felt allegiance.

In no republic was Tito's stature greater than in Bosnia, home of the Partisan movement and of his most disciplined and orthodox Party organization. Foreigners visiting Bosnia in the 1970s often found themselves surprisingly uncomfortable when they asked what would happen after Tito died, for many

8   Ramet, pp. 3-39 and 270-9.

Bosnians were offended by any mention of the possibility that Tito might one day cease to be with them.

On one of Tito's visits to Sarajevo in the 1970s, people began lining the streets hours before his scheduled arrival. By the time his motorcade arrived, the crowd was six to eight people deep along the city streets. Instead of cheers and hurrahs from the crowd, he was greeted by discreet, reverential applause and gasps of admiration more suited to a saint than a national hero. As he arrived, a children's choir sang on the steps of the Hotel Evropa and chanted, *"Mi smo Titovi; Tito je naš"* (We are Tito's; Tito is ours). Assisted from his car, he briefly greeted the choir before quickly disappearing into the hotel without a word to the assembled crowd.

The conduct of the crowd, and the general respect that Tito commanded, revealed the unparalleled position that he held in Yugoslavia and in Bosnia. He was more than popular; he was a living myth, imbued in the popular mind with mystical attributes that edged uncertainly into the spiritual realm of immortality.

Evaluating the Tito era from today's brief historical perspective is a risky enterprise. However, one must note two monumental achievements and one fatal flaw. First, Tito successfully forged a powerful resistance movement out of the most unlikely, dispirited, demoralized elements and led that movement to a triumph over the mighty German war machine. After the war, he overcame his own authoritarian instincts sufficiently to lead the Yugoslavs in creating an open, prosperous, and progressive society. Tito was as fearless a social innovator as he was a resistance organizer. Given these achievements, one can perhaps forgive his great failure, namely his reluctance to carve out a cohesive strategy for a successful Yugoslav society after his death. Most regrettable was his conscious effort to impede the emergence of an effective successor; with the hubris of many great leaders, Tito failed in his last years to bestow on others the confidence to renew or recreate the Yugoslavia that he himself had forged in the fury of war.

In a remarkably short time after his death, cautious criticism of Tito crept into public dialogue, and by the end of the decade nationalist extremists were reviling his every act, blaming him for all the sins and failures in the Yugoslav past. As with other aspects of nationalist propaganda, these ideologues found an echo in Western journalists and publicists who began to portray Tito as a tyrant who suppressed national aspirations and relied heavily on repression to stay in power. Such notions are not only false, but they are particularly ironic in the light of Tito's years-long campaign, conducted at the expense of central authority, to devolve political power to the very republics in which many of those propagandists now hold sway.

With Tito's death in May 1980, the guiding hand of a great arbitrator passed from the scene. The task was left to lesser mortals, hobbled by the complex machinery of government which Tito had enshrined in constitutional law, to confront the task of keeping the country intact. From the perspective of the 1990s, one marvels more at their ability to keep Yugoslavia functioning through a decade of rising instability than that they ultimately succumbed to disintegrative pressures in 1990 and 1991.

10

After Tito:
The Twilight of Yugoslavia

———— • ————

YUGOSLAVIA FACED SEVERE economic problems and growing national discord in the years after Tito's death. Although Bosnians shared many of these problems with other Yugoslavs, in many respects the republic of Bosnia and Hercegovina became the last bastion of genuine Yugoslavism. Its Party and government leaders, while not without their nationalist disputes, pursued the interests of Bosnia within the Yugoslav federation without yielding to the nationalistic divisiveness that typified the leadership in some other republics. The League of Communists of Bosnia and Hercegovina was noted for its conservative orthodoxy and organizational cohesion; its leaders prosecuted national extremists on several occasions. As in the royal Yugoslav era and earlier in the socialist period, Bosnians from all three major national groups supported the preservation of Yugoslavia against the forces of division and fragmentation. Those forces, however, swirled ominously around Bosnia throughout the 1980s and increasingly threatened the very existence of the Yugoslav federation.

As during Tito's lifetime, three institutions provided most of the cohesion to the increasingly disparate components of socialist Yugoslavia: the League of Communists of Yugoslavia (LCY), the Yugoslav federal government, and the Yugoslav People's Army (YPA). None of these survived the upheavals of

1991-3 in recognizable form. The LCY disintegrated in January 1990, the victim of irreconcilable differences among its constituent republican organizations. The Yugoslav federal state was reconstituted in April 1992 as the "rump Yugoslavia" (Montenegro and Serbia, including Kosovo and Vojvodina) bearing little resemblance to its predecessor. The YPA also underwent a mutation: beginning in the summer of 1991, the army abandoned its role as a defender of multinational federalism and became an agent of Serbian national aims, unrecognizable in mission and considerably different in personnel from the original YPA. In place of these institutions, two major forces emerged to contend for power: the various republican governments and the extreme nationalist forces that would prosecute the vicious wars of the Yugoslav succession.

THE ECONOMIC CRISIS

Yugoslavia's economic decline began before Tito's death in 1980 and thereafter grew more severe, reaching crisis proportions by the end of the decade. Inflation reached triple digits by the middle of the decade; productivity faltered; political gridlock blocked meaningful reforms; and a growing mountain of debt, both foreign and domestic, placed heavy burdens on enterprises and on the federal government. Although the 1984 Winter Olympics in Sarajevo brought cash and a spurt of optimism to Bosnia, a general sense of economic malaise beset Bosnians much as it did the inhabitants of other republics. As a primary center of heavy industrial production within the Yugoslav federation, Bosnia was faced with increasingly serious challenges of competitiveness and obsolescence in its core industries.

Much about the nature of Yugoslavia's economic woes in the late years of socialist Yugoslavia can be inferred from the scandal that in 1987 engulfed Agrokomerc, one of the largest enterprises in Bosnia.[1] Agrokomerc, based in the northwestern Bosnian town of Velika Kladuša, appeared to be a model of successful Yugoslav socialist enterprise. Originating in 1963 with thirty workers, the enterprise selected young Fikret Abdić as its executive director in 1967. Expanding rapidly in the production, packaging, and transport of agricultural products, Agrokomerc in 1986 was the twenty-ninth largest Yugoslav enterprise, with over 11,000 workers.

In early 1987 a fire in one of its warehouses led to an investigation that soon uncovered financial irregularities. By the spring of 1987 the Bosnian Ministry of Internal Affairs learned that Agrokomerc was built on unsecured promissory notes valued at $875 million. The Bank of Bihać had peddled the notes to other financial institutions, so the bad debt was held by a total of sixty-three banks, many located in republics outside Bosnia. In March government officials were told that Agrokomerc officials had engaged in massive illegal dealings.

The affair soon took on all the drama of a 1980s American stock market scandal. The financial irregularities were first reported in *Borba*, the organ of the Socialist Alliance of Working Peoples, on August 15, 1987. The Bank of Bihać was summarily closed, and 50,000 workers whose paychecks were drawn on the bank found themselves with worthless paper. Scattered strikes occurred in several different industries. The mountain of unsecured debt supporting Agrokomerc, it turned out, had been built up by the Bosnian Muslim families of Abdić and Pozderac. Hamdija Pozderac, patriarch of the latter, had built a political career along with his fortune. He had become the Bosnian

---

1   "Agrokomerc: The Decline of a Model Enterprise," *Radio Free Europe Situation Report*, November 19, 1987.

member of the federal Presidency and was at that time its vice president, scheduled to become president of the Presidency on May 15, 1988. As the scandal grew, Pozderac was summarily removed from the Yugoslav federal Presidency on September 12 and from the Central Committee of the LCY on October 23.

Soon the Agrokomerc affair turned into a political influence scandal. Two hundred party members in Bosnia and Croatia were removed in the next several months for complicity in Agrokomerc dealings. The Yugoslav federal Presidency was also discredited by the scandal. The Presidency had voted in July 1986, before the scandal broke, to award Fikret Abdić the "Order of the Red Flag" for "extraordinary work achievement." The official announcement was not made until after the scandal broke and Abdić had been arrested, making it appear that the federal Presidency had also been duped by Abdić's actions. Stanko Tomić, executive director of the huge Zenica Steel Works and a member of the Awards Committee, was removed from the Central Committee of the LCY in October 1987 but resisted pressure to step down from his position in the steel enterprise.

An unrepentant Abdić argued that the practices at Agrokomerc were widespread throughout Yugoslav industry, and many independent observers agreed with him. The influential Belgrade weekly *NIN* dispatched a reporter to Velika Kladuša and subsequently reported strong local support for Abdić. Faced with the prospect of massive layoffs in the wake of the scandal, most of the population in the Bihać area were grateful to Abdić for hiring many Bosnian Muslims who had previously been workers in Slovenia and felt discriminated against. Many locals felt Abdić and the Agrokomerc enterprise had been framed.

Abdić retained a substantial following in the Bihać area. In the 1990 multiparty elections, he received the most votes of any Bosnian Muslim candidate and was made a member of the Presidency of Bosnia and Hercegovina. After war broke out in 1992 he became the unchallenged leader of the "Bihać Pocket," an area in northwestern Bosnia that was not conquered by Serbian forces. In October 1993, Abdić led his followers in proclaiming an autonomous region of Bosnia centered on Bihać.

A close review of the Agrokomerc scandal reveals many characteristics of Yugoslavia's economic crisis in the 1980s. Despite the rhetoric and repeated directives from the center, workers' self-management was not a functioning system in many large enterprises such as Agrokomerc. Once in place, managers could become strongmen and virtual dictators, unfettered by controls from the workers and able to seek immense benefits and spoils from government. Seeking to eliminate ownership by capitalists and control by the state, the Yugoslav system had led to the rise of regional satrapies — entrepreneurs with enormous power, linked with power brokers in the Party, the republican and the federal governments, and other enterprises, especially banks. Many enterprises, even if accountable in theory for their financial welfare, could work their way out of a final reckoning by deals with politicians and the maze of quasi-governmental units. Even if one judges Abdić to be a friend of the workers and a booster of his community, the Agrokomerc scandal is a monument to a government that failed to govern and an enterprise that evaded financial accountability.

The economy as a whole was beset by wasteful investments, corruption, squandered resources, and runaway debt. In 1987 Yugoslavia's total foreign debt was $20 billion, with an additional $16 billion in domestic debt, or obligations between republics and enterprises. Strikes occurred on rare occasions in the early Tito years but became more common after his death in 1980; in 1989, 1,900 strikes involving 470,000 workers were reported. Workers resisted every attempt to freeze wages even if prices were simultaneously locked in. Prices tripled in 1987 and continued to rise for the next two years. Despite a temporary reduction in 1990, high inflation subsequently accelerated into absurdity owing to wholesale government credits in the sanctions-battered rump Yugoslavia (Serbia and Montenegro), where by August 1993 the dinar was losing 1% of its value every hundred minutes.

THE QUEST FOR REFORM

Over the years, a subtle but unmistakable change occurred in the movement for reform in Yugoslavia. The initial impetus for reform came from Party leaders eager to break away from the Stalinist model and define a unique Titoist path to socialism. At first this brought a welcome liberalization from the rigid statist centralization and tight political controls of the immediate postwar years; the reforms contributed to economic growth and produced a more progressive and open society than any other socialist country in the world. By the 1960s, however, the effort to formulate a unique Yugoslav path had spawned a growing controversy over how best to organize the Party, the government, and Yugoslav society as a whole. As a by-product of decentralization, the republics gained enormous power and came to be identified in each case (except for Bosnia) with a particular national viewpoint. The reform movement was gradually transformed, degenerating over time into unseemly bickering among the republics and their Party organizations as they contended for economic resources and political privileges.

By the 1980s, reform debates had themselves become an unsavory feature of Yugoslav public life. Indeed, although the proposals were about "reform," the term was something of a misnomer because decades of intensive effort produced no significant improvements in either the Party or the government. Decentralization advanced to the point of fragmentation; liberalization increased individual freedom but at times degenerated into chaos. Until the late 1980s, all debates were conducted in the abstruse code of Marxist-Leninist-Titoist jargon, so the debates were impenetrable to most outsiders and meaningless to many Yugoslavs.

PROSECUTIONS OF NATIONALISTS IN BOSNIA

Despite the growth of independent and professional news media after Tito's death, the LCY occasionally exercised a choke chain to curb dissidents whose opinions were deemed unacceptable. In Bosnia these efforts were directed principally against nationalists whose public activities were viewed as a threat to the continued existence of Bosnia and Hercegovina as a republic.

In July and August 1983, thirteen Bosnian Muslims were tried in a Sarajevo district court, accused of conspiring to transform Bosnia into an *Islamistan* (a purely Islamic polity) and of maintaining contacts with hostile exiles abroad.[2] On August 20, 1983, the defendants were convicted and given relatively harsh sentences. The longest jail term, fourteen years, was given to Alija Izetbegović, who became familiar in 1992 in the West as the first president of the Bosnian republic.

---

2 "Yugoslav 'Moslem Nationalists' Condemned," *Radio Free Europe Background Report*, September 2, 1983.

Coming at a time when many Westerners feared a recrudescence of Muslim fanaticism encouraged by Ayatollah Ruholla Khomeini's regime in Iran, the incident fueled fears that Islamic fundamentalism was rampant in Bosnia. (The trial has often been cited by Serbian and Croatian nationalists to portray the Bosnian Muslims as religious fanatics.) More accurately, the prosecutions took place because the secular Muslim leadership, as part of the Bosnian LCY establishment, wanted to assure that the newly recognized Bosnian Muslim nationality was secular rather than religious in its definition and aims. (Izetbegović served fewer than six years of his prison term. When he came to power in 1990, he espoused policies more typical of Bosnian Muslim secular leaders.)

One year later, in July 1984, the Bosnian Serb Vojislav Šešelj was tried in Sarajevo for spreading "hostile propaganda against the constitutional order."[3] In an article prepared for the Party journal *Komunist,* Šešelj attacked the national theories of Edvard Kardelj and advocated that Bosnia be partitioned between Serbia and Croatia, and that Montenegro be merged with Serbia. He was sentenced to eight years in jail. Under pressure from international human rights organizations (his trial gained a certain visibility because the 1984 Winter Olympics had just been held in Sarajevo), his sentence was reduced and he was released in March 1986. He continued to espouse his Greater Serbian views in various speeches and writings. In 1990 he openly identified himself as a Chetnik. As of early 1994 the leader of the second largest political party in the Serbian Assembly in rump Yugoslavia, he was among the most feared leaders of the vicious Serbian ethnic cleansing campaigns directed against the Muslim population of Bosnia.

3 "Vojislav Šešelj under Attack," *Radio Free Europe Situation Report,* May 4, 1987.

The trials of the Muslim nationalists and of Šešelj reveal the Bosnian Party's great concern with a revival of national extremism in the post-Tito years. But the working coalition of interests within the Party mainstream among Serbian, Croatian, and Muslim elements continued to function effectively into the final years of socialist Yugoslavia.

THE MANTLE OF LEADERSHIP

As provided in the 1974 constitution, following Tito's death the office of president of the Presidency was to rotate on May 15 of each year among the eight remaining Presidency members. After Tito died on May 4, 1980, the first occupant of the office, the Macedonian Lazar Koliševski, held office for only eleven days. For the next eleven years the institution worked much as Tito had intended, creating a strong imperative for close cooperation among Presidency members while preventing the concentration of power in the hands of a single individual. The federal Presidency, although it consistently supported Yugoslav interests against ambitions of the individual republics, was hardly a forum from which strong personalities were likely to emerge. Instead, the strongest leaders in post-Tito Yugoslavia held the office of the federal prime minister or the presidency of individual republics.

From 1946 until its demise in December 1991, socialist Yugoslavia had only nine prime ministers, five of whom were Croats. After Tito's death, the most daunting challenge facing the prime ministers was the economic decline that beset the country beginning in the late 1970s and accelerated through much of the 1980s. By 1988, a total of 400,000 workers participated in over 1,700 strikes, and Yugoslavia's inflation rate continued to rise. On December 30, 1988, Branko Mikulić, a Croat from Bosnia, resigned after a no-confidence vote in the federal Assembly; he had failed to control the rapidly escalating inflation rates that plagued the country. He was replaced in March 1989 by Ante Marković, a former president of Croatia and the last person to hold the office of federal prime minister.

MARKOVIĆ

For a time, Marković effectively addressed the country's economic problems through a comprehensive reform program. Inflation, running at 346% in March 1989 when he took office, was reduced to single digits in 1990, although it rose again to unacceptable levels in 1991. Marković was an experienced economist and an able politician. He built a broad base of political support for his program, winning the endorsement of all the republican assemblies except those of Serbia and Vojvodina for the comprehensive market-oriented reform program he introduced in December 1989. The federal Presidency and the YPA each endorsed his reform program. Marković supported political pluralism, although at first he stopped short of endorsing a multiparty system, and he encouraged privatization and an end to political interference in the economy.

By mid-1991 the Marković government was overtaken by the rise of powerful nationalist forces intent on crippling or dismantling the Yugoslav federation. Marković was unsuccessful in building long-term political support, principally because he was undermined by the Serbian strongman, Slobodan Milošević. Despite his abilities and popularity, Marković was unable to achieve a working consensus within the complex federal system Tito bequeathed to his heirs. He resigned in December 1991; by then, the notion of Yugoslavia's existence had been rendered an illusion by Slovenian and Croatian declarations of independence and the wars that followed them.

MILOŠEVIĆ

In 1987 Slobodan Milošević, a relative political newcomer, took control of the Serbian republican government, the first step in a quest for power that would transform the Yugoslav political scene.[4] Like Marković, Milošević is knowledgeable about economic and business matters, but the similarity ends there. Born in 1941, Milošević graduated from the University of Belgrade with a law degree in 1964 and was a loyal member of the League of Communists of Serbia. He was an executive at Tehnogas, a large energy concern, and then became president of a Belgrade bank. While in industry he acquired a mentor in Ivan Stambolić, who became head of the Serbian party in 1984. When Stambolić left that position in 1986 to become president of Serbia, he sponsored Milošević to assume the Party chairmanship. In December 1987, Milošević seized control of the Serbian Party organization and unseated his former mentor as president of Serbia, later (1989) assuming the post for himself.

Milošević's prosaic background provides few clues to his true character. An ambitious and opportunistic politician, he has strong authoritarian tendencies and an uncanny instinct for political survival. Despite his disarming public appearance of being utterly passionless, he is a master at manipulating the symbolism and rhetoric of Serbian nationalism and has rallied millions of followers in support of his Greater Serbian political agenda. He tolerates disorder bordering on chaos among his constituents, while showing great patience and persistence in pursuing his objectives. Most important of all, he has proven highly effective at organizing popular protests to defeat political opponents in his drive to consolidate power. In harnessing popular demonstrations to promote Serbian nationalism,

---

4 For an account of Milošević's rise to power, see Ramet, pp. 225-38.

Milošević went beyond previously accepted Yugoslav practices under socialism and contested political power in the streets rather than in the LCY or in representative assemblies.

The Milošević regime moved quickly to take over Serbia's increasingly independent media, paying particular attention to the television stations that had become influential and widely watched as the tradition of professional journalism blossomed in the 1970s and 1980s. The daily *Politika* and the weekly *NIN*, publications with wide readership throughout Yugoslavia, were purged of their independent-minded journalists and became Milošević mouthpieces.

In the summer of 1988, Milošević supporters launched a coordinated campaign to force the resignation of the Party leadership in the autonomous province of Vojvodina. After 100,000 protesters demonstrated in the streets of the capital city, Novi Sad, the entire Vojvodina political leadership resigned on October 6, 1988, and was replaced by pro-Milošević appointees. Similar tactics were employed in Kosovo and in Montenegro. Massive Serbian demonstrations in Kosovo in the summer and fall of 1988 led to the resignation of Kosovo leaders sympathetic to the Albanian position. Pro-Milošević officials were installed in their places. Further demonstrations forced the resignation of the Montenegrin leadership in January 1989. The Serbian government also dispatched agents to Bosnia, but these forays did not become known until revealed by newspapers in October 1989, touching off a crisis in relations between the two republics. In March 1989 the Serbian republic changed its constitution and made Vojvodina and Kosovo organic parts of Serbia; in the summer of 1990 their separate governments were effectively abolished in favor of central rule from Belgrade.

The rise of Milošević in Serbia meant that many of the traditional ground rules in Titoist Yugoslavia were obsolete. By employing mass demonstrations to intimidate Party and government leaders, Milošević diminished the importance of the Party apparatus and the federal Assembly in resolving inter-republican disputes. At the same time Milošević destroyed the autonomy of the two autonomous provinces, ending the de facto parity they had acquired over the years in their relations with other republics. Since he acquired control over the representatives from Vojvodina, Kosovo, and Montenegro (as well as Serbia) in the Yugoslav federal Presidency, Milošević controlled four of the eight votes. He could, and did, obstruct the workings of that institution at will.

THE PARTY WITHERS: DISSOLUTION OF THE LCY

By the late 1980s, the LCY had outgrown its roots as a small, elite force for social change and become a mass organization with about two million members; one out of every ten Yugoslavs was an LCY member. It also lost its cohesion. Republican interests had torn at the fabric of the LCY for many years, and by the late 1980s the Party was little more than a loose association of republic-based organizations. It became a comprehensive umbrella under which nearly any idea or ideology could be espoused in the name of either reform or tradition.

With growing assertiveness, Party members in the 1980s voiced opposition to "democratic centralism" (a codeword for top-down Party discipline), expressed support for political pluralism and a multiparty system, and even called for an end to the LCY's leading role in Yugoslav society. These calls came principally from Slovenia, the most Western-oriented and economically prosperous republic, but they were also heard in Croatia, Bosnia, Macedonia, and in Serbia from anti-Milošević forces.

As had been true of discussions of reform in the 1950s, the dominant theme in the 1980s within the Party, and in the increasingly freewheeling press, was economic reform. Slovenes and Croats pushed hard for market-oriented approaches and for privatization. The quest for rapid liberalization took place as democratic hopes were growing in other Eastern European socialist countries. By 1989 many Yugoslavs, having viewed with pride their country's leadership in the movement to liberalize socialism in the 1950s and 1960s, dreaded ending up as the last Communists in Europe.

In a final desperate effort to achieve a modicum of political consensus, the LCY held its Fourteenth Extraordinary Party Congress in January 1990. The congress was termed "extraordinary" because the participants hoped to agree on a major constitutional restructuring of Yugoslav society. However, compromises at the congress failed to satisfy the demands of the independent-minded Slovenian delegation. The Slovenes declared a boycott of all further proceedings. At 3:30 a.m. on January 23, 1990, only hours after the Slovene announcement, the Party congress of the LCY adjourned indefinitely. The Serbian delegation hoped to defeat the movement to adjourn, but adjournment was supported by the delegations from Bosnia, Macedonia, and the YPA. The LCY thus dissolved in a welter of bickering and contention, having introduced the extreme decentralization of political authority that would soon engulf the Yugoslav federation. While Party organizations continued to exist at the republican and local levels for some months, most reconstituted themselves and adopted new names before competing in the multiparty elections that took place in each republic during 1990.

THE YUGOSLAV PEOPLE'S ARMY: ORIENTATION AND COMPOSITION

The collapse of the Party at the Extraordinary Congress in January 1990 left the country with only one institution with a Yugoslav orientation: the Yugoslav People's Army (YPA). The YPA emerged from World War II with a proud revolutionary heritage and became a staunch supporter of Tito's socialist program. Although the YPA strongly endorsed the Yugoslav ideal of national brotherhood and unity, it never successfully eliminated the preponderance of Serbs and Montenegrins in the officer corps that developed in wartime. This persisted into the 1980s despite Tito's repeated "affirmative action" efforts to achieve national parity in the army's highest ranks. At the same time, all nationalities were well represented in the enlisted ranks, the result of widespread conscription and the notion of a republic-based citizens' army that could resist a potential foreign invader.

Unlike the party, the YPA did not fragment into feuding republican constituencies in the late socialist period, but instead retained much of its cohesion and discipline until the Yugoslav federation itself no longer existed in its original form. By tradition and inclination, Yugoslavia's socialist military leaders were averse to direct political involvement. YPA policy, dating from wartime, was to support the Party, its leadership, and the continuation of Yugoslavia "as an equal, social community of all nations and nationalities."[5] But the army was increasingly challenged by the forces of nationalism and concerned with the disintegration of the Party and the weakening of the state structure. Some political leaders, particularly Slovenes and Croats, called for an end to Party organizations within the YPA and a redefinition of the army's mission to exclude its commitment to defend socialism.

5   Ramet, p. 245.

The YPA's survival depended on the continued functioning of the federal structure; by 1989 over half of the Yugoslav federal budget was spent on the military. In numerous public policy statements in the late 1980s, military leaders deplored the growing polycentrism of the state and the fragmentation of the Party. In some policies it supported Milošević, the principal advocate of a centralist program and opponent of the looser confederation advocated by Slovenian and Croatian leaders. The YPA leadership supported Serbia's efforts in September 1989 to amend its constitution to provide for secession, yet it opposed nearly identical proposals in Slovenia and other republics.

By late 1990 it was evident that officers of the YPA held widely varying views of the army's mission. Some commanders were prepared to undermine the position of the central command. Several leading YPA officers took steps that hastened Yugoslavia's disintegration, providing arms to Serbs outside Serbia while seeking to disarm the territorial forces of the other republics. In 1990 General Ratko Mladić, a corps commander of the YPA in Croatia, provided stocks of weapons to Serbs in the Krajina region, giving them the military means to pursue autonomy from the Croatian Republic.[6] (The term *krajina* means borderland or frontier and refers specifically to the former military frontier region separating the Austrian and Ottoman empires. As early as the sixteenth century, Austria attracted Serbs to this area to defend its frontier against the Ottomans. In recent years the term *krajina* has been used widely, if not entirely correctly, to refer to all Serbian-dominated areas of the Croatian republic.) When Serbian irregulars

6 Mark Mazower, *The War in Bosnia: An Analysis* (London: Action for Bosnia, December 1992), p. 3.

and Croatian military forces clashed in the Krajina beginning in January 1991, the YPA moved in as a "peacekeeping" force. For some commanders this was a genuine effort to defuse the conflict, but for others it was an opportunity to aid Serbian irregulars.

MULTIPARTY ELECTIONS OF 1990

Multiparty elections took place in each of the six Yugoslav republics in 1990. The first elections were held in Slovenia in April and the last in Serbia in December. Although plans were drawn up for federal elections, they never took place. Outside observers generally judged these elections to be free, although the state-controlled media gave a one-sided advantage to Milošević in Serbia. In most places nationalist candidates won decisively; some winners were Communists, and many were former leaders of the League of Communists in their respective republics (Serbia, Slovenia, Macedonia, and Montenegro). Others were former dissidents who had made their political careers by opposing the LCY; these included Franjo Tudjman in Croatia and Alija Izetbegović in Bosnia.

The Bosnian elections were held in November 1990. Three ethnically based parties together won 86% of the 240 seats in the Bosnian Assembly. Eight small parties shared the remaining seats. The Serbian Democratic Party (SDP) headed by Radovan Karadžić won 72 seats, and the Croatian Democratic Community (CDC) led by Stjepan Kljuić won 44 seats. The Muslim Party for Democratic Action (PDA) won 86 seats; its two top vote-getters were Fikret Abdić, who drew heavily from his power base in northwest Bosnia, and Izetbegović. The three parties, despite sometimes harsh nationalist campaign rhetoric, agreed to rule as a coalition. Each was represented on the seven-member Bosnian State Presidency.[7] Alija Izetbegović was designated president of the Presidency for a one-year term.

The results of this election demonstrate remarkable historical consistency with previous Bosnian multiparty elections, whether in 1910 (the Austrian period) or in the 1920s (the royal Yugoslav era). In 1990, Bosnians again voted overwhelmingly for ethnically based parties, and a single party achieved an overwhelming majority among the voters of each nationality. Despite their avowed nationalist principles, the political leaders elected in 1990 briefly restored the historical pattern of coalition politics in the Bosnian Assembly in an ultimately futile effort to achieve a formula for Bosnia's political future that satisfied all parties.

The 1990 elections provided the newly elected leaders with considerable political legitimacy. By 1990 the authority of the Yugoslav federal government had eroded decisively and had been eclipsed by republican leaders. At the same time, the victory of nationalist politicians in the 1990 elections was the precursor of more serious problems, for many new leaders aroused fear and suspicion among the members of national minorities within their republics' boundaries. As the Yugoslav republics moved toward independence, the minority communities in each republic faced the prospect of losing the benefits accruing to others of their nationality who lived in a republic where they constituted a majority. The prospects for fair and equal treatment of ethnic minorities were not good.

Croatia's President Tudjman and Serbia's President Milošević actively cultivated the discontent of their fellow nationals in

7   Milan Andrejevich, "The Future of Bosnia and Hercegovina: A Sovereign Republic or Cantonization?" *Radio Free Europe Research,* July 5, 1991, p. 29.

neighboring republics. Both of them hoped to gain from dismembering Bosnia and Hercegovina. This involved each of them in a fundamental contradiction: Milošević argued for the partitioning of Croatia and Bosnia to accommodate their Serbian inhabitants, while simultaneously insisting that no one interfere with his continued repression of the Kosovo Albanians. Similarly, Tudjman demanded that no one interfere in Croatia's treatment of its Serbs at the same time that he sought to annex portions of Bosnia and Hercegovina in the name of its Croatian inhabitants. These contradictory stances seemed to bother neither of them in the least.

THE YUGOSLAV FEDERATION: THE BOSNIAN ROLE

In the absence of the LCY and with the Yugoslav federation hopelessly deadlocked, the presidents of the six republics met several times from December 1990 to June 1991 to discuss a possible compromise structure for the future of Yugoslavia. These meetings, called "YU Summits," were convened at the invitation of the federal Presidency, which participated in the first round (December 1990 - March 1991). Held in circumstances of growing acrimony and rising demands from rival republics and political groups, the talks held little hope for reconciliation.

In the second round, from March to June 1991, each of the republics hosted one meeting. Slovenia and Croatia favored making Yugoslavia into a loose confederation of sovereign states. Serbian President Milošević, having achieved a dominant position within the federation, rejected notions of confederation and greater autonomy for Slovenia and Croatia. He raised the prospect of annexing the Serb-inhabited areas of Croatia and Bosnia if those republics insisted on independence, asserting that the Serbs of Yugoslavia had a right to live together in a single state. Milošević thus held any agreement for a loose confederation (that is, greater autonomy for the republics) hostage to the Greater Serbian agenda he had promoted since his rise to power in 1987.

In June 1991, at the last YU Summit, a compromise four-point proposal for preserving the Yugoslav federation was sponsored by Macedonia and Bosnia, the latter represented by Izetbegović. Representatives of all six republics accepted the proposal in principle and agreed to negotiate further. Although nothing came of these commitments, the fact that Izetbegović was seeking a peaceful resolution to republican differences was to have fateful consequences for Bosnia. At a time when Serbian irregulars and Croatian territorial forces were rapidly arming for possible civil war, Izetbegović was acting as mediator in hopes of preserving some form of a Yugoslav polity.

Regarding Bosnia, the conference participants discussed proposals for cantonization, an approach (following the Swiss model) that would grant substantial autonomy to numerous ethnically based local government units while preserving the republic of Bosnia and Hercegovina as a weak central entity with limited authority. In the highly charged polemical press of the various republics, speculation abounded that Izetbegović had consented to a cantonization plan for Bosnia. If so, these talks represented the first of several occasions on which he agreed to a proposal for dividing Bosnia and later renounced it under pressure from others in the Bosnian government. At about the same time, in March 1991, Milošević and Tudjman met separately from the other republican presidents and secretly agreed to dismember Bosnia and partition it between Serbia and Croatia. The notorious agreement of March 1991 created a bond of common interest between the Serbian and Croatian republics that persisted and survived even the bitter 1991 fighting in Croatia.

As the inter-republican negotiations proceeded, the annual rotation for the president of the federal Presidency was approaching. The Croat Stipe Mesić was due to be selected, and the votes of five of the eight Presidency members were necessary to confirm his election. Mesić won the support of the Bosnian, Croatian, Slovenian, and Macedonian members of the Presidency. But Milošević's allies, who controlled the votes of Montenegro, Vojvodina, Kosovo, and Serbia, declined to support him despite protracted negotiations to achieve a compromise. The Presidency deadlocked in a 4-4 vote and failed to confirm Mesić. At midnight on May 15, Yugoslavia was without a titular head, and most legal experts concluded that the army had no commander in chief. Mesić was subsequently confirmed as president in July 1991 after the European Community (EC) successfully urged the key parties to keep alive hopes for some form of a Yugoslav federation. Nevertheless, the deadlock in May marked the end of the federal Presidency as a cohesive force.

By the fall of 1991, the war in Croatia meant that Yugoslavia effectively ceased to exist, but the mutation of the socialist-era Yugoslav federation into rump Yugoslavia was acknowledged in law only on April 27, 1992. By that time the EC and the United States had recognized the breakaway republics of Slovenia, Croatia, and Bosnia as independent states. On that date the Milošević regime introduced constitutional changes recognizing that rump Yugoslavia consisted only of Montenegro, Serbia, and the provinces of Kosovo and Vojvodina, which had been absorbed and stripped of their autonomy by Serbia after Milošević came to power in the late 1980s. Rump Yugoslavia, denied participation in the United Nations and subject to heavy economic sanctions owing to its activities in Bosnia, is a barely recognizable descendent of the Yugoslav federation that preceded it in the socialist era.

THE ARMS RACE

On January 25, 1991, television viewers in all republics except Croatia were shown a scratchy videotape purporting to show Croatia's defense minister, Martin Špegelj, negotiating a substantial purchase of arms from Hungary and discussing plots against YPA officers and their families. The videotapes were the work of YPA undercover security officers, who caught Špegelj in an inebriated condition on a number of occasions. Although Špegelj adamantly denied the authenticity of the tapes, Croatia's international quest to purchase arms was a poorly kept secret; in February 1991 the Hungarian Minister of Foreign Affairs publicly confirmed the sale of 10,000 rifles to Croatia. Federal Defense Minister General Veljko Kadijević demanded that Špegelj be arrested, but Croatian officials refused. Špegelj went into hiding and subsequently resigned in the summer of 1991.

Simultaneous with the triumph of nationalist politicians in all republics in the 1990 elections, the government of each republic and many political factions intensified the urgent drive to secure weapons for the civil war that many believed was inevitable. Transport of arms became an open secret. On April 9, 1991, Bosnian police stopped three trucks containing over 1,000 automatic rifles near Mostar, and Bosnians widely believed the rifles were intended for Serbian irregulars. A similar incident in May 1991 involved trucks bringing arms into Bosnia from Montenegro. In a shadowy operation known by the acronym RAM, Serbian political leaders arranged for the delivery of weapons in 1990 and 1991 to Bosnian Serb communities in eastern Hercegovina, Bosnian Krajina, and the mountainous Romanija region just outside Sarajevo. As a result of these activities, Serbs in Croatia and Bosnia were well armed by the summer of 1991.

Much of the weaponry delivered to Serbian irregulars came from the stocks of the YPA. Nevertheless, the army's commanders and spokesmen maintained a public position of impartiality and opposition to any republic or political faction acquiring arms. The evidence suggests that some YPA officers at this time genuinely opposed arming any factions while others were quite eager to hand over the armory keys to Serbian irregulars and extremists.

The growing arms race drew sharp rebukes from the federal Presidency. On January 9, 1991, the Presidency, backing the army's position, ordered that all "illegal paramilitary units" be disbanded within ten days. On January 15, taking advantage of the world's preoccupation with the first day of the US-led United Nations invasion that drove Iraq from Kuwait (Operation Desert Storm), the federal Secretariat of Defense threatened to carry out the Presidency's order if arms were not returned in the next four days. Croatian nationalists viewed this declaration as a sign of imminent attack and stepped up their preparations for conflict. Few arms were returned, but the army took no action on behalf of the federal authorities. The Presidency repeated its warning against paramilitary formations on May 9 but was again ignored by all sides.

INDEPENDENCE FOR THE REPUBLIC OF SLOVENIA

Milošević's purges in Vojvodina, Kosovo, and Montenegro contributed to the growing polarization of the republics, with Serbia and its satellites on one hand, and Slovenia and Croatia on the other. In Slovenia, the movement for a looser association with Yugoslavia gained impetus from strong opposition among Slovenes to Milošević's violations of human rights in Kosovo and resentment of his heavy-handed behavior in dominating the Yugoslav federation. In September 1989 the Slovenes amended their constitution to provide for secession from the Yugoslav federation.

The impulse for a looser relationship gained great momentum when pro-Milošević Serbs, using tactics similar to those employed in Vojvodina, Kosovo, and Montenegro, scheduled a demonstration for "Truth about Kosovo" to be held in Slovenia's capital city of Ljubljana on December 1, 1989.

Slovenian police banned the demonstration on November 19, 1989. They stopped trains entering Slovenia from the east and searched them for demonstrators before they reached Ljubljana. Prevented from staging a mass demonstration in the Slovene capital, the Serbian nationalist organizers canceled the demonstration at the last minute while bitterly denouncing the Slovenes for threatening excessive force. Serbia shortly thereafter called on its enterprises to refrain from trading with Slovenia. The boycott met with only limited success, as many Serbian enterprises valued their markets in Slovenia and would have been badly hurt by honoring a boycott.

In a Slovenian referendum in December 1990, 88% of the voters chose to separate from Yugoslavia. Speculation by Yugoslavs and foreign observers increasingly centered on whether the YPA would intervene to maintain the integrity of Yugoslavia.

On June 25, 1991, Slovenia and Croatia declared their independence from Yugoslavia. The YPA, acting on its belief that Yugoslav territorial integrity was threatened, moved on June 27 to secure Slovenia's international border-crossing points and airports, which it claimed were under federal jurisdiction. Slovene Territorial Forces fought back. By seizing caches of weapons and ammunition stockpiled within Slovenia, the Slovene forces substantially increased their armed strength. They took over 2,000 prisoners, obstructed the movement of YPA support columns, and took control of international border checkpoints from the YPA forces. The military engagement in Slovenia lasted only ten days. The Yugoslav military bombed the Ljubljana airport and attacked other targets, including a highly publicized attack on a civilian truck convoy, but YPA commanders soon experienced widespread desertion in their enlisted ranks, particularly by non-Serbs.

Responding rapidly, the EC dispatched mediators on June 28 and set in motion the process of ending financial assistance to Yugoslavia. The YPA, faced with disaster in Slovenia, decided to withdraw rather than bring in reinforcements and further challenge the Slovene Territorial Forces. The commander of the YPA, General Veljko Kadijević, was probably the prime mover in the decision not to contest the Slovene situation further.

The YPA's humiliation in Slovenia was the result of two miscalculations. First, its leadership expected the Slovenes to be sufficiently intimidated by the mere appearance of federal forces to capitulate without a fight. Secondly, the YPA believed it could easily escalate the action in the event of Slovene resistance;

such action, which under close international scrutiny was certain to be perceived as aggression, was precluded by the unexpected arrival of EC mediators. After bombing and strafing some civilian targets, the YPA quickly decided to write off Slovenia as peripheral to its efforts. On July 18, 1991, the two sides reached an agreement that allowed the remaining federal army units in Slovenia to withdraw while the republic of Slovenia was free to go its own way.

Ethnically, Slovenia was a relatively homogenous republic. It contained no significant minority population of other South Slavs and therefore faced no nationality issues as acute as those confronting Croatia, Bosnia, Macedonia, or Kosovo. The absence of any sizeable Serbian population meant that Slovenia was beyond the aspirations of Greater Serbian nationalists who wanted to unite all Serbian lands in a single state. Slovenia's separation from the Yugoslav federation was relatively painless, owing in large measure to the YPA's reluctance to engage in all-out combat to retain control over it.

The army's eagerness to avoid a protracted and costly conflict in Slovenia suggests that Milošević's Greater Serbian agenda, which excluded Slovenia from its most serious objectives, was already shared in the summer of 1991 by key commanders of the YPA. In contrast to developments in Slovenia, the YPA's relentless support for Serbian separatist movements in Croatia and Bosnia was to plunge the lands of the former Yugoslavia into full-blown war.

II

Descent Into War: Bosnia in the Wars of Yugoslav Succession

THE WAR IN Bosnia occurred against a backdrop of three important external developments that altered the prospects and alternatives of Bosnia's political leaders. First, the Yugoslav People's Army (YPA) dramatically changed its mission in the latter half of 1991 from defending Yugoslav ideals to becoming an agent of Greater Serbian nationalism. Secondly, the 1991 war in Croatia strengthened national extremists among the Bosnian Serbs and weakened those who hoped to preserve a multiethnic Bosnian state. Finally, although diplomatic representatives of the international community cited lofty principles and voiced high ideals, their actions drove the major participants in Bosnia to press separatist claims and abandon efforts for a negotiated solution.

Some observers have portrayed the Bosnian conflict as a renewal of age-old mutual hatreds that inexorably resurfaced after the collapse of Tito's Communist regime. In contrast, we assert that the current Bosnian crisis is, in the context of Bosnia's history, an *historical aberration*, albeit with a single important historical precedent: the interethnic slaughter of the World War II era. Armed conflict, ethnic cleansing, the bombardment of cities, and atrocities against civilians in Bosnia were not preordained consequences of ethnonational divisions in Bosnian society; they developed as a result of the transformation of the YPA into an instrument of Serbian nationalists, the annexationist ambitions of the Croatian and Serbian governments, and the eagerness of national extremists to conduct unsavory ethnic cleansing campaigns with the endorsement and assistance of organized armies in the region.

The armed conflict in Bosnia followed closely on the 1991 war between Croatia's Serbs (along with their allies in the YPA) and the defense forces of the republic of Croatia. We shall first survey these developments with an eye toward understanding the Bosnian situation.

THE YPA: STRATEGIC REASSESSMENT AND TRANSFORMATION

The army's defeat and withdrawal from Slovenia drove the YPA General Staff to review its strategy. This extensive review lasted through the summer of 1991.[1] Referring specifically to Operation Desert Storm (January 1991), the review concluded that such actions were a "true paradigm" for the international community to apply when intervening in local situations.[2] The YPA analysis concluded, however, that the major international players were unlikely to achieve the political consensus necessary to intervene in the Yugoslav lands.

The YPA's strategic reassessment created a high probability that "the unrest that accompanied the former Yugoslavia's disintegration would erupt into war."[3] The YPA became committed to consolidating its resources in those areas with substantial Serbian minorities, specifically Croatia and Bosnia. The

---

1 The major conclusions of this remarkable reassessment were published in *Vojno Delo* in October 1991 and analyzed by James Gow, "One Year of War in Bosnia and Herzegovina," *Radio Free Europe Research*, June 4, 1993.

2 *Ibid.*, p. 5.

3 *Ibid.*, p. 1.

YPA's overall strategy called for the army's key allies and clients to become acutely sensitive to the responses of the international community to violence and atrocities in Yugoslavia so that international intervention on the Iraqi model would never occur. The army and most of its key allies thereafter displayed extraordinary finesse, escalating their actions when the international community was preoccupied and retreating or waiting when they found themselves in the spotlight of the international media.

At the same time, the YPA in the latter half of 1991 often displayed signs of internal disagreement within its officer corps. Many commanders openly aided Serbian irregulars in Croatia; others held to a more neutral course in the Croatian war and favored a moderate, conciliatory approach. With Milošević's sponsorship and encouragement, the YPA command structure underwent a slow transition during the Croatian war, leaving in power those who favored Greater Serbian nationalism. The full transformation of the YPA, from a guardian of Yugoslav ideals and socialist ideology to an agent of Greater Serbian ambition, was a protracted process, not fully completed until the forced retirement of General Života Panić and forty-two other generals in August 1993. But the process began in the weeks following the humiliation in Slovenia and was well advanced by the end of 1991.

The development of the war in Croatia was heavily influenced by the willingness of many YPA officers to aid Serbian irregulars. Operating with the support and protection of local YPA commanders, the irregulars gained parity with, and often substantial advantages over, the Croatian Territorial Forces they were fighting. By the fall of 1991 various YPA field commanders were in effect prosecuting a civil war to unite the

Serbs of Croatia with those living in the core republics of Serbia and Montenegro.

The winners of the April 1990 multiparty elections in Croatia, Franjo Tudjman and other members of his political party, the Croatian Democratic Community, were committed Croatian nationalists. Once in power, Tudjman suppressed rival news media, and government-controlled radio and television adopted harsh nationalist rhetoric. His regime encouraged public display of the *Šahovnica*, the red and white checkerboard emblem that was welcomed by Croatian nationalists as a symbol of independence but hated by many of Croatia's Serbs as a reminder of Ustasha oppression. (The *Šahovnica*, though dating to the Middle Ages and routinely a part of Croatian symbolism under socialism, had been prominently displayed by the Ustashe in World War II.) After Tudjman's victory, Croatian-controlled enterprises dismissed thousands of Serbian workers, increasing the widespread resentment that Serbs felt toward the new regime.[4] Far from offering any hope of reconciliation, Tudjman's Croatian nationalists mounted a concerted effort to alienate and disenfranchise the Serbs of Croatia.

For their part, the Serbs of Croatia clamored for autonomy from Croatia once Tudjman came to power. They were encouraged by Milošević's actions in Kosovo. Serbian activists, showered with praise from the Milošević-controlled media in Belgrade, organized a referendum in Serb-inhabited regions of Croatia from August 9 to September 2, 1990; of 756,781 Serbs who voted, 756,549 voted for autonomy. In a direct challenge to

4 Misha Glenny, *The Fall of Yugoslavia: The Third Balkan War* (London and New York: Penguin, 1992), pp. 13, 77, and 107.

Croatian authority, a self-styled Serbian National Council proclaimed the "Serbian Autonomous Region of Krajina." The
Croatian Ministry of Internal Affairs, in response, declared its
intention to confiscate the weapons of the rebellious Serbs. The
Serbs of Croatia and the nationalist Croatian government were
firmly set on a collision course.

Beginning in 1990, officers of the YPA's Knin Corps, commanded by General Ratko Mladić, gave large numbers of
weapons from YPA stocks to Serbian paramilitary leaders in
Croatia. Mladić, a Serb from Bosnia with extreme Serbian
nationalist views, later gained notoriety as commander of Serbian
nationalist forces in Bosnia.[5] Both sides, the Croatian Defense
Forces and the restive Krajina Serbs, continued to build up their
arsenals throughout the fall and winter of 1990-1. The Serbs
declared their separation from Croatia on March 16, 1991, and
within a month clashes between armed Serbs and Croatian
police developed into a serious problem. These exchanges
assumed a much more ominous tone at the village of Borovo
Selo on May 2, 1991.

Borovo Selo was inhabited by Serbs known to harbor
particular hostility to the Croatian nationalist regime. The
Zagreb government had agreed with local Serbs to refrain from
sending Croatian police into Borovo Selo, but two Croatian
police officers entered the village on the evening of May 1. They
were greeted with automatic-weapons fire and taken into cus-
tody by local Serbs. The next day the Croatian Ministry of
Internal Affairs dispatched additional police units to Borovo
Selo. They clashed with heavily armed Serb militiamen in a
firefight that the Serbs won handily; twelve Croatian policemen
and three Serbs were killed. The precise details remain a matter

5 For a revealing interview with Mladić, see Glenny, pp. 26-9.

of considerable controversy, but Croatian propaganda claims and the bragging of Serbian extremists both suggest that Serbs slashed the throats of some of the Croatian policemen and gouged out the eyes of at least one.[6] Beyond sheer bestiality, these acts were symbolic reenactments of Chetnik reprisals against Croats in World War II, calculated to inflame ethnic hatred by rekindling the passions of wartime genocide.

Croatian media alleged that the Serbs were henchmen of the extremist Bosnian Serb Vojislav Šešelj sent to ambush Croatian policemen. As of May 1991, Šešelj was both a vocal instigator of ethnic hatred and, by his own admission, an active organizer of hate killings. At a rally in Belgrade two days after the shoot-out in Borovo Selo, Šešelj bragged to the crowd that his Chetniks had participated in that action. He threatened revenge against Croats for recent Serbian deaths as well as for Serbian deaths in World War II. The Borovo Selo incident presaged other grisly ethnic killings by Šešelj and his followers in Croatia and, during 1992, in Bosnia.

Croatia scheduled a referendum for May 19, 1991, on the question of independence from Yugoslavia. To avoid being bound by inclusion in the new Croatian independent state, the self-proclaimed "Serbian Autonomous Region of Krajina" held its own second referendum on May 12; 99% of the participants voted to leave Croatia and join Serbia. One week later, 94% of the voters in Croatia opted for independence; most Serbs boycotted the Croatian vote.

Clashes between Serbian irregulars and Croatian militiamen rapidly escalated in the summer months of 1991, and various YPA units increased their overt support for local Serbian forces. In August 1991, the YPA and Serbian irregulars sur-

6 Glenny, pp. 73-8.

rounded towns and cities in northeastern Croatia. On August 19, while the world was preoccupied with the Russian coup attempt, the YPA sharply escalated the conflict by initiating the siege and bombardment of Vukovar. On October 7, 1991, the Yugoslav air force launched an air assault on Zagreb, damaging the Presidential Palace in the city's historic heart. On November 17, Croatian forces defending Vukovar surrendered, leaving in Serbian hands the rubble and utter devastation that had once been an attractive European city. On several occasions during the war, the YPA assaulted Dubrovnik, a beautiful medieval port city with no contemporary military significance. On December 6, 1991, the YPA conducted a particularly destructive shelling of the ancient city by air, land, and sea, arousing international outrage over the wanton destruction of Dubrovnik's religious and cultural monuments.

The bombardment of cities, although apparently senseless and wanton, served a grotesque political purpose similar to that of ethnic cleansing: It frightened civilians into fleeing, leaving the military free to resettle conquered areas with Serbs or others who supported the aims of rump Yugoslavia. Since the YPA preferred to use renegades, irregulars, and clients to conduct its campaigns of terror, the bombardment and ethnic cleansing operations also allowed the perpetrators to incite additional hatred, reducing the prospects for a return to the neighborly peaceful coexistence that had prevailed in cities before the war in Croatia began.

As hostilities intensified in the summer of 1991, the EC sent observers to Croatia and sought to work out a diplomatic solution. German diplomats took the lead, declared that Yugoslavia was a relic of history, supported the secessionist republic's right to national self-determination, and demanded an end to the YPA's use of force. On October 8, 1991, the UN Secretary General appointed former US Secretary of State Cyrus Vance as his personal envoy for Yugoslavia. On January 1, 1992, Vance announced that the YPA, Serbia, and Croatia had agreed to a cease-fire and that the United Nations Protection Force (UNPROFOR) would be deployed to separate the belligerents in Croatia. On January 2, 1992, a formal agreement among the parties was signed in Sarajevo. Two weeks later UN military personnel began arriving in Croatia to inaugurate the UN's peacekeeping role in the former Yugoslavia.

With a fragile truce in place in Croatia, 1992 was to signal the onset of the brutal, bloody conflict in Bosnia.

WAR IN CROATIA: IMPACT ON BOSNIA

The Croatian war spilled over into Bosnia in two different ways. First, Serbs from the republic of Krajina and Croatian troops from the Ministry of Internal Affairs used cross-border incursions to advance their nationalist claims to Bosnia. Secondly, and more significant militarily, the YPA used Bosnia as a staging area to support the Croatian war effort. By the end of 1991, the YPA had established virtual protectorates within Bosnia, using as a cover the creation of Serbian autonomous regions in that country which called on the YPA to provide protection for their inhabitants.

The Croatian Ministry of Internal Affairs conducted maneuvers on Bosnian soil several times during the spring of 1991. These incursions were seen as provocations by Bosnian Serb politicians, who called on the YPA to protect Bosnia against Croatian aggression.

On April 26, 1991, fourteen Serbian-dominated municipal districts in northwestern Bosnia adjacent to the former Military

Frontier area of Croatia proclaimed the "Municipal Community of Bosnian Krajina" and established a headquarters in Banja Luka. On June 8, Radio Sarajevo reported that 200 Serbian militiamen from the "Serbian Autonomous Region of Krajina" had conducted military exercises in this region. Milan Martić, the Interior Minister of the Serbian Krajina, claimed that the incursion by his troops effectively dissolved the border between Bosnia and the Serbian areas of Croatia. The next day Bosnian President Izetbegović, employing Churchillian rhetoric, declared, "the battle for Bosnia has begun."[7]

Shortly after escalating its support for the Serbs in Croatia late in the summer of 1991, the YPA stepped up its activities in Bosnia. While many of the YPA's activities were undertaken in support of operations in Croatia, some of the army's movements unmistakably constituted preparations for war in Bosnia itself. In late September 1991 the army established the borders of the "Serbian Autonomous Region of Hercegovina" to support its attacks on Dubrovnik and other targets on the Dalmatian Coast. Other Serbian autonomous regions were created in Bosnian Krajina (northwestern Bosnia around Banja Luka), and Romanija (east of Sarajevo). Each requested "assistance" from federal forces in September 1991, and the YPA thereafter strengthened its presence in several Serbian-led areas of Bosnia.

In the fall of 1991, the YPA used Bosnian territory and facilities to support its mission in Croatia and moved its resources into secure locations to facilitate mobilization in the event the conflict spread to Bosnia. The YPA moved units from the cities into the Bosnian countryside, leaving only a symbolic presence in the towns. Some production facilities in Bosnia were dismantled and moved to Serbia; others were abandoned

7 *Radio Free Europe Research Report,* June 28, 1991, p. 35.

in the next several months. By the January 1992 cease-fire in Croatia, the YPA was poised to seize much of the Bosnian countryside and its major communications links.

BOSNIA'S LEADERS IN THE QUEST FOR COMPROMISE

After the Bosnian multiparty elections in November 1990, members of the three ethnically based parties that came to power began to discuss a possible compromise regarding the future of Bosnia. Muslim and Croatian politicians supported the notion of Bosnian sovereignty; Serbian leaders opposed it. On January 30, 1991, the Muslim Party for Democratic Action (PDA) submitted a proposal for a sovereign Bosnia; it was quickly endorsed by the Croatian Democratic Community (CDC) but rejected by the Serbian Democratic Party (SDP). The SDP wanted to remain in the Serbian-dominated Yugoslav federation and feared that Bosnian sovereignty would "institutionalize the minority status of Serbs in Bosnia."[8]

On June 12, 1991, representatives of all three parties asked the Bosnian state Presidency to propose a "declaration of sovereignty" that would reconcile differing views. Soon overshadowed by the war in Croatia, these efforts proved futile; no compromise was ever achieved.

In October 1991, as war raged in neighboring Croatia, the Muslim and Croatian parties abandoned their efforts to reach an agreement with the Serbs. Together they passed a resolution on October 14 demanding sovereignty for Bosnia. The assembly president — a Serb — had adjourned the session, so members of the SDP had already left. The sovereignty vote signalled an end to parliamentary efforts to reach a three-way

8 *Radio Free Europe Research Report,* July 5, 1991, p. 30.

agreement, although negotiations among leaders of the three parties continued.   On December 21, 1991, Bosnia's Serbs declared their own republic.

DIPLOMATIC INTERVENTION: THE ROAD TO RECOGNITION

In the Cold War years, Western interest in Yugoslavia was dominated by the desire to bolster Yugoslav independence against a potential Soviet invasion. Thus the United States and its allies supported a unified Yugoslavia, and they opposed separatist or breakaway elements within the country as potentially aiding or encouraging Soviet meddling.

In 1991 and 1992 both the United States and the European Community (EC) gradually abandoned their support for a united Yugoslavia in favor of recognizing the independence of most of the successor republics. The EC, however, was substantially ahead of the United States in the policy transition. While paying less attention to the problem and leaving the initiative to the EC, the United States continued in principle to support Yugoslavism until early 1992. In June 1991, Secretary of State James Baker visited Belgrade and voiced continued support for the Yugoslav federation.   YPA commanders interpreted his pronouncement as a green light for military action against Slovenian independence. The EC, on the other hand, jumped quickly into the fray when Slovenia declared independence from Yugoslavia in June 1991. By treating Slovenia and the YPA as equal contenders, the EC encouraged the Slovenes to separate from Yugoslavia. The rift between the EC and the United States thus created an opportunity for each side — the YPA centrists and the leaders of successor Yugoslav republics — to anticipate some Western support for its preferred course of action.

In an effort to create a consistent policy toward the Yugoslav lands, the EC Conference on Yugoslavia turned in November 1991 to an Arbitration Committee, headed by France's Robert Badinter and consisting of the presidents of the constitutional courts of five Western European countries, to evaluate the legal status of the Yugoslav federation. In December 1991 the Badinter Committee concluded that "Yugoslavia is in the process of dissolution."[9] It set December 23, 1991, as the deadline for applications by former Yugoslav republics seeking EC recognition of their independence; those that qualified would be recognized on January 15, 1992. By the deadline, the EC received applications for recognition from the republics of Slovenia, Croatia, Macedonia, and Bosnia and Hercegovina.

The Badinter Committee report was released on January 15, 1992.[10] The committee concluded that Slovenia and Macedonia met in full the criteria for recognition adopted by the EC on December 17, 1991. The report firmly asserted the need for the Croatian and Bosnian republics to respect fully the minority rights of the Serbian populations within their boundaries in conformity with relevant international accords, but it also insisted that existing borders between republics be maintained unless the affected parties concurred in changing them. Regarding Croatia the committee required only that the Croatian republic include in its newly drafted constitutional changes of December 4, 1991, certain guarantees for the special status of Croatia's Serbian population; otherwise, Croatia was judged to meet the EC's standards.

The Badinter Committee expressed other reservations concerning Bosnia. The report noted that the Presidency and

9   *Yugoslav Survey*, 32, no. 4 (1991), p. 19.
10 *Yugoslav Survey*, 33, no. 1 (1992), p. 121.

government of Bosnia and Hercegovina, based on its constitution and laws, had pledged to adhere to all appropriate international acts and had guaranteed observance of human rights, but that the "Serbian members of the Presidency did not join" in those declarations. The committee cited three referendums organized by Bosnia's Serbs (November 10, 1991; December 21, 1991; and January 9, 1992) in which they had expressed a desire to be excluded from any sovereign Bosnian republic that was outside the framework of Yugoslavia. (Two of these three referendums were held after the EC initiated its recognition procedures.) The report noted that both the Bosnian Constitution of 1974 and a 1990 amendment to it specifically guaranteed equal rights to the "nationalities of Bosnia-Herzegovina — Muslims, Serbs, and Croats," as well as others living in its territory.

The committee clearly felt that the EC should not recognize Bosnia as an independent state without the concurrence of Bosnia's Serbs. The report concluded that "the will of the Bosnia-Herzegovina populations" to make Bosnia a sovereign state "cannot be considered fully established." It suggested that its negative evaluation might be modified if the republic were to hold a referendum regarding independence for all its citizens, "without discrimination and under international control." Such a referendum was scheduled by the Bosnian government for February 29 and March 1, 1992.

Plans for an orderly recognition of Croatia's independence were dashed by Germany's Foreign Minister Hans-Dietrich Genscher, the leading proponent of speedy EC recognition. Germany's economic ties and cultural identification were stronger with Slovenia and Croatia than with Serbia, and German sympathies for Croatia were heightened by the YPA's escalating aggressiveness and brutality in the Croatian war. Genscher denounced the YPA's use of force in Croatia and supported Croatia's right of self-determination (that is, its right to secede from Yugoslavia) and the inviolability of Croatia's borders. Vowing not to be bound by the Badinter Committee's reservations concerning Croatia's constitutional changes and human rights commitments, Genscher forced the EC to act by announcing that Germany would unilaterally recognize Croatia's independence. Bowing to German pressure, the EC thereupon agreed to recognize the independence of Slovenia and Croatia effective January 15, 1992. The United States, on the other hand, held back, believing that premature recognition might undermine the peace process underway to end the fighting in Croatia.

The German position disregarded the Badinter Committee's insistence that Croatia fully respect the rights of the Serbian minority within its boundaries. German support for unconditional recognition thus translated into a tacit endorsement of Croatian national chauvinism at the expense of its Serbian population.

The role of Germany and the EC in pushing for recognition of the breakaway republics has been hotly debated. Some critics, particularly those with a pro-Serbian or anti-German orientation, blame the outbreak of the war in Bosnia largely or exclusively on Germany, citing historic German antipathy toward Serbia and sympathies for Croatia and Bosnia dating back at least as far as World War II. This is too simple an explanation, for the primary impetus for the Bosnian war in early 1992 came not from Western diplomats but from forces ineluctably at work within Bosnia itself. By the time Bosnia's recognition became an issue in the EC, the YPA was in the Bosnian countryside, prepared to incite and assist Serbian irregulars in dismembering Bosnia much as it had done in Croatia. The Bosnian Serbs, keenly aware of the YPA's support for a Greater Serbian agenda, were emboldened to pursue their separatist aspirations and were preparing for war. Furthermore, Croatian military units and militias, having previously intruded on several occasions into Bosnian territory, were poised to seize territory in western Hercegovina in the event the fragile political arrangements broke down.

Notwithstanding the YPA's widespread military preparations in early 1992 and the political truculence of the Bosnian Serbs, the actions of the international community were the proximate cause of the war in Bosnia.[11] The EC failed to recognize the importance of negotiation and compromise in multiethnic Bosnia, where no nationality constituted a majority and coalition politics had been the rule through much of the century. In particular, the EC's insistence on a referendum as a condition for recognition had far-reaching consequences. A referendum on independence was inherently destabilizing, for it led the Bosnian Serbs to accelerate their campaign to avoid inclusion in an independent Bosnian republic. Headed by Radovan Karadžić, the Bosnian Serb leaders complained to the EC that they were bound to be outvoted by the combination of Muslims and Croats, who favored a unified Bosnian state. To accommodate these objections, the EC invited the leaders of all three parties — Serbs, Muslims and Croats — to Lisbon in late February 1992, prior to the scheduled referendum on indepen-

---

11 Former US Secretary of State Cyrus Vance admitted as much when he stated that the "premature" recognition of Slovenia, Croatia, and Bosnia by the EC and the US "brought about the war that is now going on." *The New York Times,* April 14, 1993, p. A-6.

dence, in a last-minute effort to negotiate an agreement to "cantonize" or partition the republic. This was to be the first of many efforts by the Western powers to pressure the three sides to accept some form of ethnic division of the Bosnian republic.

In the Lisbon talks, Karadžić (representing the Bosnian Serbs) and Mate Boban (speaking for the Bosnian Croats) readily agreed on a proposal for cantonization of Bosnia. To the amazement of his Bosnian Muslim constituents and of Western diplomats, Bosnian President Izetbegović also agreed, although few specific borders or terms of the cantonization were resolved. The Lisbon agreement put Bosnia in the peculiar position of being a newly emerging independent state whose leaders had already agreed to divide it. Still, the agreement offered hope for a compromise that could potentially accommodate the aspirations of all three parties.

By late February, the EC was joined by the United States in abandoning a long-standing commitment to a united Yugoslavia and moving to support the independence of the breakaway republics. Warren Zimmerman, the US Ambassador to Yugoslavia, and others in the State Department became concerned that the multiethnic Bosnian state was about to be partitioned by Serbian and Croatian nationalists; Milošević's intentions particularly concerned them. Soon after Izetbegović returned from Lisbon, Zimmerman met personally with him and, with reference to the Lisbon cantonization agreement, urged Izetbegović to "stick by his commitments."[12] However, the shift in US policy toward recognition was itself encouraging to Izetbegović, and he

12 *The New York Times,* September 30, 1993, p. A-18, Warren Zimmerman's Letter to the Editor.   Zimmerman denied an earlier report that he encouraged Izetbegović to renounce the Lisbon agreement.   David Binder, "US Policymakers on Bosnia Admit Errors in Opposing Partition in 1992," *The New York Times,* August 29, 1993, p. 8.

also was confronted with strong pressures from within his own government to oppose cantonization or partition.

With or without encouragement from outside powers, Izetbegović renounced his support for the cantonization agreement a few days after he returned from Lisbon and met with Zimmerman. The EC promptly reconvened the talks in Sarajevo and strongly urged all three Bosnian parties to reach an agreement on cantonization. On March 18, Izetbegović again consented and agreed with representatives of Bosnia's Serbs and Croats on a map to divide the republic.

US Secretary of State James Baker met with the EC foreign ministers in Brussels on March 10. Although all parties maintained the fiction that the EC retained the lead in dealing with the Bosnian crisis, the course of events strongly suggests an American push for full recognition. The EC announced its recognition of Bosnia to take effect on April 6. On April 7, the United States followed and announced that it recognized Croatia, Slovenia, and Bosnia as sovereign, independent states.

Despite the eagerness of the US and the EC to recognize the pluralistic, multiethnic Bosnian state, Western words were not backed by the means necessary to secure the Bosnian republic against the threats of those who aspired to dismember it. The talks preceding recognition became the first of many occasions on which Western diplomats would raise Bosnian hopes by articulating noble intentions. But the US and EC were engaged in a policy of "ends without means." The Western Powers liberally offered symbolic gestures and verbal encouragement to the Bosnians but were unprepared to follow through with meaningful action to deter the obviously aggressive intentions of neighboring states and the well-positioned units of the YPA.

The Lisbon and Sarajevo agreements of early 1992, in which Izetbegović acquiesced in a plan to cantonize or partition Bosnia, raise the issue of his role in determining Bosnia's future. Elected president of the Bosnian Presidency in 1990, Izetbegović was also the leader of the Bosnian Muslim party, the Party for Democratic Action. Previously imprisoned for advocating an Islamic state, he nonetheless emerged as a consistent advocate of a multiethnic Bosnia. This was less of a contradiction than might at first appear. Izetbegović's actions followed the tradition of Mehmed Spaho and other Bosnian Muslim leaders who, while attentive to the specific interests of their Muslim constituents, often used their influence to support broader, multinational political entities that would protect the interests of the Bosnian Muslims. For earlier Muslim political leaders, this had involved participating in the ruling coalition in the Austrian-era Parliament of 1910-14, being a member of most governments in the royal Yugoslav era from 1918 to 1941, and supporting the Communist Party and government in socialist Yugoslavia. Each of these entities (except for royal Yugoslavia after 1929) preserved the integrity of Bosnia and Hercegovina, thereby providing protection for the Bosnian Muslims against partition between Serbia and Croatia.

Izetbegović consistently supported the perpetuation of multinational entities: Yugoslavia in early 1991, then Bosnia and Hercegovina after it became clear that Yugoslavia was no longer a viable political entity. Of necessity, he also adopted a fallback position: When cantonization or partition appeared to be the only option, he sought the best possible arrangement for a "rump" Bosnia and Hercegovina as a homeland for the Bosnian Muslims. Izetbegović was driven by the awareness that a Bosnian Muslim ministate, if reduced too much by partition, would not be a viable entity and could easily be devoured by the neighboring states of Croatia and Serbia.

For Radovan Karadžić and the Bosnian Serbs, the EC's pressure on Izetbegović to agree to cantonization was tantamount to collusion with their secessionist plans. Karadžić urged Bosnia's Serbs to boycott the independence referendum of February 29 and March 1, 1992; the Yugoslav air force dropped leaflets over Bosnia urging Serbs not to vote. The Bosnian Serbs were conducting themselves in a very traditional manner as well: Emboldened by the successes of their patrons in Serbia (as they had been in 1912-14 and in the royal Yugoslav era), they asserted an agenda that drew them further away from the Bosnian Muslim and Croatian parties. Few Serbs voted in the referendum; Bosnian Muslims and Croats, on the other hand, voted in large numbers and cast over 99% of their ballots for Bosnia's full independence.

Sporadic shooting took place on the day of the referendum. Two days later, Serbian irregulars shelled Bosanski Brod, a town on the Sava River in northern Bosnia. On March 27, 1992, the day the political leaders of the Bosnian Serbs proclaimed their own constitution, the YPA launched attacks against the newly declared republic of Bosnia from the south, west, and northwest. On April 6, 1992, the day the EC's recognition of Bosnia's independence took effect, Serbian snipers in the top floors of the Holiday Inn in Sarajevo sprayed peace demonstrators with machine-gun fire. By that time over 1,300 people had been killed in the burgeoning war that rapidly engulfed the nascent Bosnian state.

THE EVE OF CONFLICT: MILITARY INEQUITY OF THE BELLIGERENTS

In late March 1992, when hostilities escalated to full-scale war in Bosnia, forces supporting the Bosnian Serbs enjoyed an overwhelming advantage in weaponry and personnel. The YPA had about 90,000 troops in Bosnia: it controlled most armories and munitions stockpiles and could rely on over forty fighter planes, hundreds of tanks and heavy artillery, and many thousands more troops stationed in Serbia. Also available were the terrorist brigades of the Serbian Volunteer Guard under the control of Željko Raznjatović, known as "Arkan," occupied at the time in Vukovar (where they were widely believed to be responsible for mass killings of Croatian civilians) but available to conduct atrocities in Bosnia.

Croatian Territorial Forces had some 12,000 men in western Hercegovina. Once hostilities began, they moved quickly to occupy that territory, at first in uneasy alliance with the Bosnians but later in full-scale conflict with them. The Croatian troops were well organized and well equipped, the beneficiaries of arms acquisitions by Croatia from Hungary, Italy, and Germany that intensified during the war in Croatia. In 1991 and early 1992, Croatian forces had smuggled extensive arms into Bosnia and had a sizeable cache of weapons in western Hercegovina by the spring of 1992.

The Bosnian Territorial Forces numbered about 50,000. At the outset of the conflict, they were hopelessly outgunned by the superior forces of the YPA and its allies. They possessed mainly small arms; during much of the siege of Sarajevo in the fall and winter of 1992-3, the Bosnians possessed only a single tank. The Bosnian army was so poorly prepared partly because Izetbegović had clung until the last moment to the hope of a political settlement. Additionally, in hopes of preventing the Croatian conflict from widening, the United Nations had imposed an arms embargo in September 1991 on all of the former Yugoslavia. Since it had no borders with other countries and only a single outlet to the Adriatic Sea, Bosnia had few opportunities to violate the embargo, whereas Croatia and Serbia could easily circumvent these restrictions because of their extensive coastal and land borders. The greatest assets of the Bosnian army were its genuinely multiethnic composition (particularly in the first year of the war) and the fighting spirit of most of its soldiers. Serbs and Croats held important command positions along with Bosnian Muslims, and the ranks were made up of soldiers from all three ethnic groups who believed in, and were prepared to fight for, a multinational Bosnian state.

Serbian forces set out to capture as much of Bosnia as they could. Their efforts were initially directed against three areas: the region of eastern Bosnia (inhabited before 1992 by a mixed Serbian and Bosnian Muslim population) that borders Serbia, a large territory of northwestern Bosnia with a substantial Serbian population, and a corridor across northern Bosnia that connects the two. The corridor was essential to Serbian plans as a land bridge to the Serbs of western Bosnia and to the Serb-inhabited regions of Croatia.

The Croats' war aims likewise consisted of acquiring the maximum amount of territory. Their principal target was the region of Hercegovina west of the Neretva River and adjacent to Croatia. Consolidation of Croatian gains in this area would provide, in addition to an expansion of Croatian territory, military benefits in the event of renewed hostilities with the Serbs in Croatia. Croatian aspirations directed at Mostar, the principal city of Hercegovina, led to propagandistic claims that Mostar is a "Croatian city," an absurd claim with no basis at any time in its history.

The forces of the Bosnian government hoped, at the very minimum, to maintain control of the principal cities and the roads connecting them. The cities, with their multiethnic composition and long tradition of tolerance among ethnic groups, constituted the primary political base for preserving Bosnia as a multinational society. Controlling the roads between them in mountainous Bosnia was a major challenge, as previous military forces in Bosnia had learned. This same network of cities, towns, and principal transportion arteries had been the primary targets of the Austrian army in its initial battles to occupy Bosnia in 1878. The Germans and Italians similarly had aimed to control the towns and roads during their occupation in World War II. Against the Bosnians' compelling need to control major arteries, the Serbian and Croatian forces cut off access to the major cities, denying them essential supplies from the outside.

BOSNIA DISMEMBERED

Possessing overwhelming military superiority in Bosnia, the YPA and its paramilitary allies established control over much of Bosnia's territory in a matter of weeks. The army soon revealed a pattern of providing artillery support and enfranchising Serbian paramilitary units, principally from outside Bosnia, to terrorize and commit atrocities against non-Serbian locals. These tactics allowed the YPA to achieve its war aims but suffer few casualties and to avoid direct responsibility for the war crimes being committed by Serbian extremists.

The towns of eastern Bosnia, inhabited principally by Serbs and Muslims, were early targets of the Serbian forces. Arkan's paramilitary units, the Serbian Volunteer Guard, arrived there from Vukovar in late March 1992 to recruit and train local Serbs

Flight, IRC

FIG. 11.1 — WOMAN MOURNING A WAR VICTIM IN SARAJEVO

and to begin terror attacks against non-Serbs. In Bijeljina they opened fire on Muslims walking to the mosque for prayers on April 4 and within a few days took over the town, killing or driving out most of its Muslim inhabitants. Zvornik, further south, resisted these terrorists and was subjected to an artillery bombardment by the YPA that forced its surrender on April 10. Muslim civilians were killed in the following days as Arkan's men seized control of the town. In Višegrad and Foča, artillery barrages forced the towns to capitulate, and YPA tanks entered the towns to help subdue the local population.

Where the Serbian irregulars and their YPA backers could not force a quick surrender, they blockaded transportation arteries to choke off the flow of supplies into the towns and began intermittent artillery bombardment to terrorize the population. In eastern Bosnia, they surrounded and bombarded the refugee-swollen towns of Srebrenica, Goražde, and Žepa. (In May 1993 these towns, together with Sarajevo, Tuzla, and Bihać, were declared "safe havens" by the UN Security Council. But without UN enforcement actions, the bombardments continued.) Serbian strategy was most conspicuous in Sarajevo, where the YPA controlled all major land routes into the city by early May 1992. Serbian forces soon thereafter took control of its airport, closing off Sarajevo from the outside world.

Serbian forces were less immediately successful in their efforts to conquer a large swath of territory in northwestern Bosnia. There they ran directly into Croatian forces, since Croatia wanted to prevent the linkage of Serbian holdings in Bosnia with the areas held by the Krajina Serbs in Croatia. However, the Serbs had the advantage of having already proclaimed the "Serbian Autonomous Region of the Bosnian Krajina." They quickly consolidated their authority in and around Banja Luka. As shown in MAP 11.3, the Serbs eventually achieved control over this entire area.

THE YUGOSLAV PEOPLE'S ARMY DIVIDES

Within days of the first major actions, the role of the YPA in promoting the war lay exposed for all to see. On April 27, 1992, President Izetbegović ordered the YPA to withdraw from Bosnia or place its troops under the command of the Bosnian Territorial Forces. On May 4, under pressure from the international community to end aggression against Bosnia, the federal Presidency of rump Yugoslavia ordered the YPA to withdraw, but its order allowed soldiers from Bosnia to remain there.

What followed was a purely cosmetic operation designed to appease the international community. Only about 14,000 troops withdrew. Under the premise that they were Bosnians by origin, about 75,000 remained, and the heavy weapons of the YPA stayed with them. This action effectively split the YPA in two; the Bosnian component was renamed the Army of the Serbian Republic of Bosnia and Hercegovina (ASR). The commander of the renamed force was General Ratko Mladić, already notorious as the YPA commander who had opened the army's stockrooms to the Serbs of Croatia as early as the summer of 1990. His contempt for multiethnic Bosnia, and for the people of all nationalities who remained in its cities, became legendary after he assumed command.

The organizational division of the YPA was accompanied by the purge, through forced early retirement, of officers considered unreliable. Twenty generals were retired in March 1992 and another thirty-eight in May, including the last non-Serbs. General Kukanjac, commander of the YPA's forces in Sarajevo and noted for his willingness to seek compromise and avoid bloodshed, was withdrawn to Serbia to make way for the hardline Mladić. In August 1993 the purge resumed; forty-three generals were forcibly retired in what appeared to be the final phase in Milošević's consolidation of power and the mutation of the rump Yugoslavia's security forces into instruments of Greater Serbian nationalism.

REFUGEES AND ETHNIC CLEANSING

After only a few weeks of fighting in Bosnia, the number of refugees fleeing the Serbian onslaught grew at an astonishing rate. On April 26, less than three weeks after the EC recognized Bosnia's independence, the United Nations High Commissioner for Refugees estimated that 370,000 Bosnians had become refugees; by June 2 that number had reached 750,000. By the fall of 1992 the Bosnian war had produced two million refugees, almost half of Bosnia's population according to the 1991 census. About one million remained in Bosnia, where many fled to towns still under the control of the Bosnian government, compounding the urgent needs of civilians for food and basic supplies. Others fled to Croatia or to Serbia, where refugee camps sprang up and threatened to overwhelm the capacity of both governments to maintain them. Some refugees were accepted by Western European countries.

The rapid growth in the number of refugees highlights the deliberate strategy employed by Serbian and Croatian forces to create ethnically monolithic territories in Bosnia by driving out members of unwanted ethnic groups. They evidently wished to avoid a repetition of the "West Bank problem" faced by the Israelis — the risk of adverse international publicity that would accompany occupation of lands inhabited by a hostile population. The Serbian and Croatian national extremists also realized that the goal of a genuinely multiethnic state was the key premise of Bosnia's claim to uniqueness in the central lands of former Yugoslavia. By eradicating the pattern of ethnic intermingling and promoting hatred and intolerance among Bosnia's nationalities, they undermined the Bosnian government's potential to rebuild a political base even if it were to regain some territory in postwar negotiations. In propaganda and in deeds, Serbian and Croatian nationalists have sought to portray the Bosnian government as "Muslim," thereby seeking to devalue its claim to represent the interests of all Bosnians. To a dismaying degree, they have succeeded in the court of world public opinion.

The practice of ethnic cleansing, it should be noted, has been employed by all three sides in the conflict in Bosnia;

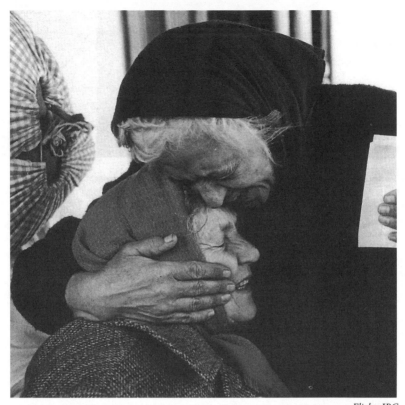

Flight, IRC

FIG. 11.2 — TWO LIFELONG BOSNIAN FRIENDS — ONE CROAT, THE OTHER
MUSLIM — WERE SENT TO DIFFERENT REFUGEE CAMPS

however, the Serbian forces and the rump Yugoslav regime bear
responsibility for recruiting, training, enfranchising, and paying the worst perpetrators of this violence, the irregular forces of
Arkan and Vojislav Šešelj. Many groups and observers, including Helsinki Watch, Amnesty International, the US State Department, and the International Court of Justice, share the
belief that Serbia has been the initiator and principal perpetra-
tor of ethnic cleansing. At the same time, Croatian armed forces
and irregulars have engaged in widespread operations of ethnic
cleansing. Muslims have also conducted ethnic cleansing op-

erations and committed atrocities, although the Bosnian government, despite the immense stress under which it operated beginning in the spring of 1992, acted on numerous occasions to curb such activities.

The methodology of ethnic cleansing is terror practiced openly and ostentatiously, calculated to drive from their homes those longtime inhabitants belonging to the "wrong" ethnic group. Ethnic cleansing thus differs from the systematic, quiet extermination procedures used by the Germans against Jews, Gypsies, and others during World War II. The Germans set out to kill people without creating public furor; the ethnic cleansers of Bosnia use killings and other atrocities to sow fear and panic and to induce flight.

Along with ethnic cleansing operations in the cities and countryside of Bosnia, the perpetrators of ethnic exclusivism used a variety of other terror tactics to impose their will on members of other ethnic groups and sow the seeds of hatred to prevent the likelihood of multiethnic reconciliation. Women of all ages were raped. While some rapes were committed by troops out of control, many rapes were deliberate, systematically encouraged by commanders to demean conquered people and to reward soldiers for acts of brutality. Prison camps were established for captured members of military units and for civilians; inmates were starved, beaten, or killed, giving Western television audiences images of emaciated prisoners not seen from Europe since World War II. As the rising tide of Bosnian refugees in the summer of 1992 attested, these tactics, deliberately employed by national extremists to destroy multiethnic society in Bosnia, achieved many of their objectives. Despite international steps to convene war crimes tribunals under the authority of Chapter VII of the United Nations Charter, no outside power did more than issue warnings to stop the atrocities while they were taking place.

THE CHANGING ROLE OF BOSNIA'S CROATS

After the multiparty elections of November 1990, the Bosnian Croats were represented by a single dominant political party, the Croatian Democratic Community (CDC). The CDC, however, contained two factions whose leaders differed sharply concerning the future of Bosnia.

Stjepan Kljuić, the leading Croatian vote-getter in the November 1990 elections and a member of the Bosnian Presidency, headed the pro-Bosnia faction. The Kljuić wing of the party supported the preservation of a unified, multiethnic Bosnian state and drew support principally from Croats living in major cities and towns. When hostilities broke out in April 1992, the pro-Bosnia faction represented the mainstream of Bosnian Croat opinion: the vast majority of Bosnian Croats voted for Bosnia's independence in the referendum of February 29 and March 1, 1992. Furthermore, many members of the Franciscan Order endorsed Bosnia's independence and urged other Croats to support the preservation of a unified, multiethnic Bosnian state. Many Croats served in the multinational units of the Bosnian army, and the forces defending Sarajevo included a purely Croatian unit under a separate commander.

The CDC's other faction favored ethnic partition of Bosnia. Its leaders hoped that Croatia would annex those portions of Bosnia with a significant Croatian population. The annexationist faction, headed by Mate Boban, had its principal base in rural western Hercegovina adjacent to the republic of Croatia, an area where the rural population was largely Croatian. More importantly, the annexationist faction espoused a program close to that favored by Croatia's President Tudjman and his followers and enjoyed Tudjman's support.

A similar split of opinion developed in the republic of Croatia regarding the appropriate Croatian policy toward Bosnia. By the spring of 1992 Croatian public opinion was bitterly anti-Serbian and obsessed with the brutality of the YPA and Serbian irregulars in conquering Vukovar and attacking Dubrovnik during the Croatian war of 1991. The first response of most Croats to the war in Bosnia was to view their neighboring republic as another victim of Serbian aggression and to support the Bosnian government in its battle against the YPA.

Croatia's President Tudjman, however, was heavily influenced by the "Hercegovinian lobby," a group of Croatian nationalists who favored the partition of Bosnia and the annexation of its Croat-inhabited regions to the Croatian republic. The Hercegovinian lobby was made up primarily of émigré Croats living in Canada and the United States who contributed heavily to Tudjman's well-financed 1990 presidential campaign. Tudjman rewarded his financial backers by fully supporting the annexationist program and by making one of them, Gojko Šušak of Ottawa, Canada, his defense minister. In addition, Tudjman personally committed himself to Bosnia's partition in March 1991 when he negotiated an agreement with Serbian President Milošević to divide Bosnia between Serbia and Croatia. As the war progressed, Tudjman and his government supported various Croatian efforts to partition Bosnia and deployed Croatian army regulars to fight alongside Bosnian Croats against the Bosnian government.

Shortly after full-scale hostilities broke out in Bosnia in March 1992, the CDC's annexationist faction gained the upper hand in the Bosnian Croat community with the military and political backing of Tudjman's regime in Zagreb. On July 3, 1992, the Hercegovinian Croats, led by Mate Boban, convened a self-styled Presidency of the "Croatian Community of Herceg-Bosna" and declared a self-governing community. Boban also commanded the loyalty of a large Croatian militia whose recruits were drawn principally from western Hercegovina. In August 1992 Boban forced the ultranationalist HOS, a rival militia organization, to disband and to integrate its personnel into his own militia. Having completed the takeover of the CDC and the consolidation of Croatian militias in Bosnia, Boban and his pro-annexationist followers controlled both the political and military organizations of the Bosnian Croats. Croatia's President Tudjman sponsored these changes, effectively ending the pretense that the forces of the Croatian republic were not involved in Bosnian affairs.

Lacking the weapons to pursue their annexationist agenda in the summer of 1992, the Bosnian Croat forces pursued a tactical alliance with the Bosnian government; however, political and military power was clearly in the hands of Croats who openly advocated the dismemberment of the Bosnian state. Soon after Boban's takeover of the CDC in the summer of 1992, his Croatian militiamen began ethnic cleansing in the Muslim villages under their control, killing and driving out Muslim inhabitants. In the fall of 1992, international mediators negotiated directly with Boban, giving him the stature of an internationally recognized leader of Bosnia's Croats.

Boban's triumph was a blow to the pro-Bosnia faction of the CDC, but many Bosnian Croats continued to support the Bosnian government and to serve in the Bosnian army. Archbishop Puljić of Sarajevo supported a multiethnic Bosnian state. In contrast to their predecessors who had collaborated with

Ustasha policies in World War II, leading Franciscans endorsed multiethnic cooperation and condemned ethnic cleansing. Stjepan Kljuić was ousted from the leadership of the CDC but remained an influential supporter of a unified Bosnia. He resigned from the Bosnian Presidency in November 1992 but rejoined that body in October 1993.

Croatian and Bosnian military units generally remained wary allies during 1992 and into the early months of 1993. Some armed conflicts took place between them, however. On May 10, 1992, Bosnian security forces clashed with Croatian troops in a skirmish over facilities abandoned by the YPA, the first instance of combat between the two forces. The dominant theme, however, was uneasy cooperation. On June 16, 1992, Croatia and Bosnia announced an agreement to cooperate more closely in the war against their common Serbian adversary, and they signed another agreement on cooperation on September 23, 1992. The ill-equipped Bosnian forces depended heavily on weapons and supplies from Croatia, and Bosnia's cities required food and other necessities that could come only through Croat-controlled territory. Although the Croats regularly extracted "taxes" from Bosnia-bound convoys that crossed their territory, they generally allowed supply lines to remain open through the winter of 1992-3.

Cooperation between Croatian and Bosnian forces broke down in the spring of 1993. Paradoxically, fighting flared in the weeks after March 1993 when both Boban's Bosnian Croats and the Bosnian government endorsed the Owen-Vance peace proposal even though the Bosnian Serbs refused to sign. Once it became evident that the international community had no intention of rolling back the victors' territorial conquests, both Croatian and Bosnian government forces hastened to consolidate their respective positions and to assume full control of regions assigned to them under the Owen-Vance plan.

Croatian commanders demanded that Bosnian army units in western Hercegovina, an area assigned to Croatian control under the peace plan, be merged into the Croatian army. In the Travnik area, another region designated as Croatian in the plan despite its large Muslim population, Croatian officers insisted that the Croatian flag fly beside the Bosnian flag. The Bosnians perceived these Croatian demands as a threat to the hope of preserving a multiethnic state even under the provisions of the Owen-Vance plan. In the spring of 1993, these and other conflicts over sovereignty and symbols ignited full-scale war between Croatian and Bosnian forces in central Bosnia and in Hercegovina.

The Croatian-Bosnian fighting in 1993 was among the war's bitterest, accompanied by vicious campaigns of ethnic cleansing by both sides. Intense combat took place in central Bosnia and in Hercegovina near the city of Mostar. Croatian forces surrounded and isolated Mostar, subjecting its civilian population to heavy bombardment and leaving thousands of its principally Muslim inhabitants trapped without basic provisions. When a United Nations aid convoy arrived with food and supplies on August 25, 1993, desperate residents refused to allow fifty-two Spanish UN peacekeepers to leave for five days, fearing (correctly) that the merciless Croatian shelling would resume as soon as the UN soldiers departed. Croatian military pressure effectively divided the city into a Croatian section to the west of the Neretva River and a Muslim section to the east, destroying a city that had been a center of multiethnic tolerance for many centuries and, early in the twentieth century, the birthplace of both the Serbian and Muslim autonomy movements.

FIG. 11.3 — NINETEENTH-CENTURY SKETCH OF THE MOSTAR BRIDGE (BUILT IN 1556), DESTROYED BY CROATIAN BOMBARDMENT ON NOV. 9, 1993

On November 9, 1993, sustained artillery barrage by Croatian forces destroyed the elegant white marble Mostar bridge spanning the Neretva River, an act of senseless and deliberate destruction on a par with the YPA's bombardment of Dubrovnik. Dating from 1556, the Mostar bridge was treasured by members of all three ethnic groups and by millions of foreign tourists who had visited it over the years. Along with the physical suffering inflicted on Mostar's civilians and the nearly total devastation of the city, the mindless destruction of the Mostar bridge deepened the despair of those who still hoped to preserve pluralism and a multiethnic society in Bosnia and Hercegovina.

Surprisingly, the fighting between Bosnian and Croatian forces in central Bosnia resulted in several significant Bosnian victories. Bosnian units successfully drove the Croats from Vareš in early November 1993. On the Bosnian side, most of the fighting was done by all-Muslim brigades, and it became evident that the Muslims benefited from military assistance that had reached Bosnia despite the continued United Nations arms embargo.

Central Bosnia was left deeply polarized by the ethnic cleansing campaigns and atrocities committed by troops of both sides. The triumph of nationalist extremists in their goal of destroying the multiethnic character of Bosnian society was exemplified by events in Fojnica, a town in the mountainous area west of Sarajevo with a mixed Muslim and Croatian population.[13]

Fojnica, home to a large Franciscan monastery and several Islamic cultural institutions, was a shining example of multiethnic cooperation in the early months of the war. Late in June 1993, General Philippe Morillon of France, Commander of United Nations Forces in Bosnia, cited Fojnica as a "model of hope." Trouble began, however, when Fojnica's Croatian leaders, backed by the brothers of the local Franciscan monastery, refused to mobilize local Croats to serve in Boban's Croatian militia against the Bosnian army. Boban's militiamen intervened, dismissed pro-Bosnian Croats from the town's government, and replaced them with Boban supporters. As fighting between Croatian and Bosnian forces increased in the summer of 1993, Croatian forces surrounded Fojnica in evident preparation for a full-scale assault. On July 2, 1993, the Bosnian army drove off the encircling Croatian units after bitter fighting. Most of Fojnica's Croatian inhabitants also fled, fearing reprisals by

13 Chuck Sudetic, "Killings in Bosnian Monastery Widen Croat-Muslim Divide," *The New York Times*, December 31, 1993, pp. A-1 and A-3, contains a detailed account of the war's impact on Fojnica.

Bettman Archive

FIG. 11.4 — REFUGEES FLEEING FOJNICA, WINTER 1993

Muslim troops of the Bosnian army. Among the few Croats who remained in the town were the leading clerics of the Franciscan monastery, who continued to promote a multiethnic solution to the war.

In an effort to recapture Fojnica, Croatian forces counterattacked on November 10, 1993. They burned two mosques in a town to the east; Muslims retaliated by burning a Catholic church in a nearby village. When Muslim forces of the Bosnian government appeared to be losing ground to the Croatian assault, rumors spread among Fojnica's Muslims that the Franciscan monastery harbored a radio transmitter and was being used as a storehouse of weapons for the Croatian forces. Four Muslim soldiers of the Bosnian army entered the monastery grounds on November 13. According to eyewitnesses, the soldiers ruthlessly executed the monastery's two leading clerics.

The Bosnian government condemned the killings and began an investigation, but its failure to apprehend any suspects for several months after the brutal murders led to Croatian accusations that the killings were either ordered or sanctioned by the Bosnian government.

Croatian-Muslim relations were further poisoned when soldiers of each side committed atrocities against civilians of the other. Croatian soldiers murdered Muslim civilians in Ahmići, near Fojnica, in April 1993; Muslim soldiers of the Bosnian army killed at least thirty-five civilians at Kriz in central Bosnia in September 1993; and Croatian soldiers killed Muslim civilians in the village of Stupni Do in October 1993.

To the amazement of both the perpetrators and victims of the Muslim-Croatian violence, hostilities ended abruptly in February 1994. This radical change grew out of US diplomatic pressure on the Tudjman regime and the threat of UN economic sanctions against Croatia if it continued military assistance to the Bosnian Croats (see further discussion on pp. 270-3). Clearly acting on instructions from Zagreb, Croatian commanders halted their attacks on Mostar, and cease-fires were hurriedly arranged between the two sides. By late March each side had ratified an agreement to join in a federation, and Croatian and Bosnian commanders met to begin merging their forces into a single army. Mostar residents emerged from their basement refuges to bask in the early spring sunshine and to savor the hope that the bitter combat might have ended permanently.

THE INTERNATIONAL COMMUNITY: AID AND ADVOCACY

Rarely in the annals of diplomacy was so much misery and suffering so universally acknowledged and yet so little effective action elicited as in the Bosnian crisis of the 1990s. Calls for military assistance to the Bosnians have been heard mostly from Western politicians *out of* office, such as former British Prime Minister Margaret Thatcher; former US Secretary of State George Shultz; Bill Clinton before he became US President; and US Senator Robert Dole after his party lost the White House. Those in power found, much as the YPA had calculated in its strategic reassessment of 1991, that the political consensus for meaningful action to support the Bosnian government was slow to emerge in the Western democracies; furthermore, no Western political leader took the lead in creating momentum for action.

In response to the war in Bosnia, the UN and its member states employed a series of symbolic gestures and low-cost cosmetic actions that addressed the consequences of the war more than its causes. Margaret Thatcher referred to this approach as a combination of "soft words and empty gestures."[14] Although an array of sovereign governments and private aid agencies worked to alleviate the suffering of war victims, the perpetrators of aggression and war crimes faced deterrent actions only in a few isolated instances when international public opinion would tolerate no more of their abuses. The actions of the UN and its member states, although numerous and costly, were therefore more effective in assuaging Western consciences than in providing a lasting solution to the crisis. These actions included humanitarian relief delivered by overland convoys and air drops, assistance for refugees, international mediation by the Owen-Vance and Owen-Stoltenberg teams, economic sanctions against rump Yugoslavia, a "no-fly-zone" over Bosnia, the

14 Margaret Thatcher, "This Week with David Brinkley," ABC Television, February 6, 1994.

creation of war crimes tribunals, and an endless succession of warnings and threats from international bodies and individual states.

During the summer of 1992, the world became increasingly aware of the atrocities being committed in the Bosnian conflict and the agony of civilians in Sarajevo and other cities subjected to bombardment by Serbian forces. In June 1992, the UN augmented its forces in the former Yugoslavia with UNPROFOR troops assigned specifically to Bosnia. Although their mission was to deliver humanitarian supplies to civilians facing starvation, UN commanders were limited to negotiating with the contending parties to achieve their goals. Serbian, Croatian, and Bosnian military commanders all proved to be obstreperous negotiating partners; supplies often sat for days and weeks in convoys or in storehouses while the warring parties held civilian populations hostage and imposed conditions on the UN's delivery of humanitarian aid.

In August 1992 the UN Security Council authorized its member states to take "all necessary measures" to ensure the delivery of humanitarian aid where needed in Bosnia.[15] As was the case in other aspects of the crisis, the key "necessary measures" to support the UN's lofty goals were employed neither by the UN itself nor by any member state. From the first days of the war, the international community tolerated an apparently bottomless reservoir of deception and broken commitments by all sides, particularly the Serbs and the ASR, regarding the delivery of humanitarian aid. Obstruction of aid convoys became a routine part of strangulation tactics used by Serbs surrounding Bosnia's cities and towns, by the Croatian forces besieging

---

15 *The United Nations and the Situation in the Former Yugoslavia.* Reference Paper, United Nations Department of Public Information, May 7, 1993.

Mostar, and by Muslim units of the Bosnian army in various circumstances. Although all three parties specifically agreed on November 18, 1993, to permit free passage of humanitarian convoys across territories under their control, the Serbs have continued (at the time of this writing in April 1994) to block convoys and to frustrate international aid workers. On December 10, 1993, UN relief spokesman Ron Wilkinson noted that the Serbs were very effective in obstructing humanitarian aid in a way that stopped just short of "bringing the wrath of the world community down on them."[16]

Because delivery of humanitarian aid was frequently obstructed by the forces besieging their cities, most Bosnian urban dwellers suffered considerable privation during the winters of 1992-3 and 1993-4. Although both winters passed without fulfilling the dire predictions that hundreds of thousands would die of starvation, life in Bosnia was miserable by any standard, and many died because they were young, elderly, disabled, or simply unable to compete in the Darwinian struggle for basic sustenance to which Bosnians of all ethnic groups were reduced. Meanwhile, the war dragged on. Sarajevo and other cities endured periodic shelling that killed and maimed thousands of civilians and annihilated cultural monuments, office buildings, and residential dwellings — from centuries-old homes to new high-rise apartments. Serbian forces cruelly targeted desperate civilians standing in bread lines or scurrying across the expansive tarmac of the Sarajevo airport.

The international community, in addition to providing humanitarian aid, followed the course it had established in Croatia and sought to mediate the conflict. UN and EC efforts

---

16 *Fort Worth Star Telegram,* Dec. 11, 1993, p. A-6. (Associated Press story by Alexander G. Higgins).

were merged at the London Conference in August 1992. Henceforth, the International Conference on the Former Yugoslavia had permanent co-chairmen to bring the warring parties together. Cyrus Vance represented the UN Secretary General, and former British Foreign Secretary David Owen was selected to succeed Lord Carrington as the EC's representative. After Vance resigned in the spring of 1993, Thorvald Stoltenberg, former Norwegian Minister of Foreign Affairs, succeeded him on May 1. The lofty principles drawn up in London, including the notion that no peace settlement should reward the practitioners of ethnic cleansing, soon vanished as the mediators pressed all sides to reach an agreement that would simply end the fighting, thus ratifying the territorial conquests of the battlefield victors.

The Owen-Vance and Owen-Stoltenberg talks have been conducted principally in Geneva, usually with representatives of Bosnia's three main factions, but at times Presidents Milošević and Tudjman also attended. Mediation, by its very nature, assumes that the parties have potentially valid and morally equal claims, and the mediators took great pains to avoid moral judgments regarding the parties in the negotiating process.

The mediators came up with two major proposals. The first plan, made public by Owen and Vance in January 1993 after protracted talks in Geneva, generally followed the Lisbon and Sarajevo agreements of February and March 1992. Under the Owen-Vance plan of January 1993, Bosnia was to be divided into ten cantons, three for each nationality, with control of the tenth — Sarajevo and environs — to be shared by all three groups (see MAP 11.1). The plan was accepted by, or forced upon, the principal representatives of all three sides. It subsequently failed to gain the endorsement of a convocation of Bosnian Serb representatives held outside Sarajevo at Pale in

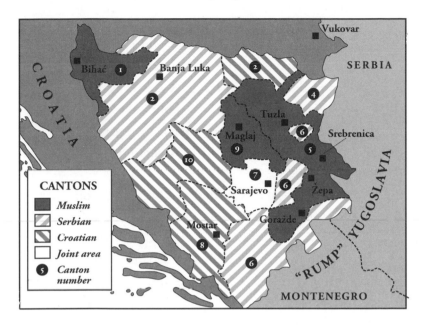

MAP 11.1 — THE OWEN-VANCE PLAN (JANUARY 1993)

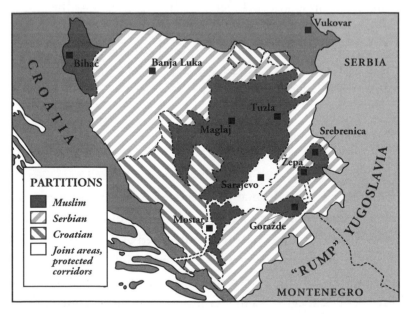

MAP 11.2 — THE OWEN-STOLTENBERG PLAN (AUGUST 1993)

May 1993. The Serbian assembly rejected the Owen-Vance proposal three times, despite being urged to accept it by Greek Prime Minister Constantine Mitsotakis, Serbian President Milošević, and Bosnian Serb leader Radovan Karadžić. In the third vote, the Bosnian Serb assembly called for a popular referendum. In the referendum, held under circumstances of dubious fairness, Bosnia's Serbs overwhelmingly rejected the proposed agreement.

A second proposal was crafted by Owen and Stoltenberg in August 1993 to accommodate Bosnian Serb objections (see MAP 11.2). Izetbegović conditionally accepted the Owen-Stoltenberg plan, but the Bosnian Parliament imposed numerous conditions on the plan and demanded a Bosnian outlet to the Adriatic Sea, in effect rejecting the Owen-Stoltenberg proposal. Despite additional talks, these negotiations under the auspices of the UN and EC remained deadlocked into early 1994 as fierce fighting continued among the belligerents. In February 1994 the efforts of Owen and Stoltenberg to achieve a consensus among the three parties were superseded by an American plan to bring the Bosnian Croats into a federation with the Muslims. At the time of this writing in April 1994, the leadership in the peace process appears to have passed from Owen and Stoltenberg to US and Russian diplomats.

THE MUSLIM ROLE IN THE BOSNIAN GOVERNMENT

By referring to the Bosnian government as the "Muslim government," some journalists have conveyed the impression that the areas under Bosnian control are inhabited and governed exclusively by Muslims. As we have noted, this is inaccurate and misleading, for the government headed (as of April 1994) by President Izetbegović is in fact made up of those from all three

MAP 11.3 — MILITARY FRONT LINES (MARCH 1994)

nationalities — Muslims, Serbs, and Croats — who favor the perpetuation of a multiethnic Bosnian state. More careful observers have, with greater accuracy, referred to the Bosnian government as "Muslim-led" or "Muslim-dominated," but the overall situation is best clarified by a review of the events that made it that way.

The Bosnian government was, in fact, "Muslim-led" beginning in November 1990, when Izetbegović became the president of the republic Presidency following the republic's first multiparty elections. His election reflected the plurality of

Bosnian Muslims in Bosnia according to the 1991 census: 44% Muslim, 31% Serb, and 17% Croat. Power, however, was shared in an unstable coalition arrangement that lasted until the spring of 1992. In April 1992 the Serbian members of the Presidency resigned, and many Serbian members of the Bosnian Parliament withdrew. As tensions grew between the Bosnian government and Boban's Croats in 1993, many Croats also withdrew from the Bosnian Parliament. As late as September 1993, however, when the Bosnian Parliament met to consider the Owen-Stoltenberg peace plan, it still contained several dozen Serbian and Croatian members. The Bosnian Presidency also continued to be a multinational body; in October 1993 it appointed replacements for those Serbs and Croats who had resigned.

The prevalence of Muslims in the Bosnian army similarly increased as conflict developed between Bosnians and Croats in central Bosnia and in Hercegovina, so that by the fall of 1993 it was possible to speak with justification of a "Muslim-led" or "Muslim-dominated" Bosnian army. The armed forces and the population in general, however, included a substantial number of Serbs and Croats who continued to share the hope that a multinational Bosnian society would somehow survive the horrors of the war.

From the war's beginning, the national extremists who instigated the conflict aimed to destroy Bosnia as a pluralistic state and extinguish the dream of mutual tolerance. We have noted how they accomplished this through campaigns of ethnic cleansing and by stoking the fires of hatred and revenge. For the Muslim leaders of the Bosnian government, who have long viewed a multinational entity as a shelter of their interests, the survival of a multiethnic Bosnian polity is crucial to their long-term survival.

FIG. 11.5 — IMAM SPAHIĆ, SPIRITUAL LEADER OF THE SARAJEVO MUSLIMS, LOST HIS DAUGHTER AND TWO GRANDDAUGHTERS IN THE WAR

The leadership of the Bosnian Muslims has often included some who wanted to create an Islamic polity rather than live within a secular, multinational state. Most leading Bosnian Muslim politicians in the twentieth century, however, have supported multinational entities as the best protection for Muslim interests. These two approaches, rather than being mutually exclusive, coexist as competing preferences in the political outlook of many Bosnian Muslims. For most Bosnian Muslims in the twentieth century, the multinational viewpoint has been the dominant trait, while the Islamic or Muslim nationalist impulse has been the recessive trait. An ample illustration is found in the career of Bosnia's President Izetbegović. Tried and imprisoned in the socialist era for advocating an Islamic state, he has consistently worked to preserve multinational polities (first

Yugoslavia, then Bosnia) since becoming president of the Bosnian Presidency in 1990.

As the Bosnian war progressed, two developments shook the traditionally dominant Muslim approach of favoring multinational polities. First was the evident reluctance of the international community and the United States to intervene militarily, or to grant an exception to the 1991 UN arms embargo, to support the preservation of a multiethnic Bosnian state. The second development was the warfare that broke out between Bosnian and Croatian forces in central Bosnia and in Hercegovina, which further contributed to the political isolation of the Bosnian Muslims and threw them back solely on their own resources.

Well into 1993, the public pronouncements of Bosnian Muslim leaders such as Izetbegović and Bosnian Foreign Minister Haris Silajdžić reflected genuine incredulity that the Western Powers, particularly the United States, would tolerate the dismemberment of a pluralistic Bosnia and validate the territorial conquests of the Serbs and Croats who were dismembering it. It became increasingly evident that the Western Powers viewed the Bosnian government only as the Muslim component of a tripartite partition plan. The Muslim leaders reacted at first with disappointment and, ultimately, with despair. As a result, some Bosnian Muslim leaders abandoned their hopes for a multiethnic Bosnian society and became more vocal in advancing exclusively Muslim aims.

The ascendancy of Muslim nationalist interests in the Bosnian government became evident when the Owen-Stoltenberg plan was under consideration in the summer of 1993. Before the Bosnian Parliament deliberated the plan, an all-Muslim *sabor* (assembly) was convened in Sarajevo by leading Muslims intellectuals and politicians to debate the peace proposal. The Muslim assembly, which had no constitutional status, recommended acceptance of the plan, albeit with extensive revisions and conditions attached. When the Bosnian Parliament assembled and considered the proposed peace plan, it followed the lead of the all-Muslim assembly, attaching such far-reaching conditions to accepting the Owen-Stoltenberg proposal that the vote was tantamount to rejecting it.

The rise of Muslim exclusivism can also be traced in the Bosnian government's approach to gangs, irregulars, and the Bosnian army. Muslim irregulars and gangs terrorized civilians in government-controlled areas since barricades were erected in the spring of 1992, and exclusively Muslim brigades were formed in the early days of the war to fight within the Bosnian army. For the most part, however, the activities of these Muslim units were restrained by the government, even though Muslim gangs were tolerated because of their contributions to the war effort.

In October 1993 the two most powerful Muslim gangs in Sarajevo were disbanded in a violent shoot-out with government troops, but in other ways the government became a more narrowly Muslim organization. Fighting against Croatian units in central Bosnia was done principally by Muslim brigades, and the Bosnian government forces in that region became almost exclusively Muslim. In November 1993, just days before the Croats destroyed the Mostar bridge, the Bosnian government disbanded a purely Croatian unit that had participated ably in the defense of Sarajevo and ordered its members to join the regular Bosnian army.

Lord David Owen, as part of the propaganda campaign to win acceptance of the Owen-Stoltenberg peace proposal, told Western nations in early 1994 that they need not fear the emergence of an Islamic state in the Balkans.   This is an invention born of wishful thinking. A Bosnian Muslim ministate, stripped of its multiethnic character by Serbian and Croatian conquests legitimized by the international community's media- tion campaign, could hardly be the secular, pro-Western entity that entered the 1990s as the republic of Bosnia and Herce- govina. It could very well seek its sources of ideology, inspira- tion, and arms from the East. Surrounded by hostile neighbors coveting its cities and industrial base, its prospects for long-term survival would be poor, and its inhabitants would experience poverty and misery compounded by isolation.

1994: NATO ULTIMATUMS AND A MUSLIM-CROATIAN FEDERATION

On February 5, 1994, a single mortar shell landed in a busy downtown Sarajevo marketplace, killing sixty-eight people and wounding two hundred others. Although the attack was only one of hundreds that had killed and maimed civilians since the war began, the concentrated and highly publicized slaughter crossed an imaginary threshold of the world's toleration for violence. American and French leaders, who had feuded pub- licly about Bosnia only days before, quickly reached an agree- ment aimed at ending the killing of civilians in Sarajevo. The French agreed that NATO should be prepared to employ air strikes against the Bosnian Serbs. In exchange, the Americans promised to become more actively involved in the Geneva negotiations. UN Secretary General Boutros Boutros-Ghali authorized the use of air strikes, and NATO issued an ultimatum to all parties (directed principally at Bosnian Serbs) demanding that all heavy weapons be brought under UN control or with- drawn from a 20-kilometer zone around Sarajevo by February 21.

These demands were not particularly new. The Bosnian Serbs had agreed to UN supervision of their heavy weapons at the London Conference of August 1992, but within hours of signing the accord they showed their disdain for such agreements by stepping up their attacks on civilian targets. NATO had been more successful in the summer of 1993 and used the threat of air strikes to force a Serbian withdrawal from Mount Igman. The Serbs evidently found the new threat of air strikes to be credible: They responded to the February ultimatum by halting their attacks, and the heavy weapons around Sarajevo fell silent on February 11 for the first time in almost two years.

For several days, few Serbian guns were removed from the exclusion zone. Then Russian diplomats intervened. Russian Deputy Foreign Minister Vitaly Churkin visited the Bosnian Serb headquarters at Pale and won a promise that the Serbs would withdraw their heavy weapons in exchange for his commitment that Russian troops would join UNPROFOR peacekeeping forces in Bosnia. The agreement allowed President Boris Yeltsin to claim a diplomatic victory and permitted the Bosnian Serbs to pretend that they had acceded to a Russian request rather than to admit that they had capitulated to NATO threats. In the days after Churkin's announcement, many Serbian heavy weapons were quickly removed from the exclusion zone for use elsewhere in Bosnia. Bosnian Serbs wildly cheered the arrival of Russian troops on February 20, in a display of Slavic brotherhood reminiscent of the greetings given Russian Pan-Slav volunteers who aided the Serbs in 1875-8. When the deadline arrived on February 21, UN commanders pronounced that the Serbs were in compliance, and the threat of NATO air strikes again receded.

NATO's willingness to use air power was soon tested when six Serbian aircraft, in blatant violation of the UN "no-fly-zone," bombed a Bosnian government munitions factory in Novi Travnik on February 28. Responding swiftly, UN and NATO commanders authorized US planes on patrol over Bosnia to fire on the offending aircraft. Four of the Serbian planes were downed by US F-16 aircraft in an aerial confrontation that was no contest.

Though the NATO ultimatum was limited to Sarajevo, its success inaugurated a new phase in the diplomatic treatment of the Bosnian conflict. Having studiously avoided meaningful engagement for almost two years, Russian and American diplomats plunged enthusiastically into the search for a durable peace in Bosnia, at times cooperating and at times appearing to compete for the leading role. After meeting with Russian leaders in Moscow, Bosnian Serb leader Radovan Karadžić announced that his forces would allow the Tuzla airport to reopen for humanitarian flights in exchange for a Russian pledge to send more troops to join UN peacekeeping forces in Bosnia.

Besides helping to end Sarajevo's bombardment, American diplomats encouraged a cessation of hostilities between the Croats and Muslims. The American initiative, led by Special Envoy Charles Redman, soon produced a cease-fire, and on March 18, 1994, President Clinton announced an agreement between the Bosnian Croats and Muslims in the Bosnian government to form a federation that would be loosely associated with Croatia.[17] Although US diplomats stressed that Serbs would be brought into the peace process later, the American initiative (perhaps unwittingly) reassembled the historical coalition between Croats and Muslims that had prevailed on several

17 For a discussion of the federation, see Patrick Moore, "The Croatian-Muslim Agreements," *RFE/RL Research Report*, April 1, 1994, pp. 20-24.

different occasions in the twentieth century, from the last years of the Austrian-era parliament to Bosnia's declaration of independence in 1992.

The Bosnian Croats' decision to make peace with the Bosnian government was a dramatic turnaround expressly directed by Croatian President Franjo Tudjman. The abrupt shift, from all-out war with the Muslims to full participation in the Bosnian state, revealed the degree to which Bosnian Croat interests had become subordinated to those of the Croatian republic and its ruling political party.

Tudjman's Bosnian policy reversal was occasioned by the deteriorating economic and political situation within Croatia and the prospect of international economic sanctions if the Croatian government continued to underwrite the war effort in Bosnia. After Croatian forces suffered substantial defeats at the hands of the lesser-equipped Muslim brigades of the Bosnian army, the Croatian military dispatched additional units into Bosnia in early 1994. These troop movements drew the attention of United Nations observers, and various Security Council members warned Croatia that economic sanctions would soon be imposed. Given Croatia's shaky economic situation, sanctions meant domestic political trouble for Tudjman and international isolation for a country that prided itself on its European character and Western heritage. On February 3, 1994, the Security Council condemned the presence of regular Croatian troops in Bosnia and demanded their withdrawal.

Tudjman unceremoniously dumped Mate Boban as the leader of the Bosnian Croats and replaced him with Krešimir Zubak, a pliable politician more acceptable to Western diplomats. Zubak and Croatian Foreign Minister Mate Granić were summoned to Washington in mid-February to negotiate a cease-fire with the Bosnian government. Tudjman endorsed the idea

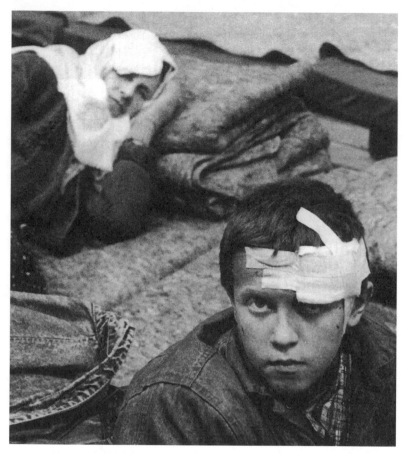

Flight, IRC

FIG. 11.6 — A REFUGEE CENTER IN MOSTAR

of a federation in late February, although his comments revealed that he was responding to pressure from the international community. Despite some squabbling over who would assume the high offices of government, negotiations between the Croats and Bosnian Prime Minister Haris Silajdžić moved swiftly. By the end of March, each side had agreed to join the newly constituted Muslim-Croatian federation. The agreement between the Muslims and Croats dramatically changed the political landscape in Bosnia. At the time of this writing in April 1994, it is too early to assess the chances for the reconstituted Muslim-Croatian alliance to endure beyond the immediate diplomatic pressures that created it. If it proves durable, the newly created Bosnian federation could reverse some of the consequences of ethnic cleansing and bitter conflicts in central Bosnia, western Hercegovina, and the city of Mostar.

Following the NATO ultimatum and the Croatian-Muslim cease-fire, the Serbian bombardment of Sarajevo and the Croatian bombardment of Mostar each came to an end. Residents of each city emerged from their basements and hiding places to survey the rubble to which their cities had been reduced. Streetcars and electrical service were partially restored in Sarajevo, and black-market prices plummeted as vital goods and services gradually became available.

Despite the cessation of daily bombardments, the siege of Sarajevo remained largely in place. The Bosnian Serbs continued to control the approaches to the city, and they limited the movements of goods and persons. Elsewhere, the Bosnian Serb forces continued to probe the limits of Western toleration. In Serbian-controlled northwestern Bosnia, where few international observers could witness their deeds, Bosnian Serbs accelerated their campaign of ethnic cleansing, using well compensated irregulars protected by local security forces.[18] Serbs also displayed growing audacity in obstructing the delivery of humanitarian aid to besieged cities. On March 23 they hijacked ten UN trucks, abducted their Danish drivers at gunpoint, and forced them to walk through a front line the Serbs said was

---

18 John Kifner, "In North Bosnia, a Rising Tide of Serbian Violence," *The New York Times*, March 27, 1994, pp. 1 and 9.

mined.[19] After two days of UN protests, the Serbs released the drivers unharmed and returned the trucks.

In the spring of 1994, the war again became a two-sided conflict between the reconstituted Bosnian government (with its Muslim-led army) and its Bosnian Serb adversaries. Bosnian government forces, freed from fighting the Croats, advanced against Serbian positions in northcentral Bosnia in a drive to recapture lands lost earlier in the war. Bosnian Serb forces, deterred from further action against Sarajevo, stepped up their bombardment of several government-controlled urban enclaves. They drove back Bosnian army units defending Goražde, a strategic Bosnian government outpost on the Drina River. Since the UN Security Council had declared Goražde a "safe haven" in May 1993, the Bosnian Serb assault on the refugee-swollen city was in open defiance of UN resolutions.

As they were defeating Goražde's military defenders, Bosnian Serb forces increased their shelling of civilian targets. In an effort to deter Serbian attacks, US warplanes under NATO command conducted "pinprick" air assaults on ASR military targets attacking Goražde on April 10 and 11, 1994. Over the next few days, Bosnian Serb forces retaliated by seizing more than 200 UN troops elsewhere in Bosnia as hostages. On April 16, a British Sea Harrier jet was shot down while attempting another air attack on ASR targets. In subsequent days the UN and NATO appeared to be powerless as the ASR intensified its shelling, even as Bosnian Serb leaders proclaimed numerous cease-fires and pledged to Russian diplomats that they would end their assaults.

The Bosnian Serbs had again crossed the international community's threshold of tolerance for systematic violence against civilians. Faced with the humiliation of the UN and

19 *The New York Times,* March 27, 1994, p. A-6.

NATO in Bosnia, the Clinton Administration on April 21 won NATO approval for an ultimatum similar to the February threat that forced an end to attacks on Sarajevo. As in August 1993 and February 1994, Serbian compliance with the ultimatum's demands was reluctant and incomplete, but the shelling eventually ceased and UNPROFOR troops entered Goražde in late April.

Developments in Goražde in March and April 1994 followed a pattern similar to those in Sarajevo in February. The Bosnian Serb leadership repeatedly tested the resolve of NATO and the UN, seeking to placate them with carefully-timed proclamations of cease-fires and expressions of peaceful intentions while intensifying their attacks on civilians. The systematic use of terror against civilians, rather than the military defeat of the Bosnian forces protecting them, served as the trip-wire of US and NATO determination to issue a credible ultimatum against the besieging ASR forces. This left the Bosnian Serbs in a position of clear military superiority in the area, deterred from complete conquest only by UN and NATO threats.

THE WAGES OF WAR

The wars of the Yugoslav succession produced no real winners. Victors and victims alike suffered, albeit in varying degrees and in different ways.

For rump Yugoslavia (Serbia and Montenegro) and the self-proclaimed "Serbian Republic of Bosnia and Hercegovina," economic devastation and the status of international pariahs accompanied military success. The conduct of their forces in Bosnia brought international condemnation and ruinous economic sanctions imposed by the United Nations. Rump Yugoslavia was beset by absurdly high inflation, around one million percent a month: The central bank revalued the currency by removing six zeroes from the dinar in October 1993 and another nine zeroes in December 1993. As of this writing, the meager civilian economy functions on German marks, barter, and black market smuggling from Bulgaria, Greece, and Hungary. For a few liters of gasoline or heating oil, residents wait in line for days.

Serbian-controlled Bosnia became a garrison state under the military control of the Army of the Serbian Republic (ASR), as the Bosnian branch of the YPA renamed itself in May 1992. After most of its Muslim inhabitants were expelled in campaigns of ethnic cleansing, Serbian-controlled Bosnia lost much of its productive capacity. Its leader, Radovan Karadžić, estimated in late 1993 that the economy was operating at only 18% of its prewar rate.[20] Most economic productivity directly supported the ASR, contributing little to the well-being of the civilian population. When Western reporters visited the area in the fall of 1993, residents covertly complained that they feared arbitrary actions by the military, comparing the regime to Stalinism in the former Soviet Union. After twenty months of war, the ASR was experiencing low morale and desertion in its ranks.

The republic of Croatia lost about a third of its territory to the YPA and its Serbian allies in the 1991 war. The direct costs of war, coupled with the war-related dearth of foreign tourists on the Dalmatian Coast and the burden of providing for hundreds of thousands of refugees, created an ongoing economic crisis in Croatia, although the situation did not become as desperate as that in rump Yugoslavia. Despite massive assistance from the republic of Croatia in men and matériel to the fighting in Hercegovina and central Bosnia in 1993, Croatian forces lost territory to Bosnian forces that outside observers assessed as

---

20 John Burns, "Bosnian Serbs Begin to Question Price of Victory," *The New York Times*, November 14, 1993, pp. 1 and 4.

lightly equipped and armed. Providing for the wave of Bosnian Croat refugees produced by the fighting increased the government's burden. Perhaps most ominous for Croatia in the long run is the challenge to the Zagreb regime that has come from autonomy movements in Istria and Dalmatia. Were these movements to succeed, the republic of Croatia could be stripped of its revenue-producing tourist regions on the Dalmatian Coast, leaving little more of Croatia than the city of Zagreb and its environs.

The war that began in April 1992 transformed the government-controlled areas of the republic of Bosnia and Hercegovina into urban islets of deprivation and misery, whose remaining inhabitants lived in subhuman conditions unknown in Europe since World War II. Most of Bosnia's inhabitants became wards of the international relief community, dependent on aid shipments that arrived erratically on humanitarian convoys and air drops from US cargo planes. After twenty-two months of war, UN doctors estimated that the average person in Sarajevo had lost twenty-five pounds of body weight since the siege began in April 1992. Although the end of daily bombardments on February 11, 1994, brought relief and cautious optimism to Sarajevo residents, the siege remained largely in effect as the ASR's encirclement of the city continued.

For most Bosnians, the war continued much as before, a stalemate with thousands of civilians trapped in the country's urban centers. A hospital in Tuzla was struck by shells the day before the UN ultimatum expired. As of April 1994, the plight of residents in the encircled cities of Goražde, Srebrenica, and Žepa in eastern Bosnia remains desperate. In addition to the estimated 200,000 Bosnians who have been killed in the fight-

FIG. II.7 — MAN MOURNING THE DEATH OF HIS MOTHER, KILLED
BY SNIPER FIRE IN SARAJEVO

ing, another estimated two million Bosnians have become refugees with little hope of returning to their homes.

Once the EC became involved in the Bosnian crisis in early 1992, mediators of the international community fully recognized the three contending parties and treated them as equal contenders with legitimate claims. Even though punitive economic sanctions were imposed on rump Yugoslavia, and both Serbian President Milošević and Bosnian Serb leader Karadžić were made the subjects of war crimes investigations, Owen and Stoltenberg extended unquestioned legitimacy to them and to Croatian leaders Franjo Tudjman and Mate Boban at the negotiating table. The willingness of the international mediators to accept all contenders on the basis of their military power served to validate the territorial conquests of the strongest parties. Coupled with the policy of tolerating a certain level of sustained violence by all sides, their approach encouraged the continuation of the war of attrition and stalemate that had begun in the spring of 1992.

The rapid dismemberment of Bosnia and Hercegovina by military force in 1992 may be compared to the events of 1941, when the disappearance of royal Yugoslavia left Bosnia at the mercy of a foreign occupying power. Then, as now, a powerful military force (the Germans in 1941, the YPA in 1992), intent on sowing discord in Bosnia, sided with a single ethnic group (the Croats in 1941, the Serbs in 1992). Then, as now, foreign occupiers allied with native collaborators engaged in genocidal campaigns with the aim of establishing an ethnically monolithic state. In 1941-5 this effort failed. The Partisans under Tito's leadership kept alive the hope of national brotherhood and unity by appealing to members of all nationalities to expel the occupying enemy. Here the similarity ends, however, for Tito and his Partisans prevailed, assisted by military aid from the Western Allies and the direct military participation of the Soviet Red Army. In the Bosnian crisis that began in 1990, international involvement neither effectively deterred ultranationalist aggressors nor offered meaningful aid to those supporting a multinational resolution.

Ethnic cleansing by Serbs, Croats, and Muslims destroyed multiethnic population patterns in many parts of Bosnia in 1992 and 1993. As the conflict progressed and national extremists conducted sustained bombardment and sieges of several Bosnian cities, hopes for a multiethnic society progressively dimmed. Of the contenders in the conflict, however, the Bosnian republic stood alone in its commitment to a multiethnic society and the principles of pluralism and mutual tolerance. Denied the opportunity to arm itself by the United Nations arms embargo, and receiving neither support nor recognition for its efforts to preserve a multiethnic society, the Bosnian government was nonetheless the refuge of choice for those of all nationalities who hoped for a pluralistic Bosnian society, particularly in Sarajevo and other besieged cities.

With its centuries-long tradition of accommodation and mutual coexistence of different religious communities and nationalities, Bosnia's historical legacy was betrayed in the conflict that began in 1992. This is not to deny that many Serbs and Croats of Bosnia have, for much of the past century, articulated a desire for political association with a neighboring state. But the historical patterns of coalition politics and compromise, coupled with deeply-rooted traditions of cooperation and coexistence in everyday life, had previously mandated that compromise take precedence over the parochial interests of any single group. In 1992, however, as representatives of the international community issued idle threats and distorted the nature of the conflict to justify inaction, armed bullies and perpetrators of vicious ethnic cleansing destroyed much of a society that shared many of the values and beliefs that are central to Western democratic life.

List of Abbreviations

ASR	Army of the Serbian Republic (Serbian-occupied Bosnia)
AVNOJ	Anti-Fascist Council for the National Liberation of Yugoslavia
CCA	Croatian Catholic Association
CDC	Croatian Democratic Community
CNU	Croatian National Union
CPY	Communist Party of Yugoslavia
EC	European Community
LCY	League of Communists of Yugoslavia
MNO	Muslim National Organization
PDA	Party for Democratic Action
SDP	Serbian Democratic Party
SNO	Serbian National Organization
UNPROFOR	United Nations Protection Force
YMO	Yugoslav Muslim Organization
YPA	Yugoslav People's Army

Chronology

EARLY MEDIEVAL PERIOD (c. 500-1180)

6th-early 7th century — Migration of Slavs into the Balkans.

Second quarter of 7th century — Migrations of Croats and Serbs into parts of northern Yugoslavia. Controversy as to degree this migration affected Bosnia. In any case, over following century or so, both Croats and Serbs were assimilated by far more numerous Slavs throughout the region.

9th-11th century — Nominal conversion of Bosnia to Christianity (Catholicism).

1180s — Hungarians asserting claim of overlordship over Bosnia resisted by Bosnia's ruler, Ban Kulin (c. 1180-1204).

MEDIEVAL PERIOD (1180-1463)

1235-41 — Hungarian "Crusade" against "heresy" in Bosnia. Fails owing to Tatar invasion of Hungary in 1241.

1252 — Hungarians persuade Pope to place Bosnia's Catholic Church under jurisdiction of a Hungarian archbishop. In years that follow, Bosnia rejects this assignment and secedes from international Catholicism, creating its own independent Church, the Bosnian Church.

c. 1318 — Stjepan Kotromanić becomes Ban of Bosnia (to rule until 1353).

c. 1322 — Kotromanić annexes Catholic lands to Bosnia's west (Bosnian Krajina and Završje).

1326 — Bosnia annexes Hum (roughly what is now Hercegovina).

1342 — Establishment of Franciscan Mission in Bosnia.

1347 — Kotromanić becomes Catholic.

1353 — Death of Kotromanić, succession of his nephew Tvrtko (1353-91) as ban.

1377 — Tvrtko crowned as king at Mileševo.

1448 — Separation of Hum under Herceg Stefan; region begins to become known as Hercegovina.

1451 — Ottomans conquer region around Sarajevo.

1459 — Under papal pressure to get Western aid against Turkish threat, King Stefan Tomaš orders Bosnian Churchmen (presumably its clerics) to accept Catholicism or leave. Majority convert, minority accept asylum from Herceg Stefan. This is Bosnia's only case of religious persecution in the Middle Ages.

1463 — Ottoman conquest of Bosnia. Though most is retained, Hungarians recover parts briefly, losing most of their gains over the next two years, but their last fortress, Jajce, holds out until 1527. Most of what is salvaged from the initial conquest of Hercegovina is retaken by Turks by 1465, though last fort in Hercegovina holds out until 1481.

OTTOMAN OCCUPATION (1463-1878)

1521-41 — Three reigns of Gazi-Husref Beg, governor of Bosnian sandžak and great builder and endower of Sarajevo's religious buildings, including its main mosque, Begova Džamija (the Beg's Mosque).

c. 1554 — Governor of Bosnia upgraded to a Beglerbeg/vizier and sandžaks of Zvornik and Hercegovina subordinated to him.

1583-1640 — Seat of Bosnian vizier in Banja Luka.

1640-98 — Seat of Bosnian vizier in Sarajevo.

1697 — Austrians burn Sarajevo.

1698-1850 — Seat of vizier in Travnik.

1826-27 — Edict to abolish Janissaries and its enforcement in Sarajevo.

1830-33 — Revolt of Husein Kapetan.

1833 — Ali Pasha Rizvanbegović rewarded for aid in putting down Husein's rebellion by becoming governor of Hercegovina, which separated from Bosnia.

1835-37 — Edict to eliminate kapetans and its enforcement.

1850 — Repression by Omar Pasha of last major Muslim resistance. Elimination of Ali Pasha. Vizier returns his residence to Sarajevo.

1875 — Major Christian peasant uprising against Muslim landlords in Bosnia.

1876 — Serbia and Montenegro declare war on Ottoman empire. Ottomans defeat Serbian forces.

1877-78 — Russia intervenes militarily on behalf of the Great Powers and conducts successful campaign against the Ottomans.

June-July 1878 — Congress of Berlin redraws boundaries in the Balkans, awards Bosnia and Hercegovina to Austria-Hungary to "occupy and administer."

AUSTRO-HUNGARIAN OCCUPATION (1878-1918)

July-Oct. 1878 — Armed resistance to Austria's entry into Bosnia, led by Bosnia's Muslims aided by some Bosnian Serbs. Austria prevails after employing 268,000 troops in four months of military operations.

1878-1918 — Bosnia is a province under Austro-Hungarian imperial rule. Serbs, Croats, and Muslims each create modern-style political parties.

1908 — Austria-Hungary formally annexes Bosnia and Hercegovina, touching off diplomatic crisis that passes without resort to war.

1910 — Constitution promulgated for Bosnia. Elections to Parliament are held, based on a limited franchise.

June 28, 1914 — Assassination of Austrian Archduke Franz Ferdinand, heir-apparent to the Habsburg throne, in Sarajevo at the hands of eight Bosnians.

1914-18 — World War I. Despite major campaigns in neighboring Serbia, no significant fighting in Bosnia. Austrian officials repress Bosnian Serbs, suspecting many of sympathizing with wartime enemy Serbia.

ROYAL YUGOSLAV PERIOD (1918-41)

Dec. 1, 1918 — Creation of the kingdom of the Serbs, Croats, and Slovenes, a constitutional monarchy under Serbia's Karadjordjević dynasty. Bosnia retained as administrative unit as part of agreement with Bosnian Muslim politicians.

Jan. 6, 1929 — Proclamation of royal dictatorship after rising national contention and assassination in Parliament of Croatian Peasant Party leader Stjepan Radić.

1929 — Bosnia is abolished as an administrative unit as Yugoslavia is reorganized into geographically-based banovinas.

WORLD WAR II (1941-45)

April 6, 1941 — German attack on Yugoslavia and aerial bombardment of Belgrade. In subsequent weeks, Yugoslavia is rapidly overrun by German and Italian forces.

1941-45 — Bosnia is incorporated into "Independent State of Croatia," under sponsorship of German and Italian occupiers. The Ustashe, Croatian fascists, engage in genocidal atrocities against Serbs, Jews, Gypsies, and political opponents from all groups.

— Bosnia becomes primary battleground between German occupiers and Communist-led Partisans of Josip Broz Tito. Partisans defeat rival Greater Serbian Chetniks under Draža Mihailović and liberate large portions of Yugoslavia, including most of Bosnia and Hercegovina, from German control.

Oct. 20, 1944 — Germans expelled from Belgrade by joint operation of Partisans and Soviet Red Army.

April 6, 1945 — Partisans enter Sarajevo.

SOCIALIST YUGOSLAV PERIOD (1945-91)

Jan. 31, 1946 — New constitution proclaimed by Communist-dominated Yugoslav government. Bosnia is restored as an administrative unit, one of six republics of socialist Yugoslavia.

1945-46 — Agrarian reform ends privileged position of Muslim landowners in Bosnia.

June 28, 1948 — Yugoslav Communist Party expelled from Soviet-led Cominform, signalling Tito's break with the international Communist movement.

1948-51 — Search for a new course, known as Titoism, as a unique Yugoslav path to socialism. Titoism emphasizes workers' self-management, nonalignment, and decentralization of political power.

1952 — Communist Party of Yugoslavia is renamed "League of Communists," reflecting change from central control to leading role in society and economy.

1954 — Milovan Djilas removed from power by Tito for espousing multiparty pluralism.

1966 — Aleksandar Ranković removed from power for opposing reforms; he is accused of using secret police to promote Serbian nationalist aims.

1971 — Croatian nationalist movement in Zagreb leads to crackdown and purge of Croatian League of Communists.

1974 — New Constitution promulgated in Yugoslavia. Tito is elected president for life; provisions for succession at his death involve collective leadership and rotation of key offices.

May 4, 1980 — Death of Josip Broz Tito.

July-Aug. 1983 — Trial and conviction of Alija Izetbegović and twelve other Bosnian Muslims in Sarajevo on charges of advocating an *Islamistan* for Bosnia.

July 1984 — Trial of Vojislav Šešelj in Sarajevo on charges of advocating Greater Serbian ideals and undermining the constitutional order.

1987 — Rise to power of Slobodan Milošević as strongman of Serbia, rallying Serbian nationalists who resent Albanian strength in Kosovo.

Jan. 1990 — League of Communists dissolves as Slovenes walk out of Party Congress when their proposals for confederation are rejected.

1990 — Multiparty elections in all republics.

Nov. 1990 — Bosnian elections result in victory for nationalist political parties and candidates Alija Izetbegović, Radovan Karadžić, and Stjepan Kljuić.

June 1991 — Slovenia and Croatia declare independence.

WARS OF YUGOSLAV SUCCESSION (1991-PRESENT)

June-July 1991 — "Ten Day War" between Slovene Defense Forces and Yugoslav People's Army (YPA). In agreement mediated by European Community, YPA withdraws and Slovenia becomes an independent republic.

July-Dec. 1991 — War in Croatia between Croatian Territorial Forces and Serbian irregulars backed by YPA. Serbs win control of one-third of the Croatian republic. First reports of "ethnic cleansing" by Serbs as they consolidate military gains.

Nov. 17, 1991 — Surrender of the last remaining Croatian forces in Vukovar. YPA artillery bombardment has reduced the city to rubble.

Jan. 1992 — Agreement between Croatia and YPA is negotiated by former US Secretary of State Cyrus Vance on behalf of the United Nations. Deployment of United Nations Protection Force (UNPROFOR) to separate belligerents is foreseen in agreement.

Mar. 1, 1992 — At insistence of European Community, Bosnia holds referendum on independence. Muslims and Croats overwhelmingly vote yes; Serbs boycott it.

Mar.-April 1992 — Violence breaks out in Bosnia between Serbian irregulars and Bosnian government troops and police. Serbian irregulars, under sponsorship of Serbian government and YPA, engage in terror and ethnic cleansing of eastern Bosnian towns.

April 1992 — YPA forces, aiding Bosnian Serbs, surround Sarajevo and consolidate control in eastern and northwestern Bosnia.

— Croatian forces consolidate control in western Hercegovina.

May 1992 — YPA ordered to withdraw from Bosnia; almost all troops and equipment remain as the "Army of the Serbian Republic of Bosnia and Hercegovina" under new commander, General Ratko Mladić.

Summer 1992 — UNPROFOR establishes security for Sarajevo airport and road to city.

Jan. 1993 — Owen-Vance Plan for "ethnic cantons" in Bosnia is made public. Bosnian Croats endorse it immediately; Bosnian government is persuaded to follow in March 1993.

April 1993 — Cooperation between Bosnian government and Croat forces breaks down. Growing Croatian-Bosnian military clashes in central Bosnia and western Hercegovina.

May 1993 — Despite intense pressure from Milošević and others, Bosnian Serbs reject Owen-Vance plan in self-proclaimed Parliament and subsequently in a referendum.

Aug. 1993 — United States threatens air strikes on Bosnian Serbs; NATO aircraft streak low over Serbian positions. Under pressure, Serbs abandon Mount Igman to UN peacekeeping forces and threat of air strikes recedes.

Nov. 9, 1993 — Sustained Croatian shelling destroys centuries-old Mostar bridge across the Neretva River.

Nov. 18, 1993 — All three parties agree to provide full access to humanitarian convoys of the international community. Obstruction of convoys continues, particularly by Serbs.

Feb. 5, 1994 — Mortar attack on Sarajevo marketplace kills sixty-eight, arousing international outrage over continued civilian deaths.

Feb. 21, 1994 — Expiration of UN and NATO ultimatum deadline for Serbian and Bosnian government forces to turn over all heavy weapons to UN control or withdraw them beyond a 20-kilometer exclusion zone around the city. Despite continued presence of some heavy weapons in the zone, the Serbs largely comply and threat of NATO air strikes recedes again.

Glossary

Autocephaly — Literally "self-headedness," adjective "autocephalous." The term is used for the status of a national Orthodox Church (e.g., the Church of Serbia), when it usurped or was awarded jurisdictional autonomy over its own territory, with its hierarchy appointing local bishops and administering its dioceses. In this position the autocephalous Church remained in communion with the other Orthodox Churches. Its independence was, moreover, limited to administrative matters. It did not have the authority to alter doctrine, which remained under the guardianship of the Patriarch of Constantinople and could only be redefined though a widely representative council of the broader Church.

Ayan — A Muslim notable in Ottoman Bosnia.

Ban — A ruler or governor of a large province, often the subordinate of a king. The title was used in the western Balkans, in Bosnia, Croatia, and Slavonia, and often became hereditary. The rulers of Bosnia were called bans from the mid-twelfth century to 1377. Bans, like those of Bosnia, often achieved considerable, if not complete, autonomy. The title was revived in twentieth-century Yugoslavia. See *Banovina*.

Banovina — A modern administrative unit ruled by a *ban* (governor). Nine Banovinas were established by King Alexander after he assumed dictatorial powers in 1929. They were based upon and named after geographical features rather than historical boundaries. Serbs made up a majority in six of the nine units.

Beg — A term of broad usage; it could refer to a landlord of a certain status, and was also used for certain fairly high officials. Thus the governor of an administrative district like a *sandžak* (comparable to a large county in an American state) was entitled *sandžak-beg*. *See also Beglerbeg.*

Beglerbeg — The governor of a major Ottoman province or *beglerbeglik* (literally the territory under a beglerbeg). In the period of initial conquests, and as late as the sixteenth century, all of Ottoman Europe was incorporated into one super-province (beglerbeglik) of Rumeli. In the sixteenth century, Ottoman Europe was divided into several provinces, so entitled, each of which was under a beglerbeg, one of which was Bosnia. The beglerbeg could also be called a *vali* or a *vizier*, and often was.

Beglerbeglik — The territory under the authority of a *beglerbeg* (see above). The *i* in the *lik* has a thick sound, so Slavs usually spell it and other Turkish words so ending as *luk*.

Bogomilism — A heretical current arising in Bulgaria in the mid-tenth century, believing in two principles (i.e., dualism) — one spiritual and good, identified with a spiritual heaven and with Christ and the New Testament; the other evil and the creator of matter and this world, identified with the God of the Old Testament. It spread beyond Bulgaria into the Byzantine empire and from there (under different names) along the Mediterranean to the south of Western Europe, including Dalmatia. Some of its adherents may have entered Bosnia. Many scholars have associated the local Bosnian Church with this sect. However, no serious evidence links that Church to dualism. Moreover, the term is not found in Dalmatia and the Western Balkans. The popular literature still frequently speaks about the medieval Bosnians being Bogomils or the present-day Bosnian Muslims being descended from Bogomils. However, it is most unlikely that this was the case.

Bosnian Church — An independent Church established in Bosnia by Bosnian Catholics when they broke with international Catholicism in the second half of the thirteenth century. Though often labeled "heretical" and even "Bogomil," it seems to have been merely schismatic (i.e., in a break with Rome), for its beliefs seem to have been in keeping with Catholic ones. Under its own independent hierarchy, it survived though the Middle Ages, only to disappear in the early years of Turkish rule.

Defters — Cadasters, the Turkish tax registers.

Divan — The council of a Turkish governor; both the sultan and the provincial governor (*vizier*) had a divan, made up of the leading officials of his entourage.

Djed — Literally "grandfather." The chief cleric of the Bosnian Church.

Janissaries — Members of a Turkish army corps (from *Yeni Çeri*, literally the "New Corps"), created to be an infantry armed with muskets in the fifteenth century. Originally recruited through the levy of Christian children, in the seventeenth century the levy ceased and membership in the corps became hereditary. Becoming involved in trade, the Janissaries became increasingly undisciplined and obsolete as an armed force; they also blocked any army reforms that threatened their privileges. The corps was finally abolished in 1826.

Kadi — A judge standing over a Turkish religious *(sheriat)* court. Since Islam penetrated every aspect of society, the kadi's court involved itself in many issues that might be thought of as being secular.

Kapetan — Commander of a fortress in Bosnia, not staffed with regular army units. The kapetan, usually a local Bosnian, was under the authority of the Bosnian *vizier*, and sometimes his direct appointee; in some cases locals got hereditary control of the position. A kapetan was also responsible for law and order in the district (*kapetanije*) around his fortress. The institution was abolished in 1837.

Krajina — Literally "borderland" or "frontier": often referred to as the Military Frontier. Krajina is a territory that once separated the Ottoman and Austrian empires. Beginning in the sixteenth century, Austrian authorities attracted Serbs to this region to provide military service in their wars against the Ottoman empire. This left a large concentration of Serbs in the borderland regions of Croatia and in northwestern Bosnia. The Serbs of Croatia adopted the name "Krajina" for the autonomous republic they declared in 1991.

Millet — The Ottomans categorized society according to religious communities, which came to be called millets. When the system was in operation (and much controversy surrounds its origins and early years), the community had self-rule in most aspects of its cultural and daily life, under its religious leader. Ottoman authorities dealt with the millet through that religious figure. The Orthodox Christians and Jews had millets; the Catholics did not. However, in Bosnia, the Franciscan leadership, having received privileges akin to those of a millet, stood over a community that greatly resembled a millet.

Mulla — A high-ranking Islamic religious figure, who might preside over a religious court.

Pasha — A Turkish rank, equivalent to "general." Like our generals, pashas had different ranks, but instead of a number of stars, a pasha was awarded a number of horse tails. One needed this rank to hold certain cabinet or provincial positions. As a result all Bosnian governors were pashas. Through the title of rank these governors bore, various contemporary diplomats and subsequent scholars have misunderstood the term's meaning; thus one frequently finds the expression "the Pasha of Bosnia." However, the governor was not the pasha of Bosnia, but the *vizier* of Bosnia who happened to hold the rank of pasha.

Pashalik (pashaluk) — The holdings of a pasha. Through the misunderstanding, noted under the word *pasha*, one often finds Bosnia, under its vizier who ranked as a pasha, referred to as a pashalik. However, it is a misusage; *beglerbeglik* or *vilayet* are more proper terms for Bosnia's status.

Reis-ul-ulema — Leader of the Bosnian Muslim religious community. The position was created in 1909 by the Austrians following a decade of Muslim demands for cultural and religious autonomy and has been retained by all regimes since 1909.

Šahovnica — Red-and-white checkerboard Croatian coat-of-arms. Dating to the medieval period, the Šahovnica was flaunted by the *Ustashe* during World War II as a symbol of extreme Croatian nationalism. Made the centerpiece of the Croatian flag in 1990, it symbolizes the revived Croatian exclusivism, resented in particular by Serbian and Jewish inhabitants of the Croatian republic.

Sandžak — A Turkish provincial district; a subdivision of a *vilayet* or *beglerbeglik*.

Sandžak-beg — The governor of a sandžak.

Sarajlije — The name used by the people of Sarajevo for themselves.

Serbo-Croatian — The language at present spoken by the Serbs, Croats, and Bosnians of former Yugoslavia. These people all speak dialects of one language which was standardized in the nineteenth century. The term, however, is a recent one; first coined in the nineteenth century, it became common only in the twentieth after the creation of Yugoslavia. Thus, although a language called "Old S-C" might accurately describe the archaic forms of the common language spoken by all these people at various points in the medieval and Ottoman periods, it is an anachronistic term for the spoken language then since its speakers would have used other terms for what they spoke. The word is now falling out of use among many ex-Yugoslavs, as chauvinist Serbs and Croats do not want to recognize the fact they share a common language with their neighbors.

Stećci — (singular *stećak)* Academic term for medieval Bosnian tombstones.

Timar — An income source (usually land and thus a form of fief) awarded to a Turkish soldier (usually a cavalryman) to support his service.

Ustashe — (adjectivally *"Ustasha"* in this work) Croatian fascists in World War II. Under German and Italian occupation, the Ustashe governed the "Independent State of Croatia," which included nearly all of Bosnia and Hercegovina, and conducted atrocities and genocide against Serbs, Jews, Gypsies, and political opponents.

Vakuf — (from the Arabic *wakf)* Endowment for the support of an Islamic religious institution such as a mosque or a religious school.

Vali — A Turkish governor over a major province; thus the governor of Bosnia could be called a vali.

Vilayet — A major Turkish province. Bosnia, for example, was a vilayet.

Vizier — An Ottoman minister. Among its usages it denoted the governors of major provinces. Thus the governor of Bosnia was the vizier of Bosnia.

Vojvoda — Slavic term for a general, also used for the leader of a pastoral clan or tribe. The leading nobleman or hegemon in Hum when Hum was under the overlordship of Bosnia bore the title "Vojvoda of Bosnia," which indicated his subordination to the Bosnian ruler.

Župa — A territorial unit (roughly equivalent to a county) found in Bosnia, Croatia, and Serbia.

Further English Readings

THE FOLLOWING WORKS are recommended to a reader seeking greater under-standing of the Bosnian conflict and its background. The list is not intended as a comprehensive bibliography.

MEDIEVAL PERIOD, (c. 500-1453)

Fine, John V.A., *The Bosnian Church: A New Interpretation*, Boulder and New York: East European Monographs, distributed by Columbia University Press, 1975.

Fine, John V.A., *The Late Medieval Balkans: A Critical Survey from the Late Twelfth Century to the Ottoman Conquest*, Ann Arbor: University of Michigan Press, 1987.

Fine, John V.A., "Bosnia," *Dictionary of the Middle Ages*, II, pp. 334-41.

Fine, John V.A., "Bosnian Church," *Dictionary of the Middle Ages*, II, pp. 341-3.

Wenzel, Marian, "Bosnian and Herzegovinian Tombstones: Who Made Them and Why?" *Südost-Forschungen*, XXI (1962), pp. 102-43.

Wenzel, Marian, *Ukrasni motivi na stećcima / Ornamental Motifs on Tomb-stones from Medieval Bosnia and Surrounding Regions*, Sarajevo: Veselin Masleša, 1965. The text is both in Serbo-Croatian and in English.

OTTOMAN PERIOD (1453-1878)

Andrić, Ivo, *Bosnian Story* (trans. Kenneth Johnstone), London: Lincolns-Prager, 1961. A magnificent novel set in early nineteenth-century Travnik, where the vizier resided.

Andrić, Ivo. *Bridge on the Drina*, University of Chicago Press, 1977 (origi-nally published 1959). A multi-generational novel about Višegrad in the Ottoman period.

Mackenzie G.M. (Lady Sebright) and A. Irby, *Travels in the Slavonic Provinces of Turkey in Europe*, 2 vols., London: 1877.

AUSTRO-HUNGARIAN PERIOD (1878-1918)

Dedijer, Vladimir, *The Road to Sarajevo*, London: MacGibbon and Key, 1967.

Donia, Robert J., *Islam under the Double Eagle: The Muslims of Bosnia and Hercegovina, 1878-1914*, Boulder and New York: East European Monographs, distributed by Columbia University Press, 1981.

Sugar, Peter F., *Industrialization of Bosnia-Hercegovina, 1878-1918*, Seattle: University of Washington Press, 1963.

ROYAL YUGOSLAV PERIOD (1918-41)

Banac, Ivo, *The National Question in Yugoslavia: Origins, History, Politics*, Ithaca: Cornell University Press, 1984.

Djilas, Aleksa, *The Contested Country: Yugoslav Unity and Communist Revolution, 1919-1953*, Cambridge: Harvard University Press, 1991. An insightful account that spans the royal Yugoslav, wartime, and socialist periods.

Rothschild, Joseph, *East Central Europe between the Two World Wars*, Seattle: University of Washington Press, 1974, pp. 201-80.

Tomasevich, Jozo, *Peasants, Politics and Economic Change in Yugoslavia*, Stanford University Press, 1957.

WORLD WAR II PERIOD (1941-45)

Auty, Phyllis, *Tito: A Biography*, Harlow, England: Longmans, 1970.

Maclean, Fitzroy, *Eastern Approaches*, London: J. Cape, 1949.

Roberts, Walter, *Tito, Mihailović and the Allies*, New Brunswick: Rutgers University Press, 1973.

Tomasevich, Jozo, *The Chetniks: War and Revolution in Yugoslavia, 1941-1945*, Stanford University Press, 1975.

SOCIALIST YUGOSLAV PERIOD (1945-91)

Radio Free Europe Research Reports.

Doder, Dusko, *The Yugoslavs*, New York: Random House, 1978.

Irvine, Jill A., *The Croat Question: Partisan Politics in the Formation of the Yugoslav Socialist State*, Boulder: Westview, 1993.

Lockwood, William, *European Moslems: Economy and Ethnicity in Western Bosnia*, New York: Academic Press, 1975.

Ramet, Sabrina P., *Nationalism and Federalism in Yugoslavia, 1962-1991*, 2nd edn., Bloomington: Indiana University Press, 1992.

Rusinow, Dennison, *The Yugoslav Experiment, 1948-1974*, London: C. Hurst, 1977.

Shoup, Paul S., *Communism and the Yugoslav National Question*, New York: Columbia University Press, 1968.

BOSNIAN WAR PERIOD (1992 -)

Balkan War Reports. Bulletins of the Institute for War and Peace Reporting, London.

Cohen, Lenard, *Broken Bonds: The Disintegration of Yugoslavia*, Boulder: Westview, 1993.

Dizdarević, Zlatko, *Sarajevo: A War Journal*, New York: Fromm International, 1993.

Filipović, Zlata, *Zlata's Diary: A Child's Life in Sarajevo*, New York: Viking, 1994.

Glenny, Misha, *The Fall of Yugoslavia: The Third Balkan War*, New York: Penguin, 1992.

Gow, James, "One Year of War in Bosnia and Herzegovina," *RFE/RL Research Report*, June 4, 1993, pp. 1-13.

Gutman, Roy, *A Witness to Genocide*, New York: Macmillan, 1993.

Hayden, Robert, "The Partition of Bosnia and Herzegovina, 1990-1993," *RFE/RL Research Report*, May 28, 1993, pp. 1-14.

Stokes, Gale, *The Walls Came Tumbling Down*, Oxford University Press, 1993, pp. 218-52.

List of Illustrations

ILLUSTRATION CREDITS

Asboth, Janos, *An Official Tour through Bosnia and Herzegovina*, London, 1890. Figures 2.1, 2.6, 5.1, 5.2, 5.3, 5.4, 5.5, 5.6, 6.1, and 11.3.

Bettmann Archive. Figures 8.1, 11.4, and 11.7

Bihalji-Merin, Oto and Alojz Benac, *Stećci*, Zagreb: Leksikografski Zavod, 1963. Figures 1.1 and 2.2.

Ćirković, Sima, *Istorija Srednjovekovne Bosanske Države*, Belgrade: Srpska Književna Zadruga, 1964. Figures 2.3, 2.4, and 2.5.

Čurčić, Vejsil, "Starinsko Oružje u Bosni i Hercegovini," *Glasnik Zemaljskog Muzeja* (Sarajevo), 1943. Figures 3.6 and 3.7.

Facts About Yugoslavia, Zagreb: 1966. Figures 8.3 and 9.1

Flight, New York: The International Rescue Committee, 1993. Figures 11.1, 11.2, 11.6, and 11.8.

Giljferding, Aleksandar, *Putovanje po Hercegovini, Bosni, i Staroj Srbiji*, Sarajevo: Veselin Masleša, 1972. Figures 3.1, 3.3, 3.5, 3.8, and 3.9.

Jokić, Gojko, *Bosnia-Hercegovina: A Tourist Guide*, Belgrade: 1969. Figure 6.2.

NYT Pictures. John Kifner. Figure 11.5.

Samardžić, Radovan, *Mehmed Sokolović*, Belgrade: Srpska Književna Zadruga, 1971. Figures 3.2 and 3.4.

List of Maps

List of Tables

Index

(Parenthetical numbers refer to illustrations, maps, or tables)